Law and the Social Work Practitioner: A Manual for Practice

Second Edition

RODGER WHITE,
GRAEME BROADBENT AND
KEITH BROWN

Series Editor: Keith Brown

LearningMatters

First published in 2007 by Learning Matters Ltd.
Second edition published in 2009

British Library Cataloguing in Publication Data
A CIP record for this book is available from the British Library.

ISBN 978 1 84445 264 4

Cover design by Code 5 Design Associates Ltd
Project management by Deer Park Productions
Typeset by PDQ Typesetting Ltd
Printed and bound in Great Britain by Cromwell Press Group, Trowbridge, Wiltshire

Learning Matters Ltd
33 Southernhay East
Exeter EX1 1NX
Tel: 01392 215560
info@learningmatters.co.uk
www.learningmatters.co.uk

Contents

Table of Cases

Table of Legislation

Statutory Instruments

About the authors

Graeme Broadbent
Graeme Broadbent has been involved in legal education for more than 25 years. He has worked in law schools in both the UK and abroad, and has taught law to students on a variety of courses. He has published work on law and legal education and is a regular contributor to conferences. He joined Kingston Law School, where he is now based, in 2002.

Keith Brown
Keith Brown holds professional qualifications in nursing, social work and teaching, and academic qualifications in nursing, social work and management. He has worked in education and training for more than 20 years, working for universities and council social work departments. Currently, Keith is the Director of the Centre for Post-Qualifying Social Work at Bournemouth University. The centre was recently recognised with the National Prize at the 2005 National Training Awards and, at the same ceremony, Keith was awarded the Linda Ammon Memorial Prize sponsored by the Department For Education and Skills, given to the person who has made the greatest contribution to education and training in the UK. Keith regularly speaks at national and international conferences. He has also published in national and international journals.

Rodger White
Rodger White was a Senior Lecturer in social work at Bournemouth University who had a passion for teaching social work law, social policy and also for the welfare of children. He taught social work law for over 15 years following an extensive career as a social work practitioner.

National Occupational Standards

This book will help you to meet the following Occupational Standards for Social Work:

- **Key Role 1**

Unit 3.1 – Assess and review the preferred options of individuals, families, carers, groups and communities

Unit 3.2 – Assess needs, risks and options taking into account legal and other requirements

Unit 3.3 – Assess and recommend an appropriate course of action for individuals, families, carers, groups and communities

- **Key Role 2**

Unit 4.2 – Identify the need for legal and procedural intervention

- **Key Role 4**

Unit 12.1 – Identify and assess the nature of the risk

Unit 12.2 – Balance the rights and responsibilities of individuals, families, carers, groups and communities with associated risk

Unit 13.2 – Work with the risk assessment and management procedures of your own and other relevant organisations and professions

- **Key Role 5**

Unit 14.2 – Carry out duties using accountable professional judgement and knowledgeable based social work practice

Unit 16.3 – Implement legal and policy framework for access to records and reports

- **Key Role 6**

Unit 18.1 – Review and update your own knowledge of legal, policy and procedural frameworks

If you are a registered social worker, this book will assist you to evidence post-registration training and learning. It relates to the national post-qualifying framework for social work education and training, especially the national criteria at the specialist level, in particular:

(i) Meet the relevant academic standards associated with social work at this level

(iv) Draw on knowledge and understanding of service users' and carers' issues to actively contribute to strategies and practice which promote service users' and carers' rights and participation in line with the goals of choice, independence and empowerment

(vii) Work effectively in a context of risk, uncertainty, conflict and contradiction

Foreword to the Post-Qualifying Social Work Practice series

All the texts in the Post-Qualifying Social Work Practice series have been written by people with a passion for excellence in social work practice. They are primarily written for social workers who are undertaking post-qualifying social work awards, but will also be useful to any social worker who wants to consider up-to-date social work practice issues.

The books in the series are also of value to social work students as they are written to inform, inspire and develop social work practice.

All the authors have a connection with the Centre for Post-Qualifying Social Work, and as a Centre we are all committed to raising the profile of the social work profession. We trust you find this text of real value to your social work practice, and that this in turn has a real impact on the service that users and carers receive.

Keith Brown
Series Editor
Centre for Post-Qualifying Social Work

Foreword

Rodger White was somebody whom we knew, respected and had a deep affection for as a colleague and friend for many years. He had a deep passion for the teaching of social work to a high standard. He frequently reminded us that he was 'ex-grammar school' and wanted to see the highest quality of social work delivered to the community.

One of Rodger's greatest qualities was that he really cared for his students and wanted them to have the best possible experience as his students. To this end, Rodger produced his law files each year, which was his way of ensuring that his students had excellent, up-to-date material on social work law.

During 2003, Rodger was diagnosed with lung cancer but, in a typical Rodger way, he continued to teach social work law during the 2003/2004 year, even though he was receiving radio- and chemotherapy. During June 2004, Rodger's health began to fail and he passed away on 11 June 2004. Right up to the final days of his life, and indeed while at the hospice, Rodger was continuing to update this social work text, with his wife Chris making notes for him as he was unable to write.

This was the nature of the man. Social work education has lost a good teacher, his family a loved relative and we have lost a great friend.

We still miss Rodger, but this text reminds us of him and the many hours that we taught together. A Rodger White Prize has been awarded at graduation to the best social work student in law since 2004, and this too reminds us of his great contribution to social work.

This text was fully updated by the two of us during the summer of 2006 and we offer it as a tribute to Rodger. Although it was originally conceived as material to support a series of classes combined together as a 'law file', we have adapted and updated the text so that it becomes a useful manual for practitioners. It is the sort of text a social worker needs close at hand in order to navigate around issues facing social workers. It therefore is also of value to social work students who are on placement or studying social work law. It is especially useful to international social workers who wish to come to the UK to practise social work and want to understand the legal system and its implications for social work practice.

We also wish to acknowledge and thank Mark Veldmeijer and Jenny Iliff for their input and advice on Chapters 8, 9 and 12.

It has at times been difficult to work on this text as Rodger is no longer with us and because the law has, in some areas, changed rapidly and significantly. A fair amount of updating has been required, though we have tried to preserve Rodger's style in making the necessary amendments. We hope that the result is a work that provides a clear overview, with suitable signposts, of law for social work practice in a way that you will find accessible and useful.

Indeed the process of updating this text has reminded us how much the law keeps changing and with it the realisation of how difficult it must be for practising social workers to keep up to date with the law. We believe you have a significant challenge in this respect and trust this text helps in some way for you to meet the challenge.

Our special thanks also need to go to Natalie Bates, our Research Assistant, for pulling together all our thoughts, ideas and notes – we couldn't do it without you.

We hope you find this text of value to you as you study and practise in social work.

Keith Brown   Graeme Broadbent
The Centre for Post-Qualifying Social Work   Kingston Law School
Bournemouth University   Kingston University

In memory of Rodger White
Friend, colleague and teacher

Introduction

This text was originally written by Rodger White with contributions from Graeme Broadbent to support student learning on a social work degree programme. It was always conceived as part of the teaching/learning package, and not a freestanding text or textbook. We have preserved this format in the belief that it will help users to structure their learning and to act as a guide to available resources. We have also preserved interactive elements which we hope will encourage readers to engage with the issues raised. With this in mind most chapters have been written in the following order:

i)   **Overview**: this will outline the rationale for the teaching material provided and a reference back to how it connects with previous material.

ii) **Objectives**: this indicates the learning objectives, which are what you should be able to do after completing the chapter that you may not have been able to do before. Your competence to use the law in practice will be achieved not just through a knowledge of law (though this is essential) but through understanding.

iii) **Reading**: there will be an indication of both essential and further reading.

iv) **Text**: the bulk of each section will consist of information and discussion about particular aspects of law.

Note: references to substantive law and to the legal system apply to England and Wales only. Though there is some shared UK legislation, social work legislation and the structure of the agencies that operate it are different in Scotland and Northern Ireland.

v)   **Exercises**: many of the sections will contain learning exercises, often in the form of case studies. Some suggestions as to issues raised by these exercises are contained in an appendix at the end of this text.

Though it was clearly written to support students undertaking a BA (Hons) Social Work course, the book is reproduced in such a way as to be of value to all social work students and practitioners.

It is especially of value to international social workers who are coming to practise in the UK and therefore need to be aware of the English legal system and its implications for social work practice in the UK.

Crown Copyright material is reproduced with the permission of the Controller of HMSO.

Chapter 1
Understanding law

Overview

It is essential that you, as a student and as a practitioner, take a critical view of social work practice. You will already be aware that there are contested perceptions of what social work is 'for' and how it should best be done, or even whether it should be done at all. Social work law is an important part of that contested terrain.

The purpose of this chapter is to take you the first few steps towards developing a sceptical, but also constructive, approach to law in social work practice. We do this, not by instructing you about particular aspects of the legal system, or bits of substantive law; instead we ask you to investigate the meaning of law and some of its underlying value assumptions. There is some useful reading you can do (see below) but firstly there is a brief exercise for you to complete, in your own time.

ACTIVITY 1.1

Very quickly, without thinking about it too much, jot down below the first five words or phrases that come to mind when you hear the word 'law'.

My five words/phrases are:

Once you have done this, don't then simply forget about it. *Reflect on what the words mean to you and why you put them there.*

Also, remember to look back at them, as your studies and your practice progress, and reconsider their meaning to you and whether you would amend them.

Objectives

In order to reach the following objectives you should:

- read through this section and complete the exercise in it
- take part in the relevant teaching session
- begin some of the essential reading.

After doing this you should be able to:

- critically discuss the notion of 'conflicting imperatives' in law

- begin to evaluate the practice-related implications of key value assumptions in law

- give an outline of what is meant by the 'rule of law'.

Two texts which deal with the highly political, professionally contentious and value-laden nature of social work law are:

Braye, S. and Preston-Shoot, M. (1997) *Practising Social Work Law* (2nd ed). Basingstoke: Macmillan

Dalrymple, J. and Burke, B. (2006) *Anti-Oppressive Practice: Social Care and the Law* (2nd ed.). Buckingham: Open University Press

You are strongly recommended to read these two books.

You are also recommended to read:

Cull, L.A. and Roche, J. (eds) (2001) *The Law and Social Work: Contemporary Issues for Practice.* Basingstoke: Palgrave

Also see the following general texts on social work law:

Ball, C. and McDonald, A. (2002) *Law for Social Workers: An Introduction* (4th ed.). Aldershot: Ashgate

Brammer, A. (2009) *Social Work Law* (3rd ed.) Harlow: Longman

Brayne, H. and Broadbent, G. (2002) *Legal Materials for Social Workers.* Oxford: Oxford University Press

Brayne, H. and Carr, H. (2008) *Law for Social Workers* (10th ed.). Oxford: Oxford University Press

Johns, R. (2007) *Using the Law in Social Work (Transforming Social Work Practice)* (3rd ed.). Exeter: Learning Matters

All social work law texts contain at least implicit assumptions about values. Many discuss them explicitly. Increasingly many 'traditional' general texts on law acknowledge that there are competing perspectives. An example is:

Fox, M. and Bell, C. (1999) *Learning Legal Skills* (3rd ed.). Oxford: Oxford University Press (Ch.1)

There is also an important and growing body of academic work, often referred to as 'critical legal theory', whose project is to investigate and contest the power relationships in law practice. This is interesting, but definitely not easy reading. An introduction to this body of work is provided in:

Mansell, W., Meteyard, B. and Thomson, A. (2004) *A Critical Introduction to Law* (3rd ed) London: Cavendish

Understanding law: values, principles and contradictions

All of us have ideas about 'law'. It is important that those who are required to put law into practice, including social workers, examine and reflect on these ideas; if we fail to do this, we run the risk of being merely 'technicians', rather than competent and reflective practitioners.

Law is complex, value-laden and contradictory. That's what makes it interesting; but it also means that simply 'knowing' the law (e.g. being able to quote what s.17 (1) of the Children Act 1989 says) is not enough: we must be able to understand it and give it meaning in practice.

Some of that understanding will derive from an awareness of contradictions in law. This is what this section is about. Below are some key points to which we will be referring.

Conflicting imperatives in law

By 'conflicting imperatives' is meant those matters with which law must be concerned but which do not readily fit together. Examples are:

- needs *vs.* rights

- welfare *vs.* justice

- individual rights to autonomy *vs.* rights of the state to intervene.

You can probably imagine that each of these imperatives and the relationship between them is complex and layered. Here is a brief example:

CASE STUDY

Mrs D. is 80 years old. Her husband died three years ago and she has no other close relatives nearby. She is physically frail and her eyesight is deteriorating. She is beginning to 'forget' to eat. Her next-door neighbour, who used to do some shopping and provide a few meals, will be leaving the area shortly. Others nearby tend to ignore her, or are actively hostile. Mrs D. wants to remain at home but is distressed about her growing inability to manage.

Some of the 'imperatives' mentioned above begin to break down into component parts. For example, how does her 'need' to remain at home equate with her 'need' to be protected? Can she resist social work intervention even if she is a danger to herself (individual rights to autonomy)? To what extent must she be in 'danger' (itself a problematic term) before intervention is inevitable, even if she is resistant? Contained within the question of the 'rights of the state to intervene' is the question of the form such intervention should take: one of the defining characteristics of social work is negotiation (perhaps, in this case, leading to home-based and/or daycare services under the range of community care legislation). But social workers are also in a position of authority and are legally empowered to take action which restricts civil liberty; in this case, for example, the use of compulsory powers under the Mental Health Act 1983, or even the little-used, but draconian, powers under s.47 of the National Assistance Act 1948.

ACTIVITY *1.2*

Clearly, law in practice is not straightforward. Can you think of other past, or possible, examples where there are 'conflicting imperatives'?

We now turn to the connected issue of value assumptions in the law. This is presented in terms of:

- images
- functions
- myths.

Value assumptions in the law

The law has a mass of value assumptions embedded in it. These are often unexamined and unspoken (that's what makes them 'assumptions'). The law is spoken of as if it is 'natural', or acts of its own volition, without human agency. You will sometimes hear people use 'common sense' statements like 'well – the law's the law isn't it', as if the operation of law is an inevitable and clear-cut process (whether they're 'for' it or 'against' it).

On the other hand, people sometimes express highly politicised ideas about law; for example, that it can be used in beneficial ways, to change attitudes and behaviour (the range of 'equal rights' legislation has this intention, if not always this effect). Or that it will tend to operate to 'put down' certain groups and favour others (we could, for example, compare law and practice in relation to social security 'scroungers' and 'tax dodgers').

As social work practitioners you will be negotiating with, and even be on the receiving end of, often very strongly expressed views about how fair, useful, confrontational, incomprehensible, etc, 'the law' is. Whatever views you are dealing with, it is important to remember that law, including law in social work practice, is only put into operation because of what people do (or don't do). As social workers, you are part of that and it is therefore important for you to reflect on how law is represented, as well as practised.

Much of this section, including the following comments, is based on Braye and Preston-Shoot, (1997, chs. 2 and 3). Read this for further discussion.

Images in law

What are the images contained in law? Examples include the following.

Competence – for example, whether a child of seven can be a 'competent' witness; whether an old person is 'competent' to live alone; whether a person with mental health problems is 'competent' to manage in the community and be released from psychiatric hospital; etc.

Promoting and preserving rights/controlling and minimising risk – the tension between 'preserving rights' and 'minimising risk' is at the heart of social work practice. It links to the issue of 'care and control': these two words are often opposed to each other, as if they were mutually contradictory. What do you think?

Moral worth – 'deservingness' – most social work services are not provided as an automatic right, but are provided (or not) following an assessment. The assessments have a legal basis and are often built around words such as 'need' and 'vulnerable'. Entitlement to a service usually only arises once a social worker (or other official) determines that certain words do apply to a particular person. Within these determinations there is very often an implied judgement about the actions of the service user (applicant/patient/claimant etc.).

An example, from the field of housing, illustrates this point. In relation to homelessness, by no means everyone who presents him/herself as homeless to a housing authority will have a right to assistance with accommodation.

This will depend on a decision by the housing authority about such issues as whether the applicant:

- is 'homeless' – that is he/she has no entitlement to accommodation which he/she can 'reasonably occupy' (or this will apply within 28 days)

- is 'eligible for assistance' (excluding persons subject to immigration controls under the range of asylum and immigration legislation)

- is in 'priority need' (the priority groups are identified in the relevant Act and a Code of Guidance)

- has not made him/herself intentionally homeless; and may also include whether or not he/she has a 'local connection'.

NB The above is a very abbreviated statement of the law. The details are to be found in Part VII of the Housing Act 1996 as amended by the Homelessness Act 2002, and the Department for Communities and Local Government Homelessness Code of Guidance for Local Authorities July 2006. This can be accessed at **www.communities.gov.uk/publications/housing/home lessnesscode**

It is only when all of these requirements are met that a (limited) right to the direct provision of accommodation arises. All of the above criteria and, in particular, that of intentional homelessness, have an element of judgement about the actions of an individual: not simply, does this person need a service, but should they have it?

As you develop your understanding, try to reflect on other practice examples where these considerations might apply.

Images of race, gender and disability

Images of 'race', 'gender' and 'disability' are contained within the race relations, sex discrimination and disability discrimination legislation and elsewhere. This range of legislation is outlined more fully later in this book, but here are a few introductory points for consideration:

- Is it contradictory to have a race relations legislation which is intended to promote harmonious race relations and immigration, and nationality legislation which has operated to keep certain minority ethnic groups (especially black and Asian) out of the UK?

- The issue of definition is extremely important: how are 'race', 'sex' and 'disability' defined? Following from this, who gets included and who gets excluded?

- What are the arrangements for enforcement of anti-discrimination legislation?

- In what circumstances is discrimination lawful ? This applies in the race relations and sex discrimination legislation concerning 'genuine occupational qualifications' (GOQs), for example. (This is a reminder that discrimination can be positive as well as negative.) There are also numerous exceptions allowing (negative) discrimination, in the more recent disability discrimination legislation (see Connolly, 2004).

All of these questions and others provide a means of investigating the meaning of these areas of law, including the images of certain social categories.

Functions of law

The law also has a range of functions (which are contested). The following are examples, but there may be others you can think of:

- **Preservation of power structures**. One representation of this lies in the frequently made observation that the majority of judges are white, male and middle class and come from very similar educational backgrounds (e.g. see *The Politics of the Judiciary*, J.A.G. Griffith (1997), and *English Legal System*, C. Elliott. and F. Quinn (2008), Ch. 10). Two dangers in this are, firstly, that it tends to assume that all white middle-class men will think and act the same. Secondly, it may divert attention from more subtle and insidious examples of concern to social workers, e.g. the involvement (or lack of it) of service users in legally based decisions.

- **Managing the relationship between 'the state' and 'the citizen'**. This is a fundamental matter. It takes us back to the example of Mrs. D, but also many others. It is important that you are alert to the operation of law in this key dynamic. Be sensitive to this in your own practice but also consider critically how such issues are dealt with in the mass media, for example.

- **Regulating different aspects of 'professionalism'**. The two aspects of this are:

  (a) the regulation of your personal and professional authority, in relation to your agency and its requirements

  (b) the regulation of your profession (or semi-profession) as a group, in relation to other professional groupings (doctors, lawyers, police, nurses, etc.).

  Another implicit consideration here is the idea of professional as 'expert' and the tension, which this may set up with the objectives of partnership and empowerment.

- **Solutions to social problems.** Does law solve them? Does it sometimes make them worse?

- **Shaping attitudes and behaviour**. Can law have this effect? To what extent can law influence behaviour and change attitudes; and to what extent is it a reflection, rather than progenitor, of such changes?

- **Avoidance**. It is often instructive to know what law does not exist, as well as what does. Where are the gaps?

- **Promoting political ideologies**. A good example would be the way in which community care legislation and associated policies have promoted the purchaser/provider arrangement, contained within a quite explicit approval of market philosophy.

Myths in law

Connected to these value assumptions, images and functions of law, is a number of myths. (Note that 'myth' has at least two meanings: something that is not true; and something that expresses a popular or fundamental idea, that is treated as if 'true'.)

Some examples of such myths are given below. In each case, one or more observations are made, but there are others you can probably think of.

Clarity – the law is often not clear (i.e. capable of only one construction) because there are different sources, which may be contradictory; and because ambiguous terms and phrases are used which are open to interpretation.

Helpfulness – the law often can be perceived as helpful, for example, when it protects the citizen, or secures the provision of a service. But the application of (an interpretation of) law can just as readily result in someone not receiving what they want. There will be occasions when certain people (e.g. the social security applicant whose claim is refused; the young offender who has just received a custodial sentence; someone who has just been compulsorily admitted to a psychiatric hospital; etc.) may perceive the law, in practice, to be unhelpful, or even destructive or oppressive.

Neutrality – the law is sometimes presented as being neutral, because it is said to be impersonal: it supposedly operates in the same way for everyone. Connected to this is the notion of 'blind justice'. However, two sets of objections may be raised to this:

- Firstly, some people are in a stronger position to use the law, for example, because they are richer, or because they are 'repeat players' who are more familiar with its institutions, such as courts. (Social workers would come into this second category though not the first!)

- Secondly, as well as the above procedural consideration, there is a structural one. In practice, the law does relatively little to address unequal social relations, such as those between rich and poor, men and women, black and white, etc.

Substantial powers – again, the law can often have an extremely powerful effect on people's lives. But it is just as likely to be perceived as insubstantial – an example might be that of the child who has disclosed serious abuse, from which criminal proceedings arise, only to find that the (alleged) perpetrator is acquitted for lack of evidence.

It must also be remembered that the purported power of the law is limited by scarce resources. This is a critical matter for health and social welfare services including social work, where the law may say that state agencies must take a particular action, but finite resources dictate that they cannot.

Law as 'solution' – the law is actually a very blunt and imprecise instrument. The extent to which this is so depends on legal processes, as much as on the substantive law itself. A good example is the way that the adversarial approach to conflict resolution in English law tends to draw up battle lines in divorce cases ('you did' – 'I didn't') that leaves ex-partners embittered and any children in the proceedings more hurt and bewildered than they might otherwise be.

Competent use of the law by social workers can be very creative and improve people's lives. It can also be done quite unobtrusively and through negotiation. For most of the time social workers are not using the formal institutions and mechanisms of law (such as courts, lawyers, the police, witness statements and so on) in order to provide a service.

You should develop a positive, as well as a critical, approach to the use of law. This will include being sceptical about the ability of law to solve problems – it is only one component, albeit an extremely important one, in a range of knowledge, skills and values that you will need to practise effectively.

ACTIVITY 1.3

- *There are two parts to this exercise. Do not take more than about 20 minutes to complete it. Firstly, read the text below on 'The rule of law'.*

The rule of law

As you develop in your understanding of law in practice there are many concepts that you may reflect on further, such as 'justice', 'law and order' (which are actually two different concepts), 'rights and duties', 'empowerment', etc.

Outlined below are six, generally positive, definitions of a notion that is well known to lawyers, but less so to social workers: the rule of law. However, as you read through these definitions you will see that, contained within them, there are many ideas that will be familiar to social workers. With a little extrapolation, we can see that some of the messages for social workers are that:

- *they should not act in an arbitrary fashion*
- *they should aim to treat people equally*
- *they are not above the law*
- *they should use the law in a reasonable way.*

Obviously, these statements are not straightforward: what does treating people equally mean? What is meant by the term 'reasonable'? And so on.

The two parts of the exercise are identified below.

Exercise One

Please will you:

i) *read through the definitions below*

ii) *then write down any further observations you may have about the implications of the 'rule of law' for social work practice.*

Six definitions of the rule of law are:

1. *The principle that everyone is subject to the law and no-one is above the law.*

   No man is above the law and every man is subject to the ordinary law of the realm and amenable to the jurisdiction of ordinary tribunals. (A.V. Dicey)

2. *That government should be carried out according to the law and not by arbitrary authority.*

   There is no more important principle in British constitutional law than the doctrine of legality under which the Government in all its guises must conform scrupulously to the letter of the law. (Prof. Graham Zellick)

3. *That a person should only be penalised for breaking the law and that the law should be made before punishment is inflicted.*

   No man is punishable or can be lawfully made to suffer in body or goods except for a distinct breach of law established in ordinary legal manner before ordinary courts of law. (A.V. Dicey)

continued

continued

4. *That everyone is equal before the law.*

5. *That law and order are preferable to anarchy.*

   All courts exist to uphold the law ... Without the rule of law and courts to enforce it, each one of us would be free to push and bully our fellow citizens and (which may be thought more important) our fellow citizens would be free to push and bully us. The justification for the law, the courts and the rule of law is that they protect us from unfair and oppressive actions by others; but if we are to have that protection we must ourselves accept that the law applies to us too and limits our freedom. (Sir John Donaldson in Heaton's Transport v. TGWU *(1972))*

6. *That rulers will only make laws which are normally reasonable and socially acceptable.*

   The sovereign cannot lay upon its subjects any burden not necessitated by the well being of the community. (J.J. Rousseau)

My observations about the implications for social work practice are . . .

Exercise Two

The notion of the 'rule of law' should be treated critically: a sceptical approach to rules and rule-based decisions is required.

Please will you:

i) *read through the quotation*

ii) *decide whether or not you agree with it and then note down up to three observations concerning the implications for social work practice.*

   In a community that aspires to a high order of legality obedience to law is not submissive compliance. The obligation to obey the law is closely tied to the defensibility of the rules themselves and of the official decisions that enforce them.
   (Selznick, P. (1979) Legality, in Campbell, C. and Wiles, P. (eds) Law and Society: Readings in the Sociology of Law. *London: Martin Robertson, p.141)*

The implications of this quotation for social work practice are:

1.   2.   3.

Conclusion

Law is not neutral. Within the text of the law itself (i.e. statutes, regulations, etc.) and through to implementation, value positions are revealed.

In order to avoid being a mere 'technician' and instead becoming a competent practitioner, it is essential that you reflect on the messages contained in this chapter and in the supplementary reading. In particular, you cannot treat 'law' as a separate entity from you. As a professional social worker you are directly involved in its interpretation and implementation and people are on the receiving end of what you do.

You should continue to reflect on this throughout the course and beyond. In that sense, this is not a 'conclusion', but an observation about what should be a continuing process.

Chapter 2

Interpreting rules: a domestic and a statutory example

Overview

The previous chapter has illustrated how important it is for social workers to have a sceptical approach to law and the values inherent within it. The underlying aim is the development of knowledge, values and skills, which leads towards you becoming a competent social work practitioner.

This chapter focuses on one very important skill: that of interpretation. This is a skill that we already have, at least to some extent. Even in non-legal contexts we spend a lot of time interpreting rules, regulations, codes of guidance, etc. We begin doing this as children.

In order to help you work on this skill there are two examples, with linked questions.

The two examples are:

- the case of the legalistic child
- the Malicious Communications Act 1988

Objectives

After completing the reading and exercises in this chapter, you should be able to:

- interpret the meanings of rules (and other forms of law)
- ask for legal advice on rules, etc., in a focused and informed manner
- outline how an Act of Parliament is set out, in order to find your way round it
- identify the main rules used by the courts for the interpretation of statutes
- appreciate the potential for ambiguity in the words used in Acts of Parliament
- apply the basic principles of interpretation to a statute
- apply statutory provisions to novel fact situations.

FURTHER READING

This whole book is about interpreting rules:

Twining, W. and Miers, D. (1999) *How to do Things with Rules: A Primer of Interpretation* (4th ed.). London: Butterworths (now published by Cambridge University Press)

The following two books have chapters on interpreting statutes. They are intended primarily for lawyers, so you need not concern yourself with the details:

Fox, M. and Bell, C. (1999) *Learning Legal Skills* (3rd ed.) Oxford: Oxford University Press (Ch. 3)

Holland, J. A. and Webb, J.S. (2006) *Learning Legal Rules: A Student's Guide to Legal Method and Reasoning* (6th ed.) Oxford: Oxford University Press (Ch. 8)

ACTIVITY 2.1

The case of the legalistic child

Please read through the facts of the case, and then attempt to answer some of the questions. The case is taken from Twining and Miers (1999, pp. 10–12).

Johnny, aged seven, is an only child. In recent months his mother has been mildly worried because he has developed a craving for sweet things and this has affected his appetite at meal times. She has commented to her husband, a practising lawyer, that Johnny 'seems to be developing a sweet tooth' and that 'he has been eating too much between meals', but until now she has done nothing about the problem. Then one afternoon she finds that Johnny has gone into the larder and helped himself to half a pot of strawberry jam. Bearing in mind her husband's insistence that discipline in the family should operate in accordance with the 'rule of law', she does not punish Johnny on this occasion. Instead she says, 'That's naughty. In future, you are never to enter the larder without my permission.' 'What does enter mean, Mummy?' asks Johnny. 'To go into,' says his Mother. 'OK,' says Johnny, relieved that he has got off so lightly.

Four incidents then follow in quick succession.

First, Johnny gets a broom and hooks out a pot of jam from the larder and helps himself. 'I didn't enter the larder,' he says.

Next, the cat enters the larder and attacks the salmon which mother has bought for a special meal to celebrate father's birthday. Mother, upstairs, hears Johnny hooting with laughter. She comes down to see him standing outside the larder door watching the cat eat the fish. 'I may not go into the larder,' he says.

The following day, at 5pm, another pot of strawberry jam is found in the larder – empty. It was half full at lunch time. Johnny, who was playing on his own downstairs for much of the afternoon, denies all knowledge of the matter. There is no other evidence.

Finally, without any attempt at concealment, Johnny enters the larder, eats another pot of jam and deliberately knocks down a pile of cans. 'It's as if he were asking to be punished,' sighs Mother.

Questions

Most, but not all, of the following questions have been taken from Twining and Miers (1999).

1. What do you think is meant, in this instance, by the phrase 'the rule of law'?

2. In How Lawyers Think (1937), Clarence Morris wrote: 'Problems occur in gross. The unit, which appears to be a single problem at a first glance, is usually a complex of related difficulties, a confluence of more specific problems. Often the initial urge is to dismiss the whole difficulty with some easy, impulsive solution.'

continued

continued

Explain how this quotation is relevant to the nature of the mother's problem in the story.

3. What is a rule?

4. In each of the four incidents referred to, has Johnny broken his mother's rule?

5. After the episodes concerning the larder, Father decides on a change of strategy. 'From now on,' he says, 'there will be only one rule that you must observe in this household: you must be reasonable at all times.'

> *a) Is this a rule? If so, is it a reasonable one?*
> *b) Give examples of practical problems of interpretation which might arise for*
> > *i) Johnny and*
> > *ii) his parents, under this provision*
>
> *c) Does father's 'rule' leave any outlet for Johnny's legalistic tendencies?*

6. Try to devise a rule, which you would consider will prevent the jam-eating problem. The rule should be:
- *watertight*
- *reasonable*
- *as simple as possible*

7. Johnny is watching his favourite television programme with his mother's agreement. Father, having just arrived home from work, walks into the room and without a word to Johnny, switches over to another channel on which a current affairs programme is in progress. Johnny protests, 'You can't do that.'

> *a) Is Johnny invoking a rule? If so, what rule?*
> *b) Are there any rules governing i) watching television and ii) the distribution of housework where you live? If so, state them. How do you know whether there are rules about these activities and what they are?*

Note: This case features parents who are trying to make and enforce explicit rules. However, as question 7 suggests, family rules are often implicit. It is worth reflecting on the fact that social workers are often called on, not just to interpret explicit, and usually written, rules (such as an Act of Parliament), but also what families' and individuals' rules for living are and how they make sense of them.

This can also be true for the social worker in an organisation, when you may not be quite clear what the rules are.

Statutory interpretation

Before going on to Activity 2.2, which involves interpretation of an Act of Parliament (the Malicious Communications Act 1988), there follows a brief introductory commentary.

We have seen that rules are not always capable of mechanical application. They are made up of words, which are not always clear: the words have to be interpreted before they can be applied to the situation in question. Legal rules are exactly the same. Contrary to popular belief, the law is not always clear, and legal rules have to be interpreted. This is one of the functions of the courts: they provide a definitive guide to the meaning of particular words and phrases in statutes. But those working with statutes need to be able to interpret them in order to carry out their functions properly. They cannot wait for a court to provide a ruling and have to predict how a court might interpret the words in any given Act. This is something you will have to do in consultation with your legal adviser who will be an expert in predicting how the courts will interpret particular provisions.

Fortunately, this task is not as daunting as it might at first appear. You have already carried out this activity in the case of the legalistic child: the rules devised by Johnny's parents needed interpreting and you will have done this in order to resolve the various disputes arising between Johnny and his parents over this. The courts work in a similar way. The main difference is that the courts follow certain rules as to how statutes are to be interpreted.

These rules, which are indicated below, only create a framework, which leaves a degree of latitude to individual judges as to the precise meaning of a legal provision. Statutory interpretation is thus a mixture of art and science and the interpretation of a particular provision is a matter of legitimate disagreement. Formally, the courts have the final word and you must follow their decisions.

You do not need to learn the detailed rules for the interpretation of statutes: we are not trying to turn you into experts on statutory interpretation, but rather trying to help you to understand how the law works and to use your legal adviser effectively. Your legal adviser will guide you as to the interpretation of particular provisions relevant to your work. However, it will help you in your dealings with your legal adviser to have some idea of the principles involved.

The basic principle that the courts follow in the interpretation of statutes is that they are giving effect to the will of Parliament as expressed in the words of the statute. This is easy to state but is more complex to apply in practice as Parliament does not always make its intentions clear, and in any event, the English language contains words that have more than one meaning.

The courts generally give words their ordinary English meaning in the context in which they are used unless:

- the context makes clear that the word is being used in a technical sense; or
- the word is defined or partially defined in the statute itself.

The prevailing approach to interpretation in recent years is to aim to give effect to the purpose of the statute by identifying that purpose and then interpreting the words accordingly. Again, this is easier to state than to apply.

The courts are also now under a duty to interpret statutes so as to give effect to the Convention Rights incorporated into English law by the Human Rights Act 1998 (see Chapter 13).

For a fuller discussion of these, and many other issues, see Holland and Webb (2006), ch. 8.

In the previous exercise, we used an everyday example. We now move on to an exercise based on a statute. We have chosen a statute from a field other than social work to enable you to concentrate on the principles of interpretation. When you have begun to understand this, we can go on to interpret statutes relevant to social work.

On the opposite page there is an example of an Act (the Malicious Communications Act 1988) which is reproduced in its original form and then, on the following page, an outline of how an Act is structured.

MALICIOUS COMMUNICATIONS ACT 1988

1988 CHAPTER 27

An Act to make provision for the punishment of persons who send or deliver letters or other articles for the purpose of causing distress or anxiety. [29th July 1988]

Be it enacted by the Queen's most Excellent Majesty, by and with the advice and consent of the Lords Spiritual and Temporal, and Commons, in this present Parliament assembled, and by the authority of the same, as follows:

1. – (1) Any person who sends to another person –

(a) a letter or other article which conveys –

(i) a message which is indecent or grossly offensive;

(ii) a threat; or

(iii) information which is false and known or believed to be false by the sender; or

(b) any other article which is, in whole or part, of an indecent or grossly offensive nature, is guilty of an offence if his purpose, or one of his purposes, in sending it is that it should, so far as falling within paragraph (a) or (b) above, cause distress or anxiety to the recipient or to any other person to whom he intends that it or its contents or nature should be communicated.

(2) A person is not guilty of an offence by virtue of subsection (1)(a)(ii) above if he shows –

(a) that the threat was used to reinforce a demand which he believed he had reasonable grounds for making; and

(b) that he believed that the use of the threat was a proper means of reinforcing the demand.

(3) In this section references to sending include references to delivering and to causing to be sent or delivered and 'sender' shall be construed accordingly.

(4) A person guilty of an offence under this section shall be liable on summary conviction to a fine not exceeding level 4 on the standard scale.

2.[Omitted]

3. – (1) This Act may be cited as the Malicious Communications Act 1988

(2) Section 1 above shall not come into force until the end of the period of two months beginning with the day on which this Act is passed.

(3) This Act does not extend to Scotland or, except for section 2, to Northern Ireland.

_____

(This Act is Crown copyright and is reproduced with permission.)

Structure of an Act of Parliament

Acts of Parliament have the same basic structure. Have a look at the Malicious Communications Act 1988 as an example on the previous page.

- Acts begin with a short title – in this case the Malicious Communications Act 1988.

- 1988 CHAPTER 27 means that this was the 27th Act passed in 1988.

- The sentence beginning 'An Act to make provision...' is called the long title. It gives some indication of the purpose of the Act and may be used to help the court interpret it.

- The date in square brackets – [29th July 1988] – is the date the Act was passed. Some Acts will come into force immediately. But the date an Act is passed is not necessarily the date the Act comes into force. The Malicious Communications Act 1988 came into force two months after it was passed: see s.3 (2). Can you suggest reasons for this? Another example would be most of the community care provisions of the National Health Service and Community Care Act 1990, which did not come fully into force until 1993: can you suggest some reasons for this?

Some Acts come into force in stages, such as the Children Act 1989. Some parts of particular Acts might never come into force: for example, certain sections of the Children and Young Persons Act 1969 were never actually implemented.

- Acts are divided into sections, which are further divided into subsections, which in turn are divided into paragraphs and sub-paragraphs. The Malicious Communications Act 1988 begins with section 1, subsection (1), paragraph (a), sub-paragraph (i).

There is a shorter way of putting this. When referring to this bit of the Act, you would simply write s.1 (1)(a)(i). Please adhere to this convention when citing legislation.

The Malicious Communications Act 1988 is a short statute. Longer Acts are divided into parts, e.g. the Children Act 1989. Each part groups together related provisions of the Act. It makes it easier to find your way round the Act if it is divided in this way. Each part of the Act is divided into sections, as above.

Longer Acts also have schedules. These are printed at the end of the Act. They are generally used to provide detail relating to more general powers and duties in the Act: e.g. s.35 of the Children Act 1989 gives a general outline of supervision orders; Schedule 3 gives more detail about requirements for the order, duration, etc.

Schedules are also used to indicate which legislation has been amended or repealed by the Act.

- The Act indicates in which parts of the United Kingdom it applies. To which countries does the Malicious Communications Act 1988 extend?

- Acts may contain a provision giving a definition of particular terms used in the Act. This may be a complete definition or a partial definition. Look at s.1 (3) of the Malicious Communications Act 1988. What is the effect of this provision?

There may seem to be a lot to learn here but, as all Acts are structured in the same basic way, the more you look at them, the more familiar you will become with their general features: don't worry if it seems a bit complicated at first.

ACTIVITY 2.2

The Malicious Communications Act 1988

Read the Malicious Communications Act 1988 and consider whether an offence under s.1 is committed in the following circumstances:

a. *Alan writes a letter to Barry which says: 'If you ever come near my house again, I will kill you.' Would your answer differ if Alan had spoken these words to Barry over the telephone?*

b. *Colin posts some excrement through the letterbox of his local councillor.*

c. *Diane, an animal rights activist, throws a firebomb at the front door of a research scientist involved in animal experiments, which Diane regards as cruel.*

d. *Eric writes to Felicity falsely stating 'Your mother is dead'.*

e. *Geraldine writes to Helen falsely stating that Helen's husband is having an affair with Irene. Geraldine thinks Helen will find this funny. She does not.*

f. *James writes to Karen, whose husband was killed recently in a much publicised industrial accident. 'You should be well satisfied, having got all that insurance money, your freedom and the chance to find yourself a new man.'*

g. *Mother, Daughter and Co., a firm of solicitors, write a letter to Linda saying: 'Unless you pay within 14 days the £500 owed to our client, a debt for which you admit you are liable, we will commence legal proceedings against you.'*

h. *Nigel, a landlord, writes to Oliver, his tenant, saying: 'If you don't pay your rent soon, you'll be in hospital for a very long time.'*

i. *Pat, a postal delivery worker, delivers a package to Quentin containing a video showing scenes of horrific violence. Quentin has not ordered this video, although it is addressed to him. Pat does not know of the contents of the package.*

j. *Your newsagent inadvertently delivers copies of the Sun, Playboy and Playgirl to your house. Would your answer differ if the newsagent had done this in order to embarrass you?*

Chapter 3
The English legal system

Overview

As you progress through this text you will acquire a great deal of knowledge about the English legal system. You will need this information for a number of reasons:

i)   You will need to have some knowledge and understanding about the legal system in order to understand the substantive law you will encounter and in order to appreciate the importance of procedure in the operation of the system.

ii) You will need to become familiar with the system, its procedures and the concepts it uses in order to function effectively as a social work practitioner with a variety of roles within the system.

iii) You will need to understand how the system works in order to help service users who come into contact with the law and legal process.

You will acquire this knowledge and understanding in a variety of ways. We do not expect you to sit down and learn vast chunks of the textbooks. This is tedious and not very productive as a form of learning. You can start by reading the textbooks and keep revisiting the relevant chapters: this will help you to become familiar with basic concepts. You can look up an individual point in a textbook or in a reference book. Your aim should be to understand the system within which you have to work. Much of the knowledge you acquire will not arise directly in your practice, but underlies the substantive law and processes which you will encounter and is necessary for your understanding of these matters. This includes knowing about the roles of other professionals within the system in order to be able to relate to them effectively.

The purpose of this chapter is to identify certain basic features of the legal system you should know about.

Identified below are those aspects of the English legal system which we consider are essential for you to know, and which you may come across in your dealings with the courts and other legal settings.

The following key areas are briefly discussed:

•   law in the United Kingdom

•   the sources of law

•   precedent

•   the differences between criminal and civil law

•   the difference between public and private law

•   burden and standards of proof

- alternative forms of dispute resolution.

Law in the United Kingdom

You will have noticed that the title of this chapter is 'the English legal system', this is because there are three separate, different legal systems in the UK – for England and Wales; Scotland; and Northern Ireland. Different legislation will usually apply to each part – for example, there is equivalent but not identical legislation to the Children Act 1989 in Scotland and Northern Ireland.

To add further complexity, there are different organisational structures in the four countries of the UK. In England and Wales what were once 'social services' departments, have split into 'adult services' and 'children and families services'; in addition, adult services particularly have 'commissioning teams' and 'provider teams'. In Scotland, social work is organised through social work departments which combine the functions of local authority social workers and probation officers. In Northern Ireland there are health and social services boards which combine the functions of local authority social services and health trusts. As can be seen from this, the boundaries between social work and other major organisational systems, such as health services and the criminal justice system, depend partly on which country you are in.

The sources of law

It is important to remember that law comes from clearly defined sources. Anything which does not fall within one of the recognised categories of law is not law. You therefore need to distinguish between law and non-law.

The sources of law also fall into a clear ranking order. Starting with the most authoritative they are:

1. European Union law

2. Acts of Parliament

3. Equity

4. Common law.

We can now briefly consider each in turn. The two you are most likely to encounter in social work practice are Acts of Parliament and common law, but it is as well to be aware of the others also.

European Union law

By virtue of the European Communities Act 1972 (as amended), if any law of any member state (the United Kingdom is, of course, a member state) is inconsistent with European Union law (as it now is), then European Union law prevails.

Although you are, at present, unlikely to encounter EU law much in practice, the EU is becoming increasingly concerned with matters of social policy and EU law may become more significant in social work practice in the future.

EU law is not the only European influence on UK law. You should also be aware and have outline knowledge of the European Convention on Human Rights. This has become (even) more important with the implementation of the Human Rights Act 1998 (see Chapter 13). The

European Union is a separate regime from that relating to the European Convention on Human Rights. Be careful not to confuse them.

Acts of Parliament

Acts of Parliament, also called statutes, are the most important modern source of law affecting social work practice. Virtually all areas of your practice are governed by statute and are subject to change by statute. As you will be only too aware, Parliament can change the law and cannot be bound by the actions of its predecessors.

An Act of Parliament starts life as a Bill. Bills may be classified according to type into:

Public Bills – these are of general application to the country as a whole.

Private Bills – these apply to a particular location, industry or project (such as the Channel Tunnel Rail Link Bill which became the Channel Tunnel Rail Link Act 1996).

Bills may also be classified according to the way in which they are introduced into Parliament:

Government Bills – these are Bills introduced by the Government and may be to implement manifesto commitments, manage the economy (there is an annual Finance Bill), promote desirable changes or respond to events.

Private Member's Bills – these are Bills introduced by an individual Member of Parliament and often deal with controversial issues of morality or social policy. Unless the government makes time available for a Private Member's Bill, it is unlikely to become law. The government always gives the majority of parliamentary time to its own Bills and the time available for Private Member's Bills is consequently very small.

A Public Bill may therefore be either a Government Bill or a Private Member's Bill. Do not confuse the classification.

It is useful to understand how a Bill becomes an Act of Parliament. In outline, the Public Bill procedure is as follows:

• Introduction and First Reading	Normally, but not necessarily, in the House of Commons – a Bill may also start in the House of Lords Introduced by Minister or Member
• Second Reading	Debate on principles of Bill
• Committee Stage	Bill examined in detail by Standing Committee
• Report Stage	Bill, as amended by Committee, reported back to House
• Third Reading	Debate on amended Bill, minor alterations possible.

The Bill then goes to 'the other House' (the House of Lords), where it goes through the same stages. In the House of Lords, the Committee Stage is normally dealt with by the whole House.

Once it has been through both Houses and the House of Commons has considered and agreed any amendments made by the House of Lords, the Bill is presented for Royal Assent.

When a Bill receives the Royal Assent, it becomes an Act and the parts into which it is divided, called clauses and subclauses when it is a Bill, are now known as sections and subsections.

Notes

1. The introduction of the Bill may have been preceded by the publication of a Green Paper, (now usually called a consultation paper), a document setting out the issues and inviting responses from the public and/or a White Paper, which will contain firmer legislative proposals (for example, there are references to Green Papers and White Papers on mental health law reform in Section 8). These documents are neither part of the Bill nor part of the formal Bill procedure and in many cases will not be published at all.

   More recently, a practice has been adopted in some instances of publishing a draft Bill, inviting comments before it is introduced into Parliament. The Mental Capacity Act 2005 started in this way.

2. Under the terms of the Parliament Acts 1911 and 1949, a Bill may, if certain conditions are satisfied, be presented for the Royal Assent, even though it has not been passed through the House of Lords. The Hunting Act 2004 was passed in this way.

Delegated legislation

Many statutes, and particularly those relating to social welfare, contain a power enabling a named individual, usually the Secretary of State, or a named organisation, such as a local authority, to make delegated legislation. Delegated legislation takes many forms, including statutory instruments and bylaws. Delegated legislation has the full force of law but can be challenged in the courts if it has been made other than in accordance with the statute giving the power for it to be made.

For social work, this delegated legislation is usually set out in the form of regulations; for example, there are regulations concerning the reviews of Looked After Children, on charging for residential accommodation for older people, and on the conduct of mental health review tribunals. It is important to stress that these regulations have the full force of the law.

Equity

The principles of equity arose to supplement the common law, which, in the 15th and 16th centuries, became incapable of remedying its own deficiencies. Its main contributions have been the trust and remedies such as the injunction. Equitable remedies are always discretionary and are granted or refused on the basis of the court's assessment of the circumstances of the case. In the early 17th century, it was established that in the event of a conflict between equity and the common law, equity would prevail. This rule is now enshrined in statute: see s.49 Supreme Court Act 1981.

You are not likely to encounter the principles of equity in social work practice.

Common law

Historically, this was the law developed by the Normans which was common to the whole country and superseded the regional laws of the Saxon kings. It is the law developed by the courts and was, until the 20th century, how most legal change occurred. In modern times, however, the number of statutes passed every year has diminished the scope for dramatic change through the common law, though it continues to develop incrementally through the decisions of the higher courts. The common law may be superseded by statute or EU law and, in the event of a conflict between the common law and equity, equity prevails.

The common law remains particularly important in relation to areas such as tort and contract.

Precedent

The idea of precedent, that is, that like cases should be treated alike, is commonplace and is something we encounter in everyday life. In the context of the law, it is a more formal matter with certain rules governing its operation.

The basic rule is that lower courts must follow the decisions of the higher courts in cases which are, in all material respects, the same. The operation of precedent, or *stare decisis* (roughly translated as 'the decision is to stand') depends on being able to find out what the higher courts have decided and on a clear system of courts in a defined relationship to each other.

The first of these is satisfied by the existence of law reports – accounts of decisions of the higher courts appearing regularly. The second was regularised in the late 19th century by the Judicature Acts 1873–75 and again under the Courts Act 1971. A diagram outlining the court structures is given in Figure 3.1. Essentially, courts are bound to follow decisions made by courts higher up the hierarchy. Thus, for example, decisions of the House of Lords bind all the courts below it in the system.

A precedent is created by the application of certain rules of law to a set of facts. Although the same facts will never recur exactly, we would expect a court encountering a situation which is materially the same, to reach the same conclusion as the previous court. This is what, in effect, the idea of precedent requires and all the courts have done is to formalise the system.

Courts create precedents in two situations:

- By developing the common law. This occurs either by creating new law where none exists or by developing existing law to meet new situations.

- By interpreting statutes. This occurs where the court rules on the meaning of the words in a particular statute. This then creates a precedent on the interpretation of that provision which has to be followed by courts lower down the system.

The system of precedent has certain advantages:

- it creates certainty, as it is dependent on rules which limit the scope for inconsistent decisions by different judges, which in turn means

- it enables lawyers to predict how a certain situation would be resolved if it went to court, thus allowing lawyers and others to administer the law without having to go to court, save in exceptional situations where a dispute arises

- it accords with the expectations of most people

- it has scope for steady growth by allowing courts to develop the law on the basis of material differences between cases.

On the other hand, there are certain disadvantages:

- it can be very rigid

- it tends toward technicality and complexity

- it can leave the law dependent on outdated decisions which are not in line with modern thinking.

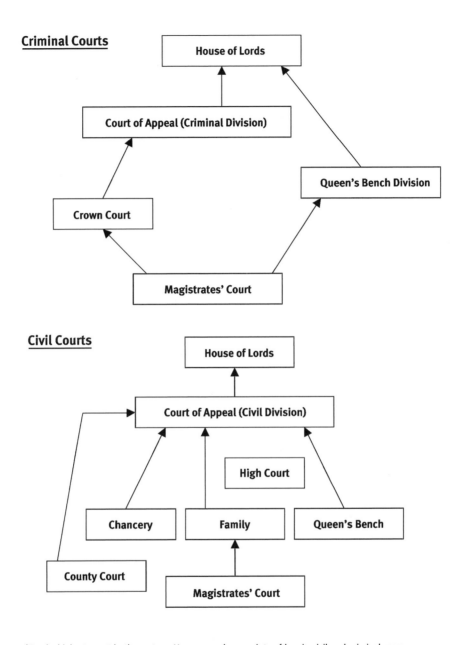

Criminal Courts

Civil Courts

House of Lords: highest court in the system. Hears appeals on points of law in civil and criminal cases.

Court of Appeal (Civil Division): hears appeals from the High Court and County Court in civil cases

Court of Appeal (Criminal Division): hears appeals against conviction and/or sentence from the Crown Court

High Court: in three divisions

– Chancery Division: hears civil cases involving land, trusts, companies, partnerships and tax

– Family Division: hears civil cases involving family matters and matters relating to children. Sits as a Divisional Court to hear appeals from magistrates' courts on family matters.

– Queen's Bench Division: hears civil cases involving contracts, torts and commercial matters. Also contains the Administrative court, which hears cases of judicial review. Sits as a Divisional Court to hear appeals from the magistrates' court in criminal cases by way of case stated.

Figure 3.1.Structure of civil and criminal courts

A court is a 'public authority' for the purposes of the Human Rights Act 1998 (s.6) (for an overview of the Human Rights Act 1998 see Chapter 13). This means that the courts must make their judgements in such a way as to be compatible with the Convention Articles contained in the Human Rights Act 1998. They must also ensure that the decisions of other public authorities (including social work agencies) that came before them are also interpreted in the light of the Convention Articles.

This means that, since the implementation of the Act in October 2000, the courts cannot simply rely on the old doctrine of precedent; they must not only look back on the past decisions of the higher courts, and treat like cases alike; they must also ensure Convention compliance.

> *Do you think, on balance, that the advantages of precedent outweigh the disadvantages?*

The differences between criminal law and civil law

Law can be classified into two categories:

- Criminal law – a crime is an offence against the state and punishable by the state, e.g. theft, murder.

- Civil law – this governs the rights and duties of individuals towards each other.

For example:

law of contract (deals with the legal effects of agreements made between individuals)

law of tort (torts are civil wrongs e.g. negligence, nuisance, defamation)

law of property (law relating to land and goods)

family law.

Table 3.1 gives, in outline, some of the basic differences between civil and criminal law.

Table 3.1 Basic differences between civil and criminal Law

	Criminal	**Civil**
Parties	Crown Defendant/Accused	Various: Claimant (formerly Plaintiff), Defendant, Complainant, Respondent, Applicant, Petitioner (Some of these terms, such as 'plaintiff' have been discarded as a result of the 1999 'Woolf' reforms of civil procedures: 'claimant' is now the preferred term.)
	R v Jones	Smith v Jones
Trial	Magistrates; Judge and Jury	Judge
Courts	Magistrates; Crown Court	County Court; High Court
Proof	Beyond reasonable doubt	Balance of probabilities
Outcome	Guilty/not guilty	liable/not liable
If case proved	Punishment	damages; equitable remedy; order

The difference between public and private law

The boundary between these two areas of law is a complicated one but essentially private law is to do with the relationship between private citizens and public law is to do with the relationship between the state (which would include social work agencies) and the citizen. An important example of a statute which includes both of these elements is the Children Act 1989. This allows the local authority to accommodate children in need, and to request the courts to make Emergency Protection Orders and Care Orders; thus the state intervenes to fundamentally affect the relationship between parents and children (this is an example of public law). The Act also empowers the courts to make Section 8 orders (residence orders, specific issues orders, contact orders and prohibited steps orders) which regulate the relationship between parents, and between parents and children (this is an example of private law).

Burden and standard of proof

Burden of proof

The phrase 'burden of proof' is often confused with 'standard of proof'. Burden of proof simply means that whoever is bringing the case has a responsibility of proving that case. For example, in care proceedings (which are civil proceedings) the local authority bringing the case has to prove that there are grounds 'on the balance of probabilities' to justify a care order (or whatever order is being requested); this proof will revolve around the very important concept of 'significant harm'. It is not for the parents/carers to prove that they have not been abusive or neglectful, or whatever is at issue.

On the other hand, in criminal proceedings it is for the prosecuting solicitor or barrister from the Crown Prosecution Service (CPS) to prove 'beyond reasonable doubt' that the defendant has committed the alleged offence(s). It is not for the defendant to prove that s/he did not commit the offence(s) – that is, the defendant is innocent until proved guilty.

Standard of proof

It is extremely important for social workers, especially those commonly involved in court proceedings, to understand the difference between civil and criminal procedures. Many of these differences are indicated above.

One very important distinction is that different standards of proof apply. In civil proceedings the court makes its decisions based on the 'balance of probabilities', meaning 'is it more likely than not?' In criminal proceedings, the court applies the more demanding standard of 'beyond reasonable doubt'.

This can lead to what appear to be anomalies. Someone may be involved in connected sets of civil and criminal proceedings (the example of child abuse is a common one) and have a decision made in civil proceedings that seems to imply 'guilty' (e.g. his/her child being made subject of a Care Order). However, in subsequent criminal proceedings, the person concerned may not be found guilty, because of the higher standard of proof that applies.

Alternative forms of dispute resolution (ADR)

Courts are not the only means of resolving legal disputes. There are alternative forms of dispute resolution (ADR). A defining feature of ADR is that it tends to be less adversarial than courts; this should not be taken as a definitive statement, though. Tribunals are probably one of the best known forms and can display adversarial characteristics. Mediation is another – at one point it was intended that all divorcing couples with children should go through a process of mediation involving a third party from a welfare services agency, but Part II of the Family Law Act 1996, which dealt with this, was never implemented.

Social workers need to make themselves aware of ADR because they may become involved in them. All of them to some degree involve the skill of negotiation, which is a central characteristic of social work.

The major forms of ADR are :

1. tribunals

2. inquiries

3. arbitration

4. mediation

5. conciliation

6. negotiation.

Find out what each involves. To what types of dispute does each of these methods seem most suited?

This brings us to the end of Chapter 3. It contains only a very brief summary of just a few key features of the English legal system. It does not deal in any detail with the hierarchical structure of the courts, nor with their various functions. It doesn't identify legal personnel. As you become more familiar with how the legal system and the courts operate, you will need to refer to the standard social work law texts and text on the English legal system itself.

FURTHER READING

Reading on the English legal system (ELS) is contained in the two standard social work law texts:

Brammer (2009) *Social Work Law* (3rd ed.) Harlow: Longman.

Brayne and Carr (2008) *Law for Social Workers* (10th ed.) Oxford: Oxford University Press.

There are scores of textbooks on the ELS. Three good examples are:

Elliott, C. and Quinn, F. (2008) *English Legal System* (9th ed.). Harlow: Pearson Longman

Partington, M. (2008) *Introduction to the English Legal System* (4th ed.). Oxford: Oxford University Press

Slapper, G. and Kelly, D. (2009) *The English Legal System* (9th ed.). London: Routledge-Cavendish.

There are also numerous law dictionaries which can help you by defining key terms. Two examples are:

Martin, E.A. and Law, J. (ed.) (2009) *A Dictionary of Law.* (7th ed.) Oxford: Oxford University Press

Stewart, W. (2006) *Collins Internet-Linked Dictionary of Law* (3rd ed.). London: Collins

Chapter 4
Children's legislation: principles of law and practice

The Children Act 1989

NB There is a persistent tendency, on the part of students and others, to refer to this legislation as the Children's Act. It is not – it is the Children Act. Accurate reference to all legislation is expected.

Overview

Having looked at the skill of interpretation, including interpreting statutes, we now turn to a major piece of social work legislation: the Children Act 1989.

For child care social workers, this is the principal piece of legislation and you must develop a detailed knowledge of it. All social workers should have some understanding of it, as well as the Mental Health Act 1983 and the range of legislation linked to the NHS and Community Care Act 1990.

The 1989 Act has recently been amended and extended by the Children Act 2004 and the Children and Young Persons Act 2008, which is gradually coming into force. The changes in the 2004 Act are mainly of an administrative nature, with the aim of giving better effect to the principles enshrined in the 1989 Act. The substantive law in the 1989 Act, described below, remains largely unaltered. The 2004 Act establishes a Children's Commissioner for each of the constituent parts of the UK and extends the duties of local authorities with regard to children and young persons, especially with regard to inter-agency cooperation. It also establishes statutory Local Safeguarding Children Boards to replace Area Child Protection Committees. It makes some detailed amendments which are noted at appropriate points in the following pages. Other measures, such as the Safeguarding Vulnerable Groups Act 2006, seek to add further protection for children, supplementing the provisions in the Children Act.

The Children and Young Persons Act 2008 also makes a number of amendments, largely administrative, to the Children Acts 1989 and 2004. It allows local authorities to delegate certain functions to other regulated providers and extends the regime relating to looked after children. A significant series of amendments to the Children Act 1989 seek to improve child protection by making the system operate more effectively with a view to preventing the recurrence of tragedies such as the death of Victoria Climbié. A positive duty to promote the well-being of children and young persons is placed on the Secretary of State by s.7, which also provides him with powers to give effect to this.

Ministerial responsibility for children has, from June 2007, been consolidated in the Department for Children, Schools and Families **www.dcsf.gov.uk**.

We have chosen to begin with the Children Act 1989 as the first area of substantive law because contained within it are certain key principles, which are, in effect, a guide to its interpretation and operation.

The information in this section is only a summary of the Children Act. It is not to be taken as a definitive statement.

As with all the subsequent sections on substantive law, this material is not intended as a substitute for referring directly to the Act itself and associated policy guidance, regulations, codes of practice, etc.

Objectives

It is extremely important that you undertake some background reading, and advice on this is given below. However, having simply read through this section, you should be able to:

• state the operating principles of the Children Act 1989

• outline the content of the Act

• distinguish between voluntary and compulsory (i.e. court-related) measures in the Act

• find out more information about the Children Acts 1989 and 2004.

ESSENTIAL READING

The literature on the Children Act and related matters is vast and growing, though some of it is now rather dated. Below is a representative sample:

i) Coverage of the Children Act and related child care matters is to be found in **Brammer** (2009) and in **Brayne and Carr** (2008)
   Also see:
   Ball and McDonald (2002) (Chs 5–10)
   Johns (2007)

ii) Particularly for those in childcare social work, it is essential to have access to one of the Children Act manuals, which contain the text of the Act, plus a commentary. Some of the older texts are good on the principles of the 1989 Act, but do not reflect the 15 years of the operation of the Act in practice and its associated case law. The more recent texts are the most reliable. An example is **White, R., Carr, P. and Lowe, N.** (2002) *The Children Act in Practice* (3rd ed.). London: Lexis Nexis

iii) In addition to the Act itself there is a series of 'Guidance and Regulations'. They are essential reading for a proper understanding of the operation of the Act. The Regulations, some of which are in the form of statutory instruments, are at the end of some of these volumes and have equal importance to the primary legislation.

An example of a full citation for each volume is as follows:

Department of Health (1991) *The Children Act 1989: Guidance and Regulations* (Vol. I), Court Orders, London: HMSO. (HMSO has since been renamed as The Stationery Office – TSO)

The volumes are:
Vol. I   Court Orders
Vol. II   Family Support, Day Care and Educational Provision for Young Children
Vol. III   Family Placements
Vol. IV   Residential Care

Vol. V   Independent Schools

Vol. VI   Children with Disabilities

Vol. VII Guardians ad Litem and other Court Related Issues

Vol. VIII Private Fostering and Miscellaneous

Vol. IX Adoption

Background on the Act

FURTHER READING

Further material about the background to the implementation of the Act is contained in the following:

Brent, London Borough of (1985) *A Child in Trust* (Jasmine Beckford Report). London: Brent LBC

Butler-Sloss, L. J. (1988) *Report to Inquiry into Child Abuse in Cleveland,* Cm 412. London: HMSO.

DHSS (1985) *Review of Child Care Law.* London: HMSO

DHSS (1987) *The Law on Child Care and Family Services* (White Paper, Cm 62). London: HMSO.

Gillick v W Norfolk and Wisbech Area Health Authority [1986] 1 AC 112 (relates to question of informed consent).

Greenwich, L.B. of (1987) *A Child in Mind* (Kimberley Carlile Report). London: Greenwich LBC

House of Commons (1984) *Children in Care* (The Short Report). London: HMSO

Lambeth, L. B. of (1987) *Whose Child?* (Tyra Henry Report). London: Lambeth LBC

Department of Health and Home Office (2003) *The Victoria Climbié Inquiry Report* (The Laming Report), Cm 5730. London: TSO

HM Treasury (2003) *Every Child Matters* (Green Paper), Cm 5860. London: TSO

House of Commons (2004). *The Bichard Inquiry Report* (The Soham murders), HC 653. London: TSO

Department for Education and Skills (2006a) *Care Matters: Transforming the Lives of Children* (Green Paper) CMB932. London: TSO.

Department for Education and Skills (2006b) *Working Together to Safeguard Children.* London: TSO.

Department for Children, Schools and Families (2007) *Care Matters: Time for Change* (White Paper), CM7137. London: TSO.

The following two texts are ancillary volumes, published before the implementation of the Act itself. They are extremely useful in providing an overview of the philosophy and general aims of the Act, but are not to be taken as definitive statements of law, particularly because the Children Act has now been operating (and therefore, interpreted) for several years since they were published.

Department of Health (1989) *An Introduction to the Children Act 1989.* London: HMSO

Department of Health (1989) *The Care of Children: Principles and Practice in Regulations and Guidance.* London: HMSO

The Department of Health publishes what were (initially) annual reports on the implementation of the Act:

Department of Health (1993) *Children Act Report 1992,* Cm 2144. London: HMSO

Department of Health (1994) *Children Act Report 1993,* Cm 2584. London: HMSO

Department of Health (1995) *Children Act Report 1994,* Cm 2878. London: HMSO

Department of Health (2000) *Children Act Report 1995–1999,* Cm 4579. London: TSO

Department of Health (2001) *Children Act Report 2000.* London: TSO

Department of Health (2002) *Children Act Report 2001*. London: TSO

The above are very important sources of information. The 1992 and 1993 Reports include references in the appendix to Department of Health sponsored childcare research programmes. The 1994 Report is a much slimmer volume and does not. The 2001 Report (obviously) indicates more recent trends, but the earlier Reports should not be disregarded.

A copy of the 2001 Report can be found at **www.dh.gov.uk/assetRoot/04/06/08/13/ 04060813.pdf**

In addition, the Children Act Advisory Committee, established in 1991, has published reports on:

- the work of the magistrates' and county courts and other court-related matters such as the appointment of guardians *ad litem*; and

- cooperation between different agencies involved in family proceedings.

The committee was disbanded in July 1997 and its work taken over by a sub-committee of the Advisory Board on Family Law, which was set up to monitor implementation of the Family Law Act 1996.

Practice-related introductions to the Children Act

There are now several books offering practice-related introductions to the Children Act. Here are three examples. (Ryan 1999 is particularly recommended as giving a clear overview of the content and operation of the Children Act):

Allen, N. (2005) *Making Sense of the Children Act 1989* (4th ed.). Chichester: John Wiley

Herbert, M. (1993) *Working with Children and the Children Act: A Practical Guide for the Helping Professionals*. Leicester: BPS Books

Ryan, M. (1999) *The Children Act 1989: Putting it into Practice* (2nd ed.). Aldershot: Ashgate

Allen provides a general introduction and is recommended for those with little or no knowledge of the Act. Ryan (1999) gives more detailed accounts and follows the components of legislation quite closely; Herbert (1993) (written by a psychologist rather than a lawyer) is less concerned with the detail of the Act and focuses instead on its implications in relation to child development and childcare work.

There are also several contributions relevant to childcare law and practice in the following strongly recommended text:

Cull, L. A. and Roche, J. (eds) (2001) *The Law and Social Work: Contemporary Issues for Practice*. Basingstoke: Palgrave

Other texts

There are several other texts which may not have 'Children Act' in the title, but which do refer to it, as well as related legislation. A couple of examples are:

Bainham, A. (2005) *Children – The Modern Law* (3rd ed.). Bristol: Family Law

Hoggett, B. (2006) *Hoggett: Parents and Children* (5th ed.). London: Sweet and Maxwell

Also available, for reference only, is the following looseleaf text, which is the major general reference work concerning children's legislation.

Hall, W.C. (1991) *Clarke Hall and Morrison on Children.* London: Lexis Nexis Butterworths (updated regularly)

You should also be aware of the following, which is a looseleaf encyclopaedia on childcare and other social work law. You will find it useful for reference.

Jones, R. M. (ed.) (1993) *Encyclopaedia of Social Services and Child Care Law*. London: Sweet and Maxwell (updated regularly)

Journals

Note that journal articles are a good way of keeping up with recent developments. Useful examples are:

- *British Journal of Social Work*
- *Child and Family Social Work*
- *Children and Society*
- *Journal of Social Welfare and Family Law*
- *Practice: Social Work in Action.*

Children's Services Plans

Local authorities have been required (since 1996) to publish Children's Services Plans. These are usually published annually, on a three-year planning cycle. This is a collaborative inter-agency process involving the social services and education departments, the health authority, police, voluntary agencies and others. (See Schedule 2, para 1A of the Children Act inserted by the Children Act 1989 (Amendment) (Children's Services Planning) Order 1990, S1 1996/785). Under s.17 Children Act 2004 these will be replaced with a new publication requirement which will include not only the former Children's Services Plans but also other education and early development plans. The contents of the new Children and Young People's Plans was specified by Regulations. Responsibility for Children's Social Services transferred from the Department of Health to the Department for Education and Skills and subsequently to the Department for Children, Schools and Families in 2007.

The remainder of this chapter consists of the following:

- Sources of information
- Developing law, policy and practice
- The scope and structure of the Children Act 1989
- Principles of the Children Act 1989
- The notion of 'parental responsibility'
- The distinction between voluntary and compulsory measures
- Key components of Part III of the Act
- Key components of Parts IV and V of the Act
- Two case studies.

Sources of information

Obviously, the reading list for this chapter gives some indication of sources, but the intention here is simply to categorise them into six groups:

1. Primary legislation: that is, the Children Act itself. This is the starting point of all interpretations of policy and practice, so make sure you do refer to it and that the version you have is up to date.

2. Secondary legislation: usually in the form of regulations e.g. the Review of Children's Cases Regulations 1991. These are usually to be found in one of the volumes of Guidance and Regulations (see under Essential Reading).

3. Government guidance and circulars.

4. Codes of practice.

5. Commentaries (see reading list). Many of these contain the full text of the Act, plus a discussion.

6. Books and journals (the latter are often more up to date, because of longer publication delays with books).

7. There are many agencies providing advice, information and material, on the Children Act (and children's services generally) but a key one is:
   The Children's Legal Centre
   University of Essex
   Wivenhoe Park
   Colchester
   Essex
   CO4 3SQ
   Tel: 01206 877910
   Website: **www.childrenslegalcentre.com**

Developing law, policy and practice

The Children Act 1989 was implemented in October 1991. It has had more than a decade in which to develop in practice and many changes have taken place over this period. Some of these changes affect social work generally – and not just childcare social work – for example increasing regulation, fragmentation and specialisation.

Some of the most relevant changes for childcare social work that influence the development of the Children Act, are as follows:

- The 'refocusing debate': this is concerned with the efforts to move 'child protection' away from investigation, 'policing' and surveillance and towards a softer approach – in effect, trying to use the compulsory powers in Parts IV and V of the Act as little as possible and instead use the supportive powers (which do not involve the courts) in Part III.

- The 'Quality Protects' programme. The Department of Health has been, increasingly rigorously, identifying and enforcing standards of practice for local authorities and other agencies. Standards are, or will be, set, for example concerning services to looked-after children; services for children with disabilities; the use of child protection conferences and registers; foster carer recruitment; after-care services, etc. (See Department of Health (1998) Quality Protects Circular: *Transforming Children's Services*, LAC (98)20.) This function has now been taken over by the Department for Education and Skills.

- The 'LACS' programme concerning 'looked-after children', i.e. those 'accommodated' and 'in care'. There are now more clearly structured processes (and numerous forms) for providing basic initial information on looked-after children and for developing action plans and reviewing progress. This is based on Department of Health and others' research (e.g. see Ward, H. (ed.) (1995) *Looking After Children: Research into Practice – The Second Report of the Department of Health on Assessing Outcomes in Child Care*, HMSO).

- The new framework for the assessment of 'children in need'. This links to the Quality Protects initiative and is an attempt to clarify and structure social work assessments of disadvantaged and vulnerable children. It supersedes the so-called 'Orange Book' (Department of Health (1988) *Protecting Children: A Guide for Social Workers undertaking a comprehensive assessment*), and has been incorporated into the government guidance on protecting children from harm (see Department for Education and Skills (2006) *Working Together to Safeguard Children,* TSO).

  This new framework was first published in March 2000. For further information see Department of Health et al. (2000) *Framework for the Assessment of Children in Need and their Families*, TSO. Also see the associated Practice Guidance (Department of Health, 2000).

- The establishment in April 2001, of the Children and Family Court Advisory and Support Service (CAFCASS) (on the basis of Chapter II of the Criminal Justice and Court Services Act 2000). This amalgamates the roles and tasks of three groups:

  - the court welfare service arm of the Probation Service

  - the guardian *ad litem* and reporting officer (GALRO) panels

  - the children's division of the Official Solicitor's Office.

Guardians *ad litem* – whose job is to protect children's interests during court proceedings – are now known as children's guardians.

- New legislation has been passed, which builds on the implementation of the Children Act. Some examples are:

  Family Law Act 1996
  Human Rights Act 1998
  Protection of Children Act 1999
  Youth Justice and Criminal Evidence Act 1999
  Carers and Disabled Children Act 2000
  Care Standards Act 2000
  Children (Leaving Care) Act 2000
  Criminal Justice and Court Services Act 2000
  Adoption and Children Act 2002
  Children Act 2004
  Children and Adoption Act 2006
  Childcare Act 2006
  Safeguarding Vulnerable Groups Act 2006
  Children and Young Persons Act 2008.

- The death of Victoria Climbié in February 2000 led to an inquiry (one of the most detailed in a depressingly long series of child abuse inquiries) which made a number of recommendations concerning child protection services.

See: Department of Health/Home Office (2003), *The Victoria Climbié Inquiry: Report of an Inquiry by Lord Laming,* Cm. 5730. TSO.

- A Green Paper *Every Child Matters* was published in Autumn 2003. A central concern of this important government document is the social exclusion of children. It therefore includes reference to failings in the child protection system, but also to the need for reforms to the youth justice system, to increasing investment in child and adolescent mental health services (CAMHS), to tackling family homelessness, and to building on the Sure Start programme by creating Sure Start Children's Centres in each of the 20 per cent most deprived neighbourhoods.

  This can only be a brief summary of the Green Paper's content. For further information see:

  HM Treasury (2003) *Every Child Matters,* Cm.5860. TSO
  Also see **www.everychildmatters.gov.uk**
  The Children Act 2004 implements many of the recommendations in this Green Paper.

- The protocol for Judicial Case Management in Public Law Children Act Cases was implemented nationally on 1 November 2003. It is a vital document, especially for those involved in care proceedings and other child-related court proceedings. The core concern of the Protocol is to reduce delays in court hearings but also to ensure fairness and that the child's voice is heard.

  The Protocol was published by the Family Policy Division of the Lord Chancellor's Department (now the Ministry of Justice). The document can be accessed at: **www.hmcourts-service.gov.uk/docs/protocol-complete.pdf**

- The Bichard Inquiry (see reading list for details) into the Soham murders looked at how child protection and information management and exchange could be improved. A series of initiatives is being considered and implemented in an effort to prevent a recurrence of this particular tragedy.

- The Children Act 2004 establishes the Children's Commissioner for England to promote awareness of the views and interests of children. The Commissioner is charged with a particular concern with the views and interests of children relating to aspects of their well being, identified in s.2(3) as:

  a) physical and mental health and emotional well-being

  b) protection from harm and neglect

  c) education, training and recreation

  d) the contribution made by them to society.

- The Childcare Act 2006 creates new duties for local authorities in relation to young children. Authorities must:

  - improve the well-being of young children in their area

  - reduce inequalities between young children in their area in relation to:

    - physical and mental health and emotional well-being

    - protection from harm and neglect

    - education training and recreation

- contribution made by them to society
- social and economic well-being.

The Secretary of State may set targets with regard to these matters. Local authorities must also make arrangements for early childhood services, ensuring early years provision, social services and health services. The Act also contains provisions to help parents, which need to be read alongside provisions contained in the Work and Families Act 2006. The combined effect of these two Acts is to provide for more extensive maternity and paternity rights; greater support for flexible working; and the provision of sufficient childcare facilities to enable parents to work.

The Children and Young Persons Act 2008 creates new duties on the Secretary of State and local authorities.

With regard to the Secretary of State, s7(1) provides:

It is the general duty of the Secretary of State to promote the well-being of children in England.

Authorities have enhanced duties with regard to

- looked-after children
- appointment and functions of independent reviewing officers
- visits to looked-after children and maintenance of contact with them.

Registration of births and deaths are required to notify the local Safeguarding Children Board of the particulars of death of a person under the age of 18.

The Childcare Act also provides for the regulation of childcare and early years providers by means of a registration/inspection model similar to that used with other institutional settings.

The scope and structure of the Children Act 1989

Scope

In the past, some children's legislation has simply drawn together different bits of earlier legislation (the Child Care Act 1980 is a good example of such 'consolidating' legislation).

The Children Act 1989 does draw together (and repeals) some aspects of earlier legislation but it also does the following:

- It introduces new concepts, in particular the notion of 'parental responsibility', but also, for example, the child 'in need' and 'significant harm'.
- It amalgamates important aspects of private law and public law. These two terms have no one definition in law generally, but, in this context, private law is to do with the regulation of relationships between parents and between parents and their children. Public law is to do with the regulation of interventions by the state (including social work agencies) into family life.

The Children Act 1989 is therefore fundamental to childcare social work practice. The only two areas it does not radically affect are adoption and youth justice (see Chapters 5 and 6).

Structure

The Children Act is split up into 12 parts, the headings for which are identified below. These parts are, in turn, separated into 108 sections, the most important of which are also identified below. There are also 15 schedules.

Here is an outline of the Parts and key sections:

Part I   Introductory
s.1   Paramountcy, welfare checklist

s.2   Parental responsibility

Part II   Orders with Respect to Children in the Family Proceedings
s.8   Orders

s.16   Family Assistance Orders

Part III   Local Authority Support for Children and Families
s.17   Provision for children in need (and Schedule 2)

s.20   Accommodation

s.22   Duty of local authority to children looked after by them

s.24   Leaving accommodation/care

s.26   Review/representations procedures

Part IV   Care and Supervision
s.31   Care and Supervision Orders; definition of harm

s.32   Delay is harmful

s.33   Effect of Care Order

s.34   Parental contact with children in care

s.35   Supervision Orders (and Schedule 3)

s.36   Education Supervision Orders

s.38   Interim Care and Supervision Orders

s.41   Guardians *ad litem* (now called children's guardians)

Part V   Protection of Children
s.43   Child Assessment Order

s.44 and 45   Emergency Protection Order

s.46   Police powers to remove children

s.47   Local authority duty to investigate

* Part VI   Community Homes
s.53   Local authority provision for community homes

* Part VII   Voluntary Homes and Voluntary Organisations
s.59   Voluntary organisations provision of accommodation

* Part VIII   Registered Children's Homes
s.63   Children accommodated in unregistered children's homes

Part IX   Private Arrangements for Fostering Children
s.66   Private fostering

* Part X   Child Minding and Day Care for Young Children
s.71–s.76   Child minding and day care for young children registration

Part XI   Secretary of State's Supervisory Functions and Responsibilities

Part XII   Miscellaneous and General
s.85   Children accommodated by health/local education authorities

s.86   Children accommodated in residential care, nursing or mental nursing homes

s.87   Welfare of children accommodated in independent schools

s.92   Jurisdiction of courts

s.96   Evidence by, or with respect to, children

s.100   Restriction on use of wardship

NB Those parts of the Act marked * have been repealed by the Care Standards Act 2000, which established the National Care Standards Commission, and which draws together the regulations for a wide range of residential and other provisions, not just those for children (see Chapter 8 on Community Care Law).

Note that the components of the schedules are not itemised here. The schedules (as in other legislation) provide more detail about how powers and duties should be implemented, e.g. Schedule 2 links to Part III (especially s.17) concerning responsibilities to children in need; Schedule 3 gives more information on what social workers' responsibilities are in relation to supervision orders (s.35); and so on.

For most childcare social workers, the most important Parts of the Act are:

Part I – this outlines the very important concepts of the paramountcy of the welfare of the child (in family proceedings) and of parental responsibility.

Part III – this deals with voluntary services (i.e. not based on a court order) from local authorities to children in 'need' and their families. Part III is at the very heart of the Children Act.

Part IV – this outlines the basis on which Care and Supervision Orders may be made by courts, and it includes (in s.31) the very important definition of 'significant harm'.

Part V – this deals with the local authority duty to investigate suspected child abuse and neglect and provides other duties concerning Emergency Protection Orders, Child Assessment Orders (very rarely used) and police powers of removal.

Note
It is very important to distinguish between Part III, which deals with voluntary services, and Parts IV and V, which deal with compulsory measures, ordered by the courts. This will be referred to later.

Key principles

This is only a brief outline of the key operating principles. One way to think about some of the major ones is to remember the six Ps and the three Cs.

The six Ps

1) Paramountcy

Section 1 states that, in certain specified proceedings, 'the child's welfare shall be the court's paramount consideration'. This should mean that the child's interests are more important than any other consideration. Note that this applies to certain court proceedings. The notion of the child's welfare is differently expressed concerning non-court-related measures (e.g. in Part III). There may be circumstances, even in court proceedings (e.g. to do with secure accommodation), where the child's welfare is not the paramount consideration (though it remains a central one).

2) Parental responsibility

Alongside the concept of paramountcy is that of parental responsibility (replacing the earlier legal and social concepts of parental rights and parental duties). This is central to the operation of the Children Act.

> *Social workers cannot fulfil their legal responsibilities to families properly unless they are quite sure who has parental responsibility for the children in them.*

Further information on the meaning of parental responsibility is given in the next section, following this one, on principles.

3) Partnership

The term 'partnership' is not used in the Act itself (though it does come up in the Guidance and Regulations and other official documentation). However, the idea of working with people, rather than on them, is both one of the most important and most problematic working principles of the Act, which refers at various points to the need for social workers to consult with, or listen to, parents, children, other interested parties (e.g. grandparents) and other local authority and voluntary organisations.

4) Provision

The whole thrust of the Act (especially Part III) is towards the provision of services. This should be done as far as possible, on a voluntary basis, with the aim of keeping families together.

5) Prevention

The prevention of deterioration of families' and children's circumstances runs throughout the Act, though the notion of promotion of children's welfare is a more positive expression of this. Such prevention will be based on sound evidence-based assessments, a clear understanding of the legal options and the most effective use of resources.

6) Protection

Parts IV and V of the Act, built around the important concept of 'significant harm', are central to social work formulations of 'child protection'. However, especially in the light of the 'refocusing' debate on child protection (i.e. trying to move this area of work away from compulsory measures, policing, control, surveillance, etc.), it may be more useful to think of the Children Act as a whole being concerned with the protection of children's interests generally.

The three Cs

1) Consultation

There are numerous points in the Act where the importance of consulting with children, parents and others is emphasised. For example, s.22 refers to the duty to 'ascertain' and 'give due consideration' to the 'wishes and feelings' of children, parents, etc., before making any decisions about 'looked-after children' or those who may be looked after. The Children Act 2004 extends the scope of statutory duties to consult.

2) Contact

There is a presumption of contact between 'looked-after' children and their parents, siblings and other interested parties. So if a child is in a residential home, or with foster carers, social workers have a duty to help them keep in touch with family members. Such contact can be refused but (except in an emergency) only by a court.

Note – do not confuse this sort of contact concerning children in the public care system (dealt with under s.34), with contact orders concerning visits by parents to children following divorce or matrimonial proceedings, etc. (s.8).

3) Consent

One of the very important themes in the Act is that of children's rights, particularly as contained in the idea that, as children get older, they are more able to make decisions for themselves. So, for example, s.44 (7) states that, where a medical examination or other assessment is ordered, in tandem with an Emergency Protection Order, the child may refuse to have the examination/ assessment if he or she is of sufficient understanding to make an informed decision. This notion of children's autonomy is extremely contentious and subject to much case law.

Other principles

A few other important principles and themes within the Act are:

The 'no-order' principle

A court should not make an order 'unless it considers that doing so would be better for the child than making no order at all' (s1(5)). This may seem obvious, but what it means for social workers is that they should not go to court simply saying 'we believe this child is suffering from significant harm', but should also state what action is proposed (including any recommendations for orders) and how making an order would improve the child's situation.

The 'no-delay' principle

A period of six months to, say, a four-year-old is a far more significant matter (usually) than to a 40-year-old. This is acknowledged in s.1(2) of the Act, which says, 'the court shall have regard to the general principle that any delay in determining the question is likely to prejudice the welfare of the child'.

Unfortunately, it has to be admitted that this principle is often not upheld in practice and that long delays in court proceedings are common.

Anti-discriminatory theme

For the first time in children's legislation, the Children Act 1989 makes specific reference to taking account of a child's race, religion, language and culture (though earlier regulations on the 'boarding out' of children in foster care had referred to the child's religious upbringing). Key points on this are referred to in the box below:

RACE, RELIGION, LANGUAGE AND CULTURE

CHILDREN BEING LOOKED AFTER
'In making any decision with respect to a child whom they are looking after, or proposing to look after, a local authority shall give due consideration . . . to the child's religious persuasion, racial origin and cultural and linguistic background' (s.2.2(5)).

DAY CARE AND FOSTER CARE
'Every local authority shall, in making any arrangements for the provision of day care within their areas; or designed to encourage persons to act as local authority foster parents have regard to the different racial groups to which children within their area who are in need belong' (sched 2 para. 11).

CANCELLATION OF REGISTRATION (CHILDMINDING AND DAY CARE)
'In considering the needs of any child . . . a local authority shall, in particular, have regard to the child's religious persuasion, racial origin and cultural and linguistic background' (s.74(6)).

CHILDREN IN CARE
'While a care order is in force with respect to a child, the local authority . . . shall not . . . cause the child to be brought up in any religious persuasion other than that in which he would have been brought up if the order had not been made' (s.33(6)(a)).

Concurrent jurisdiction

This means that family proceedings may now be heard in any one of the three levels of court (as the court of first instance). These are magistrates' courts, the county court and the High Court.

Most family proceedings are heard in the magistrates' court, but cases could be heard elsewhere if there were already related proceedings going on (e.g. concerning maintenance in the county court); or if proceedings were likely to be lengthy, complex or raise important matters of public concern, they could go to the High Court.

There are rules for the courts to adhere to in the family proceedings:

- The Family Proceedings Courts (Children Act 1989) Rules 1991 for magistrates' courts and

- Part IV of the Family Proceedings Rules 1991 for county courts and the High Court.

The notion of parental responsibility

The following section is based on extracts from two publications, each of which is cited. The first part is an outline of the components of parental responsibility in terms of parental rights and parental duties; and the second provides a helpful outline of how parental responsibility is acquired and lost.

Parental responsibility

The components of 'parental responsibility' have been summarised as follows:

Parental rights

1. The right to determine where the child should live

2. The right to determine education

3. The right to determine religion

4. The right to discipline the child

5. The right to consent to the child's marriage

6. The right to authorise medical treatment

7. The right to administer the child's property

8. The right to appoint a guardian

9. The right to agree to adoption

10. The right to consent to a change in the child's name.

Parental duties

1. The duty to protect the child

2. The duty to maintain the child

3. The duty to secure the child's education

4. The duty to control the child.

Reference: Allen, N. (2005) *Making Sense of the Children Act 1989* (4th ed.). Chichester: John Wiley, p.23

What is parental responsibility and who may have it?

The Children Act 1989 uses the term 'parental responsibility' to replace that of parental rights and duties but does not define exactly what responsibility parents and others have for children. The use of parental responsibility reflects the view that parents have power so that they can bring up their children. The law accepts that the responsibilities of parenthood change over time and according to circumstances, particularly that they diminish as children mature and become capable of making decisions for themselves. Parental responsibility is thus not an absolute but a bundle of powers and obligations, which must be fitted to the matter under consideration.

Parents generally do this quite naturally, partly by a process of trial and error relying in their knowledge of the child; when parental responsibility is exercised by someone who knows the child less well, particularly by a bureaucratic organisation, formal processes of assessment and consultation are essential.

The following table sets out how parental responsibility is acquired and lost:

Acquisition of parental responsibility		
Automatically s.2	**Mother** **Married fathers**	Including father who married the mother after the child was born
By agreement with mother s.4	**Unmarried fathers (see * below)**	
By formal appointment s.5	**Guardians**	Note – An appointment only takes effect on the death of both parents with parental responsibility or the death of a parent who had a residence order alone or with a non-parent
By Parental Responsibility Order s.4	**Unmarried fathers**	
By Residence Order	**Any individual, e.g. step-parent, relative, unmarried father, etc.**	
By Care Order/Interim Care Order s.33	**The local authority**	**Shared** with parents, or whoever already has parental responsibility.

* Following the implementation of s.111 of the Adoption and Children Act 2002 on 1 December 2003, unmarried fathers share parental responsibility (PR) with the unmarried mother provided that they register the birth jointly.

It is important to stress that this provision only applies from 1 December 2003, and an unmarried father therefore would not have parental responsibility for a child registered before that date, but would for a younger child registered after it.

Where parental responsibility is held by more than one person

Anyone with parental responsibility may exercise it without consultation with any other person unless consultation is specifically required as in cases of adoption/freeing for adoption; removal from the UK/emigration, marriage under 18; change of name; application for a residence order by a non-parent; or provision of local authority accommodation/removal from that accommodation where there is a residence order.

Following a Care Order	The local authority has the power to determine the extent to which the parents can exercise parental responsibility. (s.33)
Following a Residence Order	No one may act incompatibly with the order. (s.2 (8))

Responsibility of those without parental responsibility

A person with parental responsibility may arrange for anyone to meet their responsibility on their behalf but this does not remove their obligations to the child.

Policy issues

Parental responsibility is the term employed throughout the Act to sum up the collection of duties, rights and authority which parents have with respect to their children. People other than the parents may carry parental responsibility for a child, but this does not diminish the responsibility of the parents themselves. Parents continue to have responsibility for their children being looked after by the local authority, even where there is a court order in force.

The Act makes little reference to parental 'rights' and the choice of the term 'parental responsibility' reflects the principle that people's rights are restricted to those which they need in order to be able to discharge their parental duties adequately. Parents who are temporarily or permanently unable to discharge their parental responsibilities properly are expected to seek assistance, if necessary from the local authority.

Reference Shaw, M. et al. (1991) *Children in Need and their Families: A New Approach.* Department of Health/University of Leicester

The distinction between voluntary and compulsory measures

The pre-1989 Act legislation blurred the boundaries between voluntary and compulsory measures, for example through the mechanism of (administrative rather than 'judicial') 'parental rights resolutions' which extinguished the rights of parents to remove children who had been (voluntarily) 'received into care'.

Those boundaries are now much clearer. The points below simplify what is actually very complex, by focusing on the distinction between Parts III, IV and V.

Note the following points:

i) Services provided under Part III do not require court proceedings. They are voluntary and preventive measures, with the underlying aim of keeping families together. The key definition here is that of the 'child in need' (see s.17(10) and (11) for this definition), which is the passport to such services. Further information on Part III is provided later in this section.

ii) Compulsory measures are outlined in Part IV (Care and Supervision Orders) and Part V (Child Assessment, Emergency Protection and Recovery Orders and police protection powers). With the exception of the police protection powers (s.46), these measures can only be taken following an application to a court. The key definition here is that of 'significant harm' (see ss.31, 43 and 44). Further information is contained later in this section.

Obviously court-related measures are seen as more serious. This tends to indicate a higher perceived level of risk to the child because past or possible future events and/or parental attitudes or behaviour indicate that they will not work voluntarily with social workers.

iii) Voluntary measures under Part III are often provided to children in their own homes (though see iv) below). Compulsory measures under Parts IV and V are more likely to indicate that the child will be removed from home. However, this is not inevitable. For example, it is perfectly possible to have a Child Assessment Order with the child remaining at home; the same would usually apply if a Supervision Order is made.

iv) A child may become 'looked after' – that is looked after in the public care system either in a residential home, or in foster care – through a Care Order (s.31 in Part IV) or through being 'accommodated' (s.20 in Part III).

The standard of care for the child should be the same in either case, but there is a key distinction, to do with parental responsibility (PR):

- If a child is 'accommodated', the parents (or whoever has PR) continue to have PR. The local authority, while it has the day-to-day responsibility for the child, does not have PR. Bearing in mind that this is a voluntary measure, this means that the parent (or PR holder) can normally remove the child from the accommodation when he or she wishes to do so (s.20(8)).

- If a child is 'in care' (i.e. subject of a Care Order) the parents (or whoever has PR) continue to have PR. However, unlike 'accommodation', the local authority also has PR. Bearing in mind that this is a compulsory measure, the parent (or PR holder) cannot remove the child from care, even if he or she wishes to do so. Such decisions must be referred back to the court that made the original Care Order.

It is therefore extremely important that you do not confuse the two terms (and legal statuses) of 'accommodated' and 'in care'.

The generic term for these two distinct categories is 'looked after'.

Key components of Part III of the Children Act 1989

The title of Part III (ss.17–30) is 'Local Authority Support for Children and Families'. Its key components are:

1. General duty of local authorities and definition of 'child in need' (s.17)

2. Identification of local authority services (e.g. pre-school and out of school services, family centres, counselling, etc.) (ss.17,18 and Schedule 2)

3. Provision of accommodation (ss.20 and 21) and duties towards looked-after children (s.22)

4. Advice and assistance ('after-care') (s.24)

5. Secure accommodation (s.25)

6. Reviews; representations procedures (s.26)

7. Cooperation between and within, authorities (s.27) and consultation with LEA (s.28)

8. Recouping of costs (s.29).

Though you should refer to the Act itself, in order to develop a detailed understanding of Part III, further information is given below on:

- the general duty of local authorities

- the definition of a child 'in need'

- accommodation.

General duty

The general duty of local authorities (s.17 (1)) is:

a) 'to safeguard and promote the welfare of the children within their area who are in need; and

b) so far as is consistent with that duty, to promote the upbringing of such children by their families, by providing a range and level of services appropriate to those children's needs.'

Section 53 of the Children Act 2004 (inserting a new s.17(4A) into the 1989 Act) creates a new statutory duty requiring local authorities, before determining what services to provide, to ascertain the relevant child's wishes with regard to those services and to take the child's views into account ('give due consideration') when deciding what services to provide.

These services are referred to in more detail in s.18 (day care) and in Schedule 2, but they also include 'accommodation' (see iii below). Services may include giving assistance in kind or, in exceptional circumstances, in cash (s.17 (6)). (This is the equivalent to what used to be termed 'Section 1 payments' under the now repealed Child Care Act 1980.)

The general duty under this section of the Act is broader than in previous legislation, in that it is written in terms of promoting children's welfare rather than (more negatively) keeping them out of care, but it applies to a restricted group of children, that is 'children in need'.

Child 'in need'

A child is taken to be 'in need' (see s.17 (10)) if:

a) 'he is unlikely to achieve or maintain, or to have the opportunity of achieving or maintaining, a reasonable standard of health or development without the provision for him of services by a local authority under this Part;

b) his health or development is likely to be significantly impaired, or further impaired without the provision for him of such services; or

c) he is disabled;

and "family" in relation to such a child, includes any person who has parental responsibility for the child and any other person with whom he has been living.'

The terms are further defined in s.17 (11).

> *a child is disabled if he is blind, deaf, dumb or suffers from mental disorder of any kind or is substantially and permanently handicapped by illness, injury or congenital deformity or such disability as may be described; and in this Part – 'development' means physical, intellectual, emotional, social or behavioural development; and 'health' means physical or mental health.*

The above definitions (which are, obviously, open to interpretation) are extremely important: being defined as a child 'in need' provides the 'passport' to services outlined in Part III and elsewhere.

Accommodation

Local authorities have a duty to provide accommodation to a child in need who appears to require accommodation, if this is the result of any of the following (see s.20 (1)):

a) 'There being no person who has parental responsibility for him

b) His being lost or having been abandoned; or

c) The person who has been caring for him being prevented (whether or not permanently and for whatever reason) from providing him with suitable accommodation or care.'

NB Section 20 should be read as a whole, since it details further, more specific, powers and duties concerning accommodation and also outlines matters to do with consultation and agreement.

NB If a child is accommodated, parental responsibility remains with the parent (or whoever has PR) and does not rest with the local authority.

Note that there are particular powers and duties concerning children of 16 and above. These are:

s.20(3) 'Every local authority shall provide accommodation for any child in need within their area who has reached the age of 16 and whose welfare the authority consider is likely to be seriously prejudiced if they do not provide him with accommodation.'

NB This duty is a narrower one than for younger children; there is no reference, in respect of younger children, to the authority having to consider whether or not providing accommodation would 'seriously prejudice' their welfare.

s.20(5) 'A local authority may provide accommodation for any person who has reached the age of 16 but is under 21 in a community home which takes children who have reached the age of 16 if they consider that to do so would safeguard or promote his welfare.'

s.20(11) 'Subsections (7) and (8) [which refer, respectively, to the right of PR holders to object to accommodation being provided in certain circumstances and to the right of PR holders to

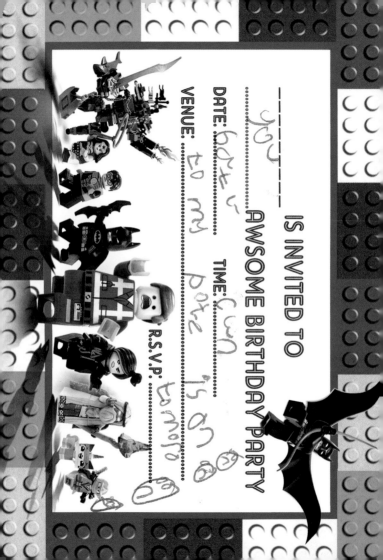

—— JoJ —— IS INVITED TO AWSOME BIRTHDAYPARTY

DATE: boxes

TIME: C w

VENUE: to my

pore is on

R.S.V.P: tomoro

remove a child from accommodation] do not apply where a child who has reached the age of 16 agrees to being provided with accommodation under this section.'

Key components of Parts IV and V of the Children Act 1989

The title of Part IV is 'Care and Supervision' and Part V is 'Protection of Children'. Remember that, as distinct from Part III, much of these two parts of the Act are concerned with compulsory measures. Their key components are:

Part IV   (ss.31–42)

s.31	Grounds for care and supervision orders (contains definition of 'significant harm')
s.33	Effects of care order
s.34	Parental contact, etc., with the children in care
s.35	Supervision orders (supervisor's duties, to be read in tandem with Parts 1 and 2 of Schedule 3.)
s.37	Powers of the Court in certain family proceedings (to direct local authorities to investigate child's circumstances)
s.41	Representation of children by guardians *ad litem*. (Now known as guardians.)

Part V   (ss. 43–52)

s.43	Child assessment orders
s.44	Emergency protection orders
s.46	Police powers to remove children in an emergency
s.47	Local authority's duty to investigate
s.50	Recovery orders

The notes on the following pages refer to some major aspects of Part V, then of Part IV.

Part V   Protection of Children

This deals with the protection of children. At its core is the s.47, duty to investigate. This states (s.47(1)) that if a local authority is informed that a child in their area is on an emergency protection order, or in police protection, or they have 'reasonable cause' to suspect that the child is suffering, or is likely to suffer, 'significant harm', then that authority 'shall make, or cause to be made, such enquiries as they consider necessary to enable them to decide whether they should take any action to safeguard or promote the child's welfare'.

The initial home visit, following a call to a social services duty officer/child-care assessment team to express concern about an allegedly abused or neglected child, would therefore derive its legal authority from this section.

Section 53 of the Children Act 2004 (inserting a new s.47(5A) into the 1989 Act) requires local authorities, when making a decision under s.47, to 'ascertain the child's wishes and feelings with regard to the action to be taken with respect to him' and to take these into account ('give due consideration') when reaching a decision.

Note also that Part II of the Children Act 2004 establishes statutory Local Safeguarding Children Boards to replace Area Child Protection Committees.

The notes in the following boxes, briefly outline the Emergency Protection Order (s.44) and also (though it has been very little used) the Child Assessment Order (s.43).

Emergency Protection Order (s.44)

Purpose	To enable the child, in a genuine emergency, to be removed from where he is or to be kept where he is, if and only if this is necessary to provide immediate short-term protection
Duration	8 days, with a possible extension of 7 days
Appeals and discharges	No appeal allowed, but an application for discharge may be heard after 72 hours unless the interested party was given notice of the hearing at which the order was made and was present at that hearing
	Order may be challenged by the child and parent of the child, any person with parental responsibility and any person with whom the child was living before the order was made
Applications	Anyone may apply

Ground for application

The court may make an order if, but only if, it is satisfied that –

a) there is reasonable cause to believe that the child is likely to suffer significant harm (s.44 (1)(a)) (if he is not removed or remains in present accommodation)

b) in the case of an application made by a local authority

   (i) enquiries are being made with respect to the child under Section 47 (1)(b) (Local authority duty to investigate) and

   (ii) those enquiries are being frustrated by access to the child being unreasonably refused to a person authorised to seek access and that the applicant has reasonable cause to believe that the access to the child is required as a matter of urgency (s.44(1)(b))

The police may apply for an EPO, but have separate powers under s.46 to take a child into police protection.

The welfare principle and presumption of no order both apply. However, the 'welfare check-list' does not (on the basis that not enough is yet likely to be known in order to apply it).

The Court may make directions about contact with the child and/or medical or psychiatric examination or assessment.

The applicant acquires limited parental responsibility.

Section 44(1)(c) covers applications by an authorised person (currently only the NSPCC is an 'authorised' agency) who has reasonable cause to suspect a child is suffering, or likely to suffer significant harm, is making enquiries about the child's welfare and where access to the child is frustrated.

Child Assessment Orders (s.43)

Purpose
This is a provision to enable an assessment of a child to be made where:
- Significant harm is suspected
- Child is not thought to be at immediate risk
- LA or authorised person considers an assessment is required
- Parent or other persons responsible for child have refused to co-operate.

Aim is to allow LA/authorised person to find out enough about the state of a child's health or development or way he has been treated to decide what further action, if any, is required

Welfare principle and no order principle apply. Welfare checklist does not apply. Holder of order does not acquire parental responsibility.

Duration
Seven days allowed for the assessment, from a date specified by the order. Necessary arrangements therefore ought to be made in advance of the application so that initial multi-disciplinary assessment can take place within the seven-day period allowed.

Effect of an order
1. Any person in a position to do so (usually with parental responsibility or having a child in care) produces the child to the person named in the order and complies with directions or requirements in the order.
2. The carrying out of the assessment in accordance with the terms of the order is authorised.

Note
a) A child of sufficient understanding to make an informed decision may refuse to consent to the assessment.

b) Child may be kept away from home for purposes of assessment but only if the Court is satisfied it is necessary and it is done in accordance with the directions and limited to periods specified.

Department of Health Regulations and Guidance Vol. 1 Court Orders states:

The child assessment order is emphatically not for emergencies. It is a lesser, heavily Court controlled order dealing with the narrow issue of examination of assessment of the child in specific circumstances of non co-operation by the parent and lack of evidence of the need for a different type of order or other action (para 4.4).

However, the Court may, of its own action, make an Emergency Protection Order if it is satisfied that there are sufficient grounds (e.g. Court decides situation is more serious than applicant judges; new information emerges during CAO application, perhaps from a children's guardian) (previously known as a guardian *ad litem*) (s43(4)).

Part IV   Care and Supervision

This deals with compulsory measures relating to care and supervision orders (including education supervision orders, which are not specifically referred to below; for this, see s.36).

The outline below is based on 13 points:

i) The principles of the Children Act apply (as they do with any other part of the Act).

ii) This Part (and also Part V) sets limits on state intervention, with an underlying assumption of the avoidance of court proceedings if possible.

iii) A central consideration, in making (or not) a care or supervision order, is the concept of 'significant harm' (s.31(2) – see box below). But the welfare checklist (s.1(3) – see box below) and the 'no-order principle' (s.1(5)) also apply.

iv) There is concurrent jurisdiction – that is, family proceedings may be heard in a magistrates' court, county court or the High Court.

v) There is an enhanced role (in comparison with pre-1989 Act legislation) for the children's guardian.

vi) Applications for a Care Order (CO) or Supervision Order (SO) can only be made by a local authority, or 'authorised person' (at present, only the NSPCC is authorised – see s.31(9)).

vii) Following an application for a CO, an SO may be made and vice versa (s.31(5)).

viii) A CO can only be made on a child up to the age of 17 (or 16 if married) (s.31(3)).

ix) When a CO is made, the local authority has parental responsibility (s.33(3)(a)), but shares it with the parent, or whoever has PR.

x) There is an assumption of continued parental contact for children 'in care' (s.34), which can only be wholly terminated by a court.

xi) Detailed requirements for SOs (s.31(1)(b)) are contained in Parts 1 and 2 of Schedule 3. Key points to note are:

- SOs are made initially, for up to 1 year (Schedule 3, para 6(1))

- they may be extended to up to 3 years (para 6(4))

- they do not continue past the age of 18 (s.91(3))

xii) Interim orders (s.38) can now include interim SOs as well as COs. The maximum initial period is up to eight weeks and thereafter up to four weeks (s.38(4) and (5)). There is no limit on the number of interim orders but timetabling provisions (s.32) would apply with a view to making decisions as quickly as possible.

xiii) Applications for the discharge of a CO or discharge/variation of an SO (s.39) may be made by

- the person with parental responsibility

- the child

- the local authority.

That outlines some major points about Part IV. What you must appreciate is that decisions about care and supervision orders are based on two sets of considerations:

- significant harm

- the welfare of the child.

The two boxes below give further information:

Significant harm

A central consideration for courts (and, therefore, for social workers) in deciding whether care orders (and also EPOs and CAOs) are appropriate, is that of significant harm. The key definition is to be found in s.31 of the Children Act 1989. Section 31 (2) reads as follows:

'A court may only make a care order or supervision order if it is satisfied:

a) that the child concerned is suffering, or is likely to suffer, significant harm; and that the harm, or likelihood of harm, is attributable to:

    (i)   the care given to the child, or likely to be given to him if the order were not made, not being what it would be reasonable to expect a parent to give him; or
    (ii) the child being beyond parental control.'

s.31 (9) and (10) then states:

s.31 (9) '"harm" means ill treatment or the impairment of health or development; "development" means physical, intellectual, emotional, social or behavioural development; "health" means physical or mental health; and

---

> ''ill treatment'' includes sexual abuse and forms of ill-treatment, which are not physical.'
> s.120 Adoption and Children Act 2002 adds: 'impairment suffered from seeing or hearing the ill treatment of another'.

s.31(10) 'Where the question of whether harm suffered by the child is significant and turns on the child's health or development, his health or development shall be compared to that which could reasonably be expected of a similar child.'

Welfare of the child

The other core consideration in family proceedings, alongside that of significant harm, is the welfare of the child. Even if the threshold criteria for significant harm are established, a care or supervision order may not be made. The 'welfare checklist' (s.1(3)) must be considered – with the welfare of the child continuing to be the paramount consideration. The matters to be considered (by the court and – by implication – by the social worker) are contained in s.1.

Paramountcy
s.1(1)   'the child's welfare shall be the court's paramount consideration'
'No delay'
s.1(2)   'any delay in determining the question is likely to prejudice the welfare of the child'.

The welfare checklist
s.1(3)   The court shall have regard to:

- the ascertainable wishes and feeling of the child
- his physical, emotional and educational needs
- the likely effect on him of any change of circumstances
- age, sex, background and any characteristics court considers relevant
- any harm which he has suffered or is at risk of suffering
- the range of powers available to the court under this Act.

'No order' principle
s.1(5) 'Where a court is considering whether or not to make one or more orders under this Act with respect to a child, it shall not make the order or any of the orders unless it considers that doing so would be better for the child than making no order at all.'

It has been suggested (Adcock, 1991, p.23) that a possible sequence for considering this checklist would be as follows:

1. Define the child's present and future needs in the light of past significant harm, normal child development and racial, cultural and any other specific considerations.
2. Identify the child's wishes and feelings.
3. Define the changes required to meet the child's future needs, taking into account his or her wishes.
4. Assess parental capacity to do this and conditions required to achieve any change.

5. Consider the effects, both positive and negative, on a child of any change and identify the least detrimental alternative.
6. Consider whether any changes can be achieved without an order. If not, make an appropriate recommendation for an order.

Reference: **Adcock, M.** (1991) Significant harm: implications for the exercise of statutory responsibilities, in **Adcock, M. et al.** (eds) *Significant Harm: Its Management and Outcome*. Croydon: Significant Publications, p.23 (this book is now in a second edition which does not contain the above information in the same form).

Postscript – the Children Act 1989: the orders

As you will now appreciate, there are numerous orders that can be made by courts under the Children Act. Most, but not all, are contained in Parts IV and V. They are itemised below, beginning with the relevant section.

Section 8. There are four types of s.8 orders. These are 'private law' orders, intended to regulate the relationship between parents (and others) and their children. The four types are:

- Residence orders

- Contact orders

- Prohibited steps orders

- Specific issue orders.

The Children and Adoption Act 2006 and Children and Young Persons Act 2008 contain provisions designed to make s.8 orders more effective in practice.

Section 10	Family Assistance Orders – to advise, assist and befriend any person named in the order (usually a parent). Most likely to occur in divorce or matrimonial proceedings.
Section 31	Care orders
Section 32	Supervision orders
Section 34	Orders relating to contact with children in care
Section 36	Education supervision orders
Section 38	Interim care orders and interim supervision orders
Section 43	Child assessment orders
Section 44	Emergency protection orders
Section 46	Police protection powers (not an 'order' since the intervention of the court is not required). Also see s.48 (9) relating to warrants for entry, which can only be exercised by the police.
Section 50	Recovery orders – this authorises the recovery of children who have been abducted, or who have run away from 'care'. Note that this section does not apply to certificated 'refuges' (see s.51). Refuges are residential establishments, usually provided by voluntary agencies, e.g. the Children's

Society, for children who have run away from fostering and residential care, as well as their own families.

ACTIVITY *4.1*

You can work on your understanding of the Children Act by considering the following two case studies, which focus particularly on the use of Parts III and V of the Act.

Case study 1

A health visitor colleague describes the following situation to you.

Josie Taylor lives with her two children, Joe, aged 7, and Linda, aged 4. Joe attends the local primary school, Linda is not yet at school and does not attend any form of day care provision. Josie is white and her two children are of 'dual heritage'. Dennis, the father, is Afro-Caribbean and is divorced from Josie. There is a residence order in favour of Josie; however, Dennis lives nearby and is in almost daily contact with the children. The maternal grandparents also live near and see the children frequently.

The health visitor states that the children appear to be happy and well cared for. However, she is worried that, in the past, Josie has had periods of serious depressive illness and that she is heading that way again. Your colleague is trying to plan for a situation that might arise, in which Josie may be temporarily unable to care for the children.

The health visitor asks for information on:

i) The legal positions of Josie, Dennis and the grandparents in respect of the children and the means whereby (where the individuals concerned do not already have it) they could apply for parental responsibility.

ii) Whether or not the local authority would need to take court action if Josie becomes ill again.

What advice would you give?

Case study 2

You have received a telephone call from a concerned neighbour to say that she has heard the husband and wife next door shouting and a child crying very loudly. She is worried about the child's safety.

When you visit, you are allowed by the parents to see the child, Cheryl, a 12-year-old girl. Cheryl has bruising to her left cheek. The father admits to having hit her and says that this has happened before. He says this is because she persists in staying out late. The atmosphere remains quite heated, with Cheryl saying she can 'do what she likes'. In spite of their agitation both parents are saying that they don't want their daughter to be 'taken away', but Cheryl is saying she's 'had enough of being at home'.

What are the key issues in this situation, in the light of the Children Act 1989? Outline the legal alternatives available to the local authority and their relative merits.

Chapter 5
Adoption

Overview

The outline below is intended to give an understanding of developments in adoption law, from the Adoption Act 1976 to the (not yet fully implemented) Children and Adoption Act 2006 and associated regulations. The primary legislation on adoption is:

Adoption Act 1976

Adoption Agencies Regulations 1983

Adoption Rules 1984

Adoption and Children Act 2002

Children and Adoption Act 2006

Children and Young Persons Act 2008.

Proposals for amendments to adoption law were made but, until the Adoption and Children Act 2002, not implemented, in a number of government publications, including a series of inter-departmental review discussion papers from 1990 to 1994 which are referenced below. These include:

Department of Health (1992) *Review of Adoption Law: Report to Ministers of an Inter-Departmental Working Group*

Department of Health (1993) *Adoption: The Future*, Cm.2288 (White Paper)

Department of Health (1996) *Adoption: A Service for Children*

The latter consultation document contained a draft bill (the Adoption Bill 1996) including the following proposals for change:

- the introduction of a 'placement order'
- a new welfare principle
- changes to the grounds for dispensing with parental consent to adoption.

This was then followed by the Adoption Law Review (1998–99) and, in turn, a White Paper published in December 2000:

Department of Health (2000) *Adoption: A New Approach*, Cm 5017

The content of this White Paper is available at the following website:

www.dh.gov.uk/assetRoot/04/08/05/12/04080512.pdf

The Adoption and Children Act 2002

Following the White Paper, the government published the Adoption and Children Bill 2001. The Adoption and Children Act 2002 has now been enacted and is being implemented incrementally. When implemented this will repeal the Adoption Act 1976. There are associated National Adoption Standards for England (see LAC (2001), 22).

The Children and Adoption Act 2006 makes some amendments to the 2002 Act with regard to inter-country adoptions.

Guides to the new adoption legislation will become available. See, for example, the following.

Bridge, C. and Swindells, H. (2003) *Adoption: the Modern Law*. Bristol: Family Law

Bevan, H. (ed.) (2007) *The Adoption and Children Act 2002*. London: Lexis Nexis Butterworths

Swindells, H. and Heaton, C. (2006) *Adoption: The Modern Procedure*. Bristol: Family Law

Further information on developments in this area can be found at the government's adoption website: **www.everychildmatters.gov.uk/socialcare/childrenincare.adoption**

British Association for Adoption and Fostering (BAAF)
Saffron House
6–10 Kirby Street
London EC1N 8TS
Tel: 020 7421 2600
E-mail: mail@baaf.org.uk
Website: www.baaf.org.uk

See also the journal *Family Law*.

FURTHER READING

As a general guide see:

Triseliotis, J. et al. (1997) *Adoption: Theory, Policy and Practice*. London: Cassell (though note that it is now dated with regard to the law)

Also the following very important DoH publication:

Dept. of Health (1999) *Adoption Now: Messages from Research*. Chichester: John Wiley

For adoption law specifically see:

Bainham, A. (2005) *Children: The Modern Law* (3rd ed.). Bristol: Family Law (Ch.7)

Cretney, S., Masson, J. and Bailey-Harris, R. (2003) *Principles of Family Law*. London: Sweet and Maxwell (Ch.23)

Chapter 6
Youth justice

Provided below is a list of youth justice legislation; an outline of some key developments; information on useful sources; and advice on follow-up reading.

Youth justice legislation, and the system for which it provides a framework, is extremely complex and volatile. Frequent amendments to the legislation are made (as in criminal justice as a whole); these changes are often a response to 'public opinion' frequently driven by the mass media.

This is an area in which perception (of crime) is more influential than the reality. It has also been noted that young offenders have low social value (they are not one of society's favourite groups) but high political significance (they are the site of concerns about law and order, the failure of the family, falling educational standards, etc.).

Youth justice legislation

Youth justice legislation is extremely complex and dynamic. It reflects the frequent amendments in criminal justice policy generally. The Crime and Disorder Act 1998 is particularly important because it instituted a number of new court sentences, led to the establishment of 'Youth Offender Teams' (YOTS) and the national Youth Justice Board. The following is a list of some of the key legislation.

Children and Young Persons Act 1933

Children and Young Persons Act 1969

Criminal Justice Act 1982

Criminal Justice Act 1991 (as amended by the Criminal Justice Act 1993)

Criminal Justice and Public Order Act 1994

Crime and Disorder Act 1998

Youth Justice and Criminal Evidence Act 1999

Powers of Criminal Courts (Sentencing) Act 2000

Criminal Justice and Court Services Act 2000

Criminal Justice and Police Act 2001

Anti-social Behaviour Act 2003

Criminal Justice Act 2003

Children Act 2004

Serious Organised Crime and Police Act 2005

Police and Justice Act 2006

Violent Crime Reduction Act 2006

Serious Crime Act 2007

Criminal Justice and Immigration Act 2008

A useful source of information is:

National Association for the Care and Resettlement of Offenders (NACRO)
Park Place
10-12 Lawn Lane
London SW8 1UD
Tel: 020 7840 7200
Website: **www.nacro.org.uk**

Also see the website of the National Association for Youth Justice: **www.nayj.org.uk**

The NAYJ now publishes a journal entitled *Youth Justice* (first edition July 2001).

**ESSENTIAL
READING**

There are chapters on youth justice in the two standard social work law texts:

Brammer (2009) *Social Work Law* (3rd ed.). Harlow: Longman.
Brayne and Carr (2008) *Law for Social Workers* (10th ed.). Oxford: Oxford University Press.

**FURTHER
READING**

There is a wealth of literature on youth justice. A key text is:

Ball, C. et al. (2001) *Young Offenders: Law, Policy and Practice* (2nd ed.). London: Sweet and Maxwell

The following book is a standard text on criminology and criminal justice. In particular see:

Newburn, T. (2007) Youth Crime and Youth Culture, in Maguire, M., Morgan, R. and Reiner, R. (eds) *The Oxford Handbook of Criminology* (4th ed.). Oxford: Oxford University Press

Also see:

Goldson, B. (ed.) (1999) *Youth Justice: Contemporary Policy and Practice*. Aldershot: Ashgate

Goldson, B. (ed.) (2000) *The New Youth Justice*. Lyme Regis: Russell House

Gordon, W. et al. (1999) *Introduction to Youth Justice* (2nd ed.). Winchester: Waterside Press

Muncie, J. et al. (eds) (2002) *Youth Justice: Critical Readings*. London: Sage

Muncie, J. (2009) *Youth and Crime* (3rd ed.). London: Sage

Pitts, J. (1999) *Working with Young Offenders* (2nd ed.). Basingstoke: Macmillan

What is a child?

Returning now to the Children Act itself, an important legal (and social) question is raised: what is a child?

A child, as far as the Children Act 1989 is concerned, means someone from 0 up to 18. Earlier legislative distinctions between 'child' and 'young person' and terms such as 'minor' or 'infants', are not used.

Note that legal responsibilities in the Act have been cited with references to concerns about (as yet) unborn children, and there are responsibilities in the Act towards those over 18, e.g. concerning 'advice and assistance' to certain people 'under 21' (see s.24). However, the principal focus of the Children Act is on those from birth to (legal) adulthood.

Chapter 7

Mental health law: an outline

Overview

Even if you do not specialise in mental health and do not aspire to become an Approved Mental Health Professional or an Approved Clinician, you still need to have an awareness of the basic concepts and procedures under the Mental Health Act 1983 (MHA) in order to inform your decision-making in dealing with your clients. However, for an in-depth insight into mental health law, we recommend you look at Barber, P., Brown, R. and Martin, D. (2008) *Mental Health Law in England and Wales*, Exeter: Learning Matters, which contains the text of the Mental Health Act 1983 as amended.

The legislation is complex, as it deals with a number of different situations, which require different treatment. At this stage, you should try to understand the main features of the legislation. We focus on two aspects in particular: first, the main concepts used in the legislation, which in turn depend on the exercise of professional judgement on the part of those using the legislation and, secondly, a selection of the procedures the Act requires those wishing to invoke the provisions of the Act to follow. As the Act allows professionals to take actions in respect of an individual without that person's consent, a key feature of the Act is the provision of safeguards for the individual to reduce the risk of abuse of power. In assessing the values underlying this legislation, you will need to consider whether an adequate balance is achieved between authorising intervention in appropriate cases and protecting the individual from unwarranted interference. A further feature of this area is the Code of Practice, which explains how the provisions of the Act should be implemented.

This chapter is meant to introduce you to the main concepts and procedures contained in the legislation and you should not, at this stage, expect to acquire a working knowledge of the legislation. We are looking at the legislation in outline only.

Objectives

After completing the reading, you should be able to:

*   identify, in outline, the framework of mental health legislation;

*   understand the relationship between the Mental Health Act and the Code of Practice;

*   critically assess the key concepts and procedures in the Mental Health Act;

*   have an awareness of the options available in respect of those suffering from mental disorder;

*   have a working knowledge of the recent reforms in mental health law.

ESSENTIAL READING

An excellent overview of this area of law is to be found in Brammer (2009) *Social Work Law* (3rd ed.). Harlow: Longman. (Ch.10 on 'Mental health and mental incapacity').

Also see:

Ball and McDonald (2002, Ch.13)

Brayne and Carr (2008, Ch.17)

Brown, R. (2009) *The Approved Mental Health Professional's Guide to the Mental Health Act 1983*. Exeter: Learning Matters.

Brown, R., Barber, P., Martin, D. (2009) *Mental Health Law in England and Wales*. Exeter: Learning Matters.

Johns (2007, Ch.5 on 'Community care'; also Ch.2 on 'Human rights')

Rashid, S.P. et al. (1996) *Mental Health Law* (3rd ed.). Norwich: University of East Anglia.

Useful background material on mental health legislation, case law, government policy documents, etc., is contained in:

Brayne and Broadbent (2002) *Legal Materials for Social Workers*. Oxford: Oxford University Press (Ch.5)

A key authority on mental health legislation which contains the text of the MHA and related regulations and commentary is:

Jones, R. (2008) *Mental Health Act Manual* (11th ed.). London: Sweet and Maxwell.

FURTHER READING

You are also strongly recommended to consult the following book, which attempts very successfully to put mental health law and policy into a political and theoretical context:

Bartlett, P. and Sandland, R. (2007) *Mental Health Law, Policy and Practice* (3rd ed.). Oxford: Oxford University Press

The following book contains an analytical discussion of the development of mental health law from the Lunacy Act 1890 to the Mental Health Act 1983:

Unsworth, C. (1987) *The Politics of Mental Health Legislation*. Oxford: Clarendon Press

The following is the lead agency in the field of children's mental health services:

Young Minds
48–50 St John Street
London EC1M 4DG
020 7336 8445
Website: **www.youngminds.org.uk**

Journals

You are strongly encouraged to use journals for *all* your work. In the field of mental health law, policy and practice you may find useful material in mainstream social work journals, but examples of other journals that often contain relevant material are:

British Journal of Psychiatry
Journal of Mental Health
Journal of Mental Health Law
New Law Journal
Psychiatric Bulletin

Websites

The following two websites provide sources of material on mental health law and related matters:

www.imhap.org.uk
www.mhac.org.uk

(if you click on 'Links to other sites' you can then get access to hundreds of other mental health-related websites)

You can also access the websites of (and use publications from) the following voluntary agencies:
MIND – National Association for Mental Health
Granta House
15–19 Broadway
London E15 4BQ
Tel: 020 8519 2122
E-mail: **contact@mind.org.uk**
Website: **www.mind.org.uk**

MENCAP
123 Golden Lane
London EC1Y 0RT
Tel: 020 7454 0454
E-mail: **help@mencap.org.uk**
Website: **www.mencap.org.uk**

Rethink (previously National Schizophrenia Fellowship)
89 Albert Embankment
London SE1 7TP
Tel: 0845 456 0455
Website: **www.rethink.org**

SANE
1st Floor, Cityside House
40 Adler Street
London E1 1EE
Tel: 020 7375 1002
(Also branches in Bristol and Macclesfield)
Website: **www.sane.org.uk**

The Mental Health Act Commission
Maid Marion House
56 Hounds Gate
Nottingham
NG1 6BG
Tel: 0115 943 7100
Website: **www.mhac.org.uk**

There are biennial reports from the Mental Health Act Commission and also occasional reports from the Department of Health and the Social Services Inspectorate.

Particularly important is:

Department of Health (2008) *Refocusing the Care Programme Approach*. London: The Stationery Office

This publication emphasises the importance of the 'Care Programme Approach' – CPA which is to do with the provision of more systematic and co-ordinated assessments, care treatment and support for people with mental health problems living in the community.

The remainder of this section includes:

- Sources of mental health law
- Principles of interpretation and application
- Key definitions
- Informal patients
- Compulsory admission
- Discharge from hospital
- After-care
- Criminal proceedings
- Mental health law reform
- Two case studies.

Sources

Legislation

Mental Health Act 1983 (MHA)

Mental Health (Patients in the Community) Act 1995 (MHPCA)

Mental Health Act 2007

Background to the MHA

A brief outline of the diverse roots of contemporary mental health law is provided in Bartlett and Sandland (2003, pp.21–28). These roots go back to 18th and 19th century legislation on 'lunacy', 'madhouses', 'idiocy', etc.; but a more recent starting point is the Mental Health Act 1959, 'which repealed all existing legislation dealing with mental illness and mental deficiency' (Jones, 2008, p.7) and which was based on the 1957 Report of the Royal Commission on the Law Relating to Mental Illness (Cmnd.169).

An emphasis in the MHA 1959 (retained in the 1983 Act) was on the avoidance of compulsory measures, where possible, and on community – rather than hospital-based – provision, where available and preferable.

A series of reports and White Papers during the 1970s (outlined in Jones, 2008, pp.7–8) led to changes in mental health law, initially in the Mental Health (Amendment) Act 1982 and then in the consolidating MHA 1983, which is the current primary legislation.

Very fundamental reforms of mental health law were then proposed in 1998. There are several reasons for this, but particularly the development of community care policy and associated deinstitutionalisation, which has meant that there are far fewer people receiving mental health treatment/services in hospital and far more 'in the community'.

These reforms to the MHA 1983 were withdrawn in March 2006, with the government favouring alterations to the current Mental Health Act 1983. The government faced opposition to implementing the draft Mental Health Bill from a wide range of groups representing the views of both service users and professionals involved in the implementation of mental health law. In announcing the withdrawal of the draft bill, the government had 'taken into account concerns over the length and complexity of the earlier draft as well as pressures on, parliamentary time'.

The result was the amendment Act of 2007. This contains many of the controversial aspects included in the draft bill, including compulsory treatment in the community, broadening definitions of mental disorder and the removal of the 'treatability test', which had at times been seen as problematic when considering detention of some people with personality disorders.

However, as Vernon notes, social work with service users with a mental disorder does not just involve this Act – it 'may involve other legislation concerning people who are elderly, those who have a chronic illness, a disability, people who are homeless, welfare rights issues, aspects of community care provision and criminal justice matters' (1998, p. 188). Many of these areas are referred to elsewhere in this manual and in the texts cited in the reading list.

The MHA now contains 176 sections, which are structured into the following ten parts:

Part I	Application of the Act (s.1)
Part II	Compulsory Admission to Hospital and Guardianship (ss.2–34)
Part III	Patients Concerned in Criminal Proceedings or Under Sentence (ss.35–55)
Part IV	Consent to Treatment (ss.56–64)
Part IV(A)	Treatment of community patients not recalled to hospital (ss.64A–64K)
Part V	Mental Health Review Tribunals (ss.65–79)
Part VI	Removals and Return of Patients within United Kingdom, etc. (ss.80–92)
Part VII	repealed
Part VIII	Miscellaneous Functions of Local Authorities and the Secretary of State (ss.114–125)
Part IX	Offences (ss.126–130)
Part X	Miscellaneous and Supplementary (ss.130A–149)

There are also five schedules. In particular, note schedule 1 on hospital and guardianship orders and schedule 2 on the membership of Mental Health Review Tribunals (MHRT).

Other sources

Knowledge of the Code of Practice is essential to an understanding of mental health legislation. A fourth edition was published in 2008 for England.

*__Department of Health__ (2008) *Mental Health Act 1983: Code of Practice* (4th ed.). TSO.

There is a separate Code of Practice for Wales.

There are also regulations in the form of statutory instruments (as for the Children Act):

*Mental Health (Hospital, Guardianship and Consent to Treatment) (England) Regulations 2008

*First Tier Tribunal Rules 2008

(All items marked * for both England and Wales are contained in Barber, Brown and Martin, 2008.)

Principles of interpretation and application of the legislation

The Code of Practice for England, which is now in a fourth edition, outlines the broad principles for administering the Act (para. 1-1) in a new 'Statement of guiding principles'.

From the English Code of Practice to the Mental Health Act 1983: 'Guiding Principles

Purpose principle
1.2 Decisions under the Act must be taken with a view to minimising the undesirable effects of mental disorder, by maximising the safety and wellbeing (mental and physical) of patients, promoting their recovery and protecting other people from harm.

Least restriction principle
1.3 People taking action without a patient's consent must attempt to keep to a minimum the restrictions they impose on the patient's liberty, having regard to the purpose for which the restrictions are imposed.

Respect principle
1.4 People taking decisions under the Act must recognise and respect the diverse needs, values and circumstances of each patient, including their race, religion, culture, gender, age, sexual orientation and any disability. They must consider the patient's views, wishes and feelings (whether expressed at the time or in advance), so far as they are reasonably ascertainable, and follow those wishes wherever practicable and consistent with the purpose of the decision. There must be no unlawful discrimination.

Participation principle
1.5 Patients must be given the opportunity to be involved, as far as is practicable in the circumstances, in planning, developing and reviewing their own treatment and care to help ensure that it is delivered in a way that is as appropriate and effective for them as possible. The involvement of carers, family members and other people who have an interest in the patient's welfare should be encouraged (unless there are particular reasons to the contrary) and their views taken seriously.

Effectiveness, efficiency and equity principle
1.6 People taking decisions under the Act must seek to use the resources available to them and to patients in the most effective, efficient and equitable way, to meet the needs of patients and achieve the purpose for which the decision was taken.

Using the principles
1.7 All decisions must, of course, be lawful and informed by good professional practice. Lawfulness necessarily includes compliance with the Human Rights Act 1998.

1.8 The principles inform decisions, they do not determine them. Although all the principles must inform every decision made under the Act, the weight given to each principle in reaching a particular decision will depend on the context.

1.9 That is not to say that in making a decision any of the principles should be disregarded. It is rather that the principles as a whole need to be balanced in different ways according to the particular circumstances of each individual decision.'

The authority of the code was recently considered in *R (Munjaz)* v *Mersey Care NHS Trust* [2005] HRLR 42. In this case, the House of Lords had to consider whether the policy and practice of a hospital with regard to the seclusion of patients was lawful. Part of the evidence against the hospital was that it had departed from the code. However, it was held that the trust had shown good reasons for departing from the code: the code is guidance and not instruction. In emphasising that such departures should be exceptional, Lord Bingham said (para. 21):

> It is guidance which any hospital should consider with great care, and from which it should depart only if it has cogent reasons for doing so. Where, which is not this case, the guidance addresses a matter covered by section 118(2), any departure would call for even stronger reasons. In reviewing any challenge to a departure from the Code, the court should scrutinise the reasons given by the hospital for departure with the intensity which the importance and sensitivity of the subject matter requires.

Courts may even decide that the code does not explain concepts in the Mental Health Act accurately. In *R(E)* v *Bristol City Council* [2005] EWHC 74 (Admin), which is discussed more fully later, the judge said that the code, in explaining the word 'practicability', had confused this concept with 'possibility' and that in this respect the code was wrong. Something may be possible but not practicable, and the Act, in s.11(4), is concerned with the practicability of consulting the nearest relative and not with the possibility of doing so. Practitioners need to be aware of judgements such as this which supplement the Mental Health Act and the code. This revised position is adopted in the 2008 edition of the Code.

As the above highlights, there are many areas where practitioners will face dilemmas where guidance is not totally satisfactory. As a practitioner these dilemmas can either cause personal and professional uncertainty, or assist in the development of sound practice through keeping up to date with legal developments, having access to professional supervision and working in environments that allow the development of sound practice.

Key definitions

Mental disorder

The amendments contained in the Mental Health Act 2007 mean that there is now a very broad definition of 'mental disorder'. It is 'any disorder or disability of the mind'.

There is some crossover in the application of the MHA between those with a mental disorder and those with a learning disability (the latter being people with 'arrested or incomplete development of mind', in the terms of the Act). However, people with a learning disability are not subject to compulsory admission to, and detention in, hospital for treatment under section 3 (see 'Compulsory admission', below), unless they behave in an 'abnormally aggressive' or 'seriously irresponsible manner'. They can, however, be admitted for assessment, and assessment followed by medical treatment, under section 2.

Section 1(3) says that dependence on alcohol or drugs is not to be considered to be a disorder or disability of the mind.

It may be helpful to bring special attention to s.1(3) for this reason:
the previous exclusions for promiscuity, other immoral conduct or sexual deviancy have now gone.

Patient

'Patient' for the purposes of the Act is defined in s.145(1) as a person 'suffering or appearing to be suffering from mental disorder'.

Nearest relative

'Relative' is defined in s.26, in descending order of seniority, as follows:

a)   husband or wife or civil partner (but not if deserted/permanently separated)

b)   cohabitor of six months or more; this includes same-sex partners

c)   son or daughter

d)   father or mother

e)   brother or sister

f)   grandparent

g)   grandchild

h)   uncle or aunt

i)   nephew or niece

j)   any other person who has lived with the patient for at least five years.

'Nearest relative' is the person highest in the list subject to some additional rules if there are two of the same standing, the elder is nearest. If the patient ordinarily resides with or is cared for by one or more relatives or was cared for by such person immediately before admission to hospital, these would be given preference over all others (s.26 (4)).

Note that, by virtue of s.29, a person can apply to a county court, which can order that the functions of the nearest relative are to be carried out 'by the applicant, or any other person specified in the application, being a person who, in the opinion of the court, is a proper person to act as the patient's nearest relative and is willing to do so'. The following may apply to the court: the patient, any relative, anyone living with the patient, an AMHP.

The nearest relative may apply for a patient's compulsory admission to hospital (ss.2, 3, 4), or reception into guardianship (s.7). The Code of Practice recommends giving preference to the AMHP taking on the role, however, because of their greater professional knowledge and distance from the patient (para. 4.28).

Note the following additional points:

• the nearest relative has the right to object to admission for treatment, or guardianship

• the nearest relative has the power to discharge a civil patient from detention, or guardianship, though discharge from hospital may be prevented if the patient would be likely to behave dangerously

• the nearest relative has no right to object to a Community Treatment Order but has powers of discharge

• whenever he/she cannot discharge the patient, except when prevented from discharging a patient admitted for assessment, he/she may apply to a Mental Health Review Tribunal.

On nearest relative definition and role, see Brown (2009).

Approved Mental Health Professional

Section 114 states that a local social services authority may approve a person to act as an approved mental health professional for the purposes of this Act. This can now include social workers, nurses, psychologists or occupational therapists, but not doctors. Before approving a person a local social service authority shall 'be satisfied that he has appropriate competence in dealing with persons who are suffering from mental disorder'.

Courses are approved by the General Social Care Council in England or in Wales. So under subsection (10) an 'approved mental health professional' means:

'(a) in relation to acting on behalf of a local social services authority whose area is in England, a person approved under subsection (1) above by any local social services authority whose area is in England, and

(b) in relation to acting on behalf of a local social services authority whose area is in Wales, a person approved under that subsection by any local social services authority whose area is in Wales'.

Note the following point:

the AMHP acts in a personal capacity and must exercise his/her own judgement and should not rely on direction from senior officers. However, though the AMHP does act in such a capacity, he will be protected by the doctrine of vicarious liability.

Under the amended 2008 legislation, this role has been broadened to include other professions such as nurses and occupational therapists and the title changed to 'Approved Mental Health Professional'. This was seen as a way of easing difficulties in the recruitment of ASWs, whilst still providing an alternative to the medical view. The training of AMHPs will remain the responsibility of local authorities although they will not necessarily need to be employed by a local authority.

Responsible clinician

By section 34 'the responsible clinician' means –

(a) in relation to a patient liable to be detained by virtue of an application for admission for assessment or an application for admission for treatment, or a community patient, the approved clinician with overall responsibility for the patient's case;

(b) in relation to a patient subject to guardianship, the approved clinician authorised by the responsible local social services authority to act (either generally or in any particular case or for any particular purpose) as the responsible clinician;

The responsible clinician does not need to be a doctor (as used to be the case with the 'responsible medical officer' (RMO). They could be a doctor or a nurse, social worker, occupational therapist or psychologist.

Hospital

'Hospital' for the purposes of MHA is defined in s.145(1) as any health service hospital within the meaning of the National Health Service Act 2006 and any accommodation provided by a local authority and used as a hospital or on behalf of the Secretary of State.

Informal patients

Section 131(1) states:

> Nothing in this Act shall be construed as preventing a patient who requests treatment for mental disorder from being admitted to any hospital or mental nursing home in pursuance of arrangements made in that behalf and without any application, order or direction rendering him liable to be detained under this Act or from remaining in any hospital or mental nursing home in pursuance of such arrangements after he has ceased to be so liable to be detained.

This is an extremely important provision: it reinforces that hospital treatment should be provided on an informal basis wherever possible. Compulsion should only be used in certain prescribed circumstances.

Section 131 replicates a provision in the earlier Mental Health Act 1959, which was part of an increasing emphasis on informal admissions. However, the question of informal admissions is problematic: a distinction has been made between a fully voluntary arrangement where the patient clearly consents to admission and an informal admission where the patient does not dissent.

The case of *HL* v *UK* [2005] 40 EHRR 32 considered this principle with regard to patients lacking capacity. The European Court of Human Rights ruled that in admissions where patients lacked capacity, the common law principle of acting in the 'best interests' of the patient did not include sufficient procedural safeguards. The Department of Health have issued guidance on the ruling and its impact on informal admissions (**www.dh.gov.uk/assetRoot/04/09/79/92/ 04097992.pdf**).

Compulsory admission

Part II of the Act deals with 'Compulsory admission to hospital and guardianship'. This is an extremely important aspect of mental health legislation and is the focus of much of the work of AMHPs. You should set the earlier reference to the importance of informal admissions against the fact that detained patients form an increasing percentage of all admissions.

Statistics for 2004–05 show that there were 26,752 formal admissions that year. Of these 25,052 were admissions under Sections 2–4 and the rest were under forensic (Part III) sections.

An AMHP assessing for any of the following sections has a duty to satisfy himself that detention in hospital is in all circumstances of the case the most appropriate way of providing care and medical treatment of which the patient stands in need (s.13(2)).

Some AMHPs are concerned that there are few alternatives to admission or preventative services to avoid compulsory admission. Linked with this is an emphasis on a safety-first approach (Titterton, 2005), which can make it increasingly difficult for mental health practitioners to seek a 'least restrictive alternative' as they are guided in the Code of Practice (para. 2.6).

Brown, R. (2009, p.59) lists alternatives to compulsory admission:

> Informal admission, day-care, out-patient treatment, community psychiatric nursing support, crisis intervention centres, primary health care support, local authority social services provision, support from friends, relatives, voluntary agencies.

The three key sections concerning compulsory admission are:

Section 2 – admission for assessment

Section 4 – admission for assessment in an emergency

Section 3 – admission for treatment

These three sections are outlined quite fully below.

Admission for assessment – Section 2

i) Grounds for admission

s.2 (2) 'An application for admission for assessment may be made in respect of a patient on the grounds that –

a) he is suffering from mental disorder of a nature or degree which warrants the detention of the patient in a hospital for assessment (or for assessment followed by medical treatment) for at least a limited period; and

b) he ought to be so detained in the interests of his own health or safety or with a view to the protection of other persons.'

Here any form of mental disorder may furnish grounds for an application. Therefore a person with learning disability may be detained under this section.

ii) Procedure

An application for admission for assessment may be made either by the nearest relative of the patient or by an approved mental health professional.

Section 11(3) requires that

> 'Before or within reasonable time after an application for the admission of a patient for assessment is made by an approved mental health professional, that professional shall take such steps as are practicable to inform the person (if any) appearing to be the nearest relative of the patient that the application is to be or has been made and of the power of the nearest relative under section 23 (2)(a) below'. (This is the power to discharge the patient from hospital.)

The application needs to be based on the written recommendations in the prescribed form of two doctors.

> A patient admitted to hospital in pursuance of an application for admission for assessment may be detained for a period not exceeding 28 days beginning with the day on which he is admitted.

iii) Discharge

s.23 (2) 'An order for discharge may be made in respect of a patient –

(a) where the patient is liable to be detained in pursuance of an application for admission for assessment ... by the responsible clinician, by the managers or by the nearest relative of the patient.'

A patient detained under s.2 may also be discharged by a Mental Health Review Tribunal, if an application to a tribunal has been made by the patient within 14 days of the patient's admission to hospital (s.66 (1) (a) and (2) (a) and s.72 (1) (a)).

An order for discharge by the nearest relative may be blocked by the responsible clinician on the grounds that the patient, if discharged, would be likely to act in a manner dangerous to other persons or to himself. (s.25). The nearest relative has no right of appeal.

Admission for assessment in cases of emergency – Section 4

i) Grounds for admission

s.4(2) 'It is of urgent necessity for the patient to be admitted and detained under section 2 above and that compliance with the provisions of this part of this Act relating to applications under that section would involve undesirable delay.'

ii) Procedure

s.4 (2) 'An emergency application may be made either by an approved mental health professional or by the patient's nearest relative.'

(3)   'An emergency application shall be sufficient in the first instance if founded on one of the medical recommendations required by section 2 above, given, if practicable, by a practitioner who has previous acquaintance with the patient.'

(4)   'An emergency application shall cease to have effect on the expiration of a period of 72 hours from the time when the patient is admitted to the hospital unless –

   a) the second medical recommendation required by section 2 above is given and received by the managers within that period.'

Under section 4(5) the applicant must have seen the patient within the previous 24 hours of the application being made.

iii) Discharge

In effect, only the responsible clinician and the hospital manager can discharge the patient.

Practice issues

Admission under section 2 is the *normal* procedure; admission under section 4 should be in exceptional cases only. Given the consistent misuse of emergency admission powers under the previous legislation, it is vital to resist misuse of section 4 on the grounds of administrative convenience, reluctance of a second doctor to attend, or local policies by hospitals regarding 'out of hours' admissions.

3. Admission for treatment – Section 3

i) Grounds for admission

s.3 (2) 'An application for admission for treatment may be made in respect of a patient on the grounds that –

a)   he is suffering from mental disorder of a nature or degree which makes it appropriate for him to receive medical treatment in a hospital; and

b)   . . .

c)   it is necessary for the health or safety of the patient or for the protection of other persons that he should receive such treatment and it cannot be provided unless he is detained under this section; and

d)   appropriate medical treatment is available for him.'

A person with learning disability who is not abnormally aggressive or seriously irresponsible cannot be detained under this section.

ii) Procedure

s.11 (1) 'An application for admission for treatment may be made either by the nearest relative of the patient or by an approved mental health professional.'

Note
Under s.11 (4) such an application shall not be made by an AMHP 'if the nearest relative of the patient has notified that professional or the local social services authority on whose behalf the professional is acting, that he objects to the application being made'. No application should be made except after consultation with the person (if any) appearing to be the nearest relative of the patient unless it appears to the professional that in the circumstances such consultation is not reasonably practicable or would involve unreasonable delay.

The issue of 'practicability' is dealt with in the Bristol case referred to earlier. In this case the patient sought assurances that her nearest relative (NR) under the Act would not be contacted by an AMHP in the event that an admission under section was required. It was put to the court that this would cause undue distress to the patient, a view supported by her psychiatrist. In this case the court decided that in these circumstances it would not be practicable to contact the NR.

Prior to this judgement, the practicability of contacting the nearest relative was explained by the Code of Practice. It was impracticable to contact the NR when an ASW could not establish contact with the NR due to lack of information and referred to the 'availability of the nearest relative, not the appropriateness of informing or consulting the person concerned' (Code of Practice, para. 2.16).

The judge discussed the interpretation of 'practicability':

> *To confine practicability, as does the Code of Practice, is far too restrictive and could lead and, in my judgement, would lead to positive injustice in the breach of the claimant's rights under Article 8.*

The Bristol case is still relevant to the context of the revised Mental Health Act.

s.11 (5) No application 'shall be made by any person in respect of a patient unless that person has personally seen the patient within the period of 14 days'.

The application needs to be based on two medical recommendations.

A patient admitted under section 3 may be detained in a hospital for a period not exceeding six months. This can be renewed for 6 months and then annually.

Where renewal of s.3 is contemplated, the responsible clinician must examine the patient within two months of expiry of the section (s.20 (3)) and decide whether grounds for renewal exist. These are set out in s.20 (4) and are substantially the same as grounds for admission in s.3 (2).

Under s.20 (5) the RC must 'consult one or more other persons who have been professionally concerned with the patient's medical treatment' before the order is renewed.

iii) Discharge

s.23 (2) 'An order for discharge may be made in respect of a patient –

a) where the patient is liable to be detained in a hospital in pursuance of an application for admission for treatment by the responsible clinician, by the managers, or by the nearest relative of the patient.'

NB A patient detained under s.3 may also be discharged by a Mental Health Review Tribunal if he applies to the tribunal within the first six months of detention, then once during each period of renewal (MHA 1983, s.66 (1)(b) and (2)(b), s.72(1)(b)).

The nearest relative may apply to the tribunal if his order for discharge under s.23 (2) has been barred under s.25 (1) on the grounds that 'the patient if discharged would be likely to act in a manner dangerous to other persons or to himself'.

Practice issues

The choice between appropriately using section 2 or section 3 for compulsory admission is discussed in the Codes of Practice. The guidance varies between England and Wales.

Other compulsory powers (very briefly) are as follows:

4. Reception into guardianship (ss.7–10)

This applies only to patients 16 and over. If a patient is suffering from mental disorder of a nature or degree which warrants reception into guardianship and it is necessary in the interests of the welfare of the patient or protection of others, that patient should be received into guardianship. The application is made by an AMHP or the NR, with recommendations by two registered medical practitioners. The application is made to the relevant Social Services Department rather than hospital.

(See s.7 and the commentary on it in Barber, Brown and Martin, 2008; this contains references for further reading.)

5. Compulsory detention of informal patients (s.5(2))

The clinician in charge or person designated by them can detain an informal patient for up to 72 hours by reporting that a compulsory admission 'ought to be made' to the hospital managers.

A nurse (suitably qualified) can detain an informal patient who is receiving treatment for up to six hours (s.5(4)) or until a clinician with the authority to detain him/her arrives, whichever is the earlier.

6. Mentally disordered persons found in public places (s.136)

A police officer may take a person to a 'place of safety', usually a hospital, if that person 'appears to be suffering from mental disorder' and is 'in need of immediate care or control'.

Within 72 hours the person is to be examined by an AMHP and doctor and a decision made to release the detained person or make other necessary arrangements such as admission or support in the community.

7. Warrant to search for and remove patients (s.135(1))

An AMHP may obtain a warrant from a magistrate to search and remove a person from premises to a place of safety if there is reason to suspect that he or she is suffering from a mental disorder and a) is being neglected or ill-treated or not kept under control or b) lives alone and is unable to care for himself. A doctor and AMHP must accompany the police officer. As with s.136, the timescale for this is 72 hours.

If a patient is admitted under any of the short-term/emergency sections (ss.4, 135. 136), compulsory treatment does not apply. Any treatment for mental disorder of a patient detained under these sections would be under the Mental Capacity Act in the 'best interests' of the patient or possibly, in an emergency, under common law. This could include sedation or tranquillisation for patients who are highly aroused or distressed or who may be putting their own or others' health or safety at risk by their behaviour.

Discharge from hospital

Informal patients

An informal patient may discharge him/herself.

Section 5(2) allows a clinician to prevent an in-patient leaving hospital and to detain that person for up to 72 hours for assessment.

Section 5(4) allows a nurse to prevent an in-patient leaving hospital and to detain that person for up to six hours.

Detained patients

Discharge by responsible clinician or hospital managers

A person must be discharged when he is no longer suffering from mental disorder and from any order where it is no longer necessary.

Discharge by nearest relative

The NR may apply to hospital managers for the discharge of a person detained for treatment or assessment: ss.23, 25. The nearest relative must give 72 hours' notice – the RC can then certify that in his/her opinion the patient would be likely to act in a manner dangerous to other persons or himself if discharged – this has the effect of preventing discharge.

The NR would then have to apply to the Mental Health Review Tribunal requesting discharge.

Discharge by Mental Health Review Tribunal (MHRT)

Each MHRT has three members, comprising a legal chair, one medical member and one lay member. The relevant individual has a right to free legal representation in proceedings before the MHRT. MHRT proceedings are governed by Mental Health Tribunal Rules.

The function of the MHRT is to review the justification for the patient continuing to be detained or in guardianship: it is not concerned with the lawfulness of the initial admission.

The functions of MHRTs are dealt with in Part V of the MHA. (For a commentary see Jones, 2008; also Bartlett and Sandland, 2007, pp.373–429.)

A patient wishing to challenge the legality of his initial admission would normally do so by one of:

i)   *Habeas corpus* proceedings

or

ii)   judicial review

or

iii) action for damages for torts of false imprisonment and/or assault.

MHRT can order discharge on application from:

•   patient

•   nearest relative

•   Secretary of State

•   automatically in the case of a person who has not had a tribunal hearing within six months of admission.

A person dissatisfied with a decision of MHRT can:

i)   ask the MHRT to state a case for the High Court (s.78)

or

ii)   apply for judicial review of the MHRT decision.

After-care

After-care, following hospital discharge, is a recurrent concern, arousing much mass media attention and public anxiety, often focused on those diagnosed as psychopathic, the issue of 'treatability' and the tension between public protection and individual liberty.

For patients detained on section 3 after-care service will be free.

Criminal proceedings

Even though social workers in mental health services may not be involved with people made subject of court orders in criminal proceedings, it is very much more likely for those employed in the probation service and certain for those employed in special hospitals.

Criminal proceedings are dealt with under Part III of the Act. No attempt is made to summarise the legislation here.

(For further information see the commentary in Barber, Brown and Martin, 2008.

Section 17 leave

Section 17 of the Act allows a responsible clinician to grant leave to a patient who is liable to be detained in hospital, thereby providing a means for a detained patient to be absent from hospital. Leave can be granted for specified or for indefinite periods or time. The RC can attach conditions if thought necessary in the interests of the patient or for the protection of others. While on leave the patient remains liable to be detained, subject to Part 4 consent to treatment provisions and can be required to receive treatment for mental disorder.

An RC has the power to revoke leave of absence and recall a patient to hospital if they think it necessary in the interests of the patient's health or safety or for the protection of others.

Barber, Brown and Martin (2008, p.50) point out that 'there have been several cases before the courts, where patients have challenged the lawfulness of their continued detention where their care and treatment was largely managed outside of a hospital environment. The outcomes of the cases to date have established that detention can continue to be renewed, and that leave of absence can continue to be granted long term provided that there is a significant component of the patient's care and treatment plan taking place at a hospital. There is no requirement for the patient to be re-admitted or to be treated as an in-patient'.

However, with the introduction of Community Treatment Orders there is now a requirement that RCs consider the use of a CTO where leave of absence will exceed 7 consecutive days.

The English Code of Practice states at Para 21.10:

> *The requirement to consider SCT does not mean that the responsible clinician cannot use longer-term leave if that is the more suitable option, but the responsible clinician will need to be able to show that both options have been duly considered. The decision, and the reasons for it, should be recorded in the patient's notes.*

Community Treatment Orders (CTO). Section 17A

The CTO replaces after-care under supervision, s25A. As with after-care under supervision, a CTO cannot be made unless a patient is liable to be detained in a hospital for treatment. Thus patients who are liable to be detained under section 3, 37, and unrestricted Part 3 patients, can be made subject to a CTO by their RC, with the agreement of an AMHP as long as the following criteria are met as set out in s17a(5):

(a) *the patient is suffering from mental disorder of a nature or degree which makes it appropriate for him to receive medical treatment;*

(b) *it is necessary for his health or safety or for the protection of other persons that he should receive such treatment;*

(c) *subject to his being liable to be recalled as mentioned in paragraph (d) below, such treatment can be provided without his continuing to be detained in a hospital;*

(d) *it is necessary that the responsible clinician should be able to exercise the power under section 17E(1) below to recall the patient to hospital;*

(e) *appropriate medical treatment is available for him.*

The RC and AMHP must agree that the above criteria are met. The AMHP must also state that it is appropriate to make the CTO, and where discretionary conditions are set, agree that these are necessary or appropriate.

There are two kinds of condition:

Mandatory conditions
All patients made subject to a CTO will have the following two conditions attached to the order. These require them to make themselves available for:

1. examination by the RC for the purpose of extending the CTO, and
2. examination by the SOAD for the purpose of consent to treatment provisions.

Discretionary conditions
The RC may, if they can obtain the agreement of an AMHP, specify further discretionary conditions. These must be considered necessary or appropriate to:

*   ensure the patient receives medical treatment, or

*   prevent risk of harm to the patient health or safety, or

*   protect others.

Section 20A of the Act sets out the provisions and criteria for extending CTOs. The CTO will last for an initial period of six months, and can then be extended for a further six months and then yearly. The RC, with the agreement of an AMHP, can extend a CTO if he is satisfied that the initial criteria are still met, and the AMHP agrees that it is necessary to extend the order.

Patients who are subject to CTOs may be recalled to hospital by their RC. Recall must be in writing and can only take place if either the patient has failed to comply with a mandatory condition or they require medical treatment in hospital for their mental disorder, and there would be a risk of harm to the health or safety of the patient or to others if they were not recalled to hospital for treatment of their mental disorder. After recalling the patient the RC will consider whether, within the 72 hour period, any problems can be resolved and the patient returned to the community. During the period of recall a patient is subject to Part 4 of the Act, which may allow compulsory treatment.

If a patient needs care and treatment as an in-patient for a longer period the RC could consider revoking the CTO. The RC, with the agreement of an AMHP, may revoke a CTO if the criteria for detention under s3 are met. This would mean that:

*   the patient is suffering from a mental disorder of a nature or degree which makes it appropriate for him to receive medical treatment in a hospital; and

*   it is necessary for the health or safety of the patient or for the protection of other persons that he should receive such treatment and it cannot be provided unless he is detained under this section; and

*   appropriate medical treatment is available for him.

A patient may be discharged from a CTO by their RC, NR (subject to the restrictions set out in section 25 of the Act whereby the RC can bar the discharge if the patient is dangerous), a Tribunal or the hospital managers.

(This case study is taken from Brammer, 2009, p.368.)

CASE STUDY

George, aged 47, is susceptible to periods of depression and self-harming. He has been admitted to the local psychiatric hospital on a voluntary basis a number of times over the years. He recently lost his job, became depressed, stopped taking his medication and started to drink heavily. He refused to go back into hospital on a voluntary basis and has been detained for five months. His only relative, a sister whom he sees infrequently, has contacted the hospital and insists George should be allowed home. His living accommodation is very poor and he has very few links in the community. He would also like to be discharged. The hospital are concerned that if discharged he will fail to take his medication and may start to self-harm again.

Consider any option that would enable George to return safely to the community.

Chapter 8
Community care law: an introduction

Overview

We have already considered examples of social work service operating within a statutory framework in relation to children and mental health services. We have also seen that the law in these areas is not value-neutral.

In this chapter we look at the legal framework of community care and in particular the framework for community care decisions. This involves the interaction of the statutory rules in the relevant legislation (with the NHS and Community Care Act 1990 as the starting point for assessments) and the general common law rules applicable to decision-making. These rules for decision-making – generically known as administrative law – are outlined in Chapter 9.

The law therefore contributes in a substantive and a procedural way to social work assessments and service provision (in this context, by substantive we mean, roughly 'what you can do', and by 'procedural', roughly, 'how you should do it'). It is essential that you grasp the connection between these two elements, to ensure that your decisions not only accord with principles of good social work practice, but are also lawful.

This chapter is only intended to be an introduction to community care law. However, you will find much useful advice and guidance on work in the community care field in Brown, K. (2006) *Vulnerable Adults and Community Care*. Exeter: Learning Matters. This text is written by practitioners to support and illuminate social work practice issues in this field.

Objectives

After completing the reading and exercises, you should be able to:

- identify the legal framework for community care and the values underlying it
- appreciate the complexity of the law in this area
- understand the community care decision-making process
- apply the law to novel fact situations.

ESSENTIAL READING

There is a useful outline of this complex area of law in **Brammer** (2007), Ch. 14 'Community Care'; also see Ch.17 on 'Adult Protection').

Alternatives are:

Ball and McDonald (2002, Ch.12)

Brayne and Carr (2008, Ch.16) overview – community care services and service users

Johns (2007, Ch.5)

Vernon (1998), Ch.6 – this chapter contains a brief chronological outline of community care legislation, but obviously only up to 1998.

For background material on community care law and policy see: **Brayne and Broadbent** (2002) Ch.4

There are chapters in the following book relevant to community care law (in particular, Ch. 16 – 'Care in the community; Ch. 29 'The Court of Protection'; Ch. 32 'Elder abuse'):

Cull, L. A. and Roche, J. (eds) (2001) *The Law and Social Work: Contemporary Issues for Practice*. Basingstoke: Palgrave

FURTHER READING

Clements, L. and Thompson, P. (2007) *Community Care and the Law* (4th ed.). Legal Action Group. This book is particularly recommended for practitioners in community care: it provides a well-structured discussion of a very complex area of law, policy and practice; in addition, appendix A contains key provisions from relevant legislation.

Cooper, J. (ed.) (2000) *Law, Rights and Disability*. London: Jessica Kingsley

Department of Health (2000) *No Secrets: The protection of vulnerable adults – Guidance on the development and implementation of multi-agency policy and procedures*. London: HMSO

Gordon, R. and Mackintosh, N. (1996) *Community Care Assessments: A Practical Legal Framework* (2nd ed.). London: Sweet and Maxwell

Griffiths, G. and Roberts, G. (1995) *The Law and Elderly People* (2nd ed.). London: Routledge

Johns, R. and Sedgwick, G. (1999) *Law for Social Work Practice: Working with Vulnerable Adults*. Basingstoke: Macmillan

McDonald, A. (2000) *Community Care Law*. Norwich: University of East Anglia

Mandelstam, M. (1998) *An A–Z of Community Care Law*. London: Jessica Kingsley

Mandelstam, M. (2009) *Community Care Practice and the Law* (4th ed.). London: Jessica Kingsley. (The above text contains, among other things, summaries of key cases affecting community care decisions.)

Taylor, M. and MacDonald, A. (1995) *The Law and Elderly People*. London: Sweet and Maxwell

Journals

As for other aspects of social work law you should use mainstream social work journals, but a few other examples of journals which sometimes contain material on community care law are:

British Medical Journal
Disability and Society
Health Service Journal
Legal Action (frequent articles)
Modern Law Review
Nursing Standard (and other nursing journals)

Websites

Use the website of (and publications from) the following:

Age Concern (England)
Astral House
1268 London Road
London SW16 4ER
Tel: 0800 009966
Website: **www.ageconcern.org.uk**

The Disability Alliance
Universal House
88–94 Wentworth Street
London E1 7SA
Tel: 020 7247 8776
E-mail: **office.da@dial.pipex.com**
Website: **www.disabilityalliance.org**

Help the Aged
207–221 Pentonville Road
London N1 9UZ
Tel: 020 7278 1114
Website: **www.helptheaged.org.uk**

MENCAP
123 Golden Lane
London EC1Y 0RT
Tel: 020 7608 3254
Website: **www.mencap.org.uk**

The Royal Association for Disability and Rehabilitation (RADAR)
12 City Forum
250 City Road
London EC1V 8AF
Tel: 020 7250 3222
E-mail: **radar@radar.org.uk**
Website: **www.radar.org.uk**

Carers UK (Carers National Association)
Website: **www.carersonline.org.uk**

You can also get relevant information on the following government website: **www.dh.gov.uk**

The rest of this chapter contains:

- Sources of community care law

- Community care law – general considerations

- Community care – the legal framework

- The importance of case law

- Making connections

- Case studies.

Sources
Legislation

Below is a list of key community care legislation, in chronological order. Further references to these Acts are made in this section.

National Assistance Act 1948 (NAA)

Health Services and Public Health Act 1968 (HSPHA)

Chronically Sick and Disabled Persons Act 1970 (CSDPA)

Local Authorities Social Services Act 1970 (LASSA)

National Health Service Act 1977 (NHSA)

Health and Social Services and Social Security Adjudications Act 1983 (HASSASSA)

Mental Health Act 1983 (MHA)

Disabled Persons (Services, Consultation and Representation) Act 1986 (DPSCRA)

National Health Service and Community Care Act 1990 (NHSCCA)

Carers (Recognition and Services) Act 1995 (CRSA)

Community Care (Direct Payments) Act 1996 (CCDPA)

Mental Capacity Act 2005

Recent legislation
There is other more recent legislation which will, increasingly, have an impact on community care services, in particular the following:

Health Act 1999
This abolishes the previous law on fund-holding GP practices (s.1) and establishes Primary Care Trusts (s.2). Very importantly for local authority social work agencies, it establishes a framework for closer cooperation between the NHS and local authorities (see ss. 26–32 on 'Partnerships'). This will fundamentally affect the structure and organisation of community care services.

Care Standards Act 2000
This Act, now fully implemented, will have a wide ranging impact on social work and social care services.

It establishes a National Care Standards Commission (s.6 – already implemented). It provides national minimum standards for, and leads to greater co-ordination and uniformity of, registration and inspection of a wide range of 'public care' services such as nursing and residential homes for older people, children's homes and fostering and adoption services. It will also impact directly on the social work profession itself by establishing a General Social Care Council (s.54) and requiring the registration of social workers.

Health and Social Care Act 2001
This is the legislative means of implementing the NHS Plan (the White Paper (Cm. 4818 – I) published in July 2000) and the government response to the Royal Commission on Long Term Care (Cm. 4818 – II). It is in five parts.

Part III enables the establishment of Care Trusts (s.45) and therefore builds on those aspects of the Health Act 1999 which require closer co-operation between health authorities and local authorities.

Part IV deals with the funding of long term care. Very importantly the responsibility for care in nursing homes passes to local authority social services departments. 'Preserved rights' to funding through income support and job seekers allowance end.

The complexity of community care legislation

Part III of the NHS and Community Care Act 1990 (fully implemented in April 1993) provides the legislative framework for community care in England and Wales. However, as Brayne and Martin note (1997: 276), 'this area of law is, to put it mildly, not user friendly. The opportunity in the NHSCCA to bring all the principles into one understandable piece of legislation was thrown away.' Unlike the Children Act, the NHSCCA is certainly not consolidating legislation: instead, it provides a bare framework, to which is attached a complex range of legislation (much of which is referred to above).

The quotation above (in the 5th edition) is replaced in the 9th edition by the following 'warning' (Brayne and Carr, 2005, p.525) which explains why this is 'difficult territory':

- 'There are many different types of vulnerable people needing support within the community or residential care
- You may owe different types of duty depending on the service user's needs
- You will find descriptions of the types of service users, the range of needs, and the powers and duties you must exercise in different pieces of legislation, regulations, and circulars
- Courts interpret your powers and duties in ways that may be hard to comprehend.'

The complexity of community care law means that government circulars are frequently issued, in an attempt to clarify and develop law, policy and practice. It is therefore essential that social work practitioners working in the broad field of community care are aware of such guidance. This is particularly important in relation to what are termed 'local authority circulars' (LACs) (e.g. Dept. of Health Circular *Community Care: Review of Residential Homes Provision and Transfers* – LAC (91)12). When LACs are issued under s.7(1) of the Local Authority (Social Services) Act 1970 (LASSA), it 'places a duty on Local Authorities, in the exercise of their service functions, to act under the guidance of the Secretary of State. Such guidance should must normally be followed by local authorities; deviation would only be permissible for good reason, and even then without substantial departure from guidance (*Robertson* v *Fife Council*)' (Mandelstam, 2005, p.64).

At the same time you must also be aware of the court's responses to the practice generated through this policy guidance, especially by means of judicial review.

Some leading cases are referred to in the section on case law later in this chapter. The relationship between legislation policy guidance, practice and judicial decisions is complex, dynamic – and very difficult to keep up with.

Policy guidance

As indicated above, policy guidance is an extremely important means of clarifying (and sometimes, in effect, extending) a very complex area of law. A distinction is drawn between:

- **Policy guidance**: though not 'law' (only Acts, regulations and case law) as indicated above, this is formal guidance issued under s.7(1) of LASSA 1970 and must be adhered to
- **Practice guidance**: 'Such guidance is advice on how an authority might go about implementing or interpreting a particular statutory responsibility' (Clements, 2004, p.19).

A key thing to know, therefore, is whether guidance is issued under s.7(1) LASSA 1970. Most Department of Health guidance on community care law is not issued under this Act, i.e. it is practice guidance.

Guidance is issued in the form of local authority circulars (LAC), local authority social services letters (LASSL) and letters or advice notes from the Chief Inspector of the SSI (Social Services Inspectorate) (CI). An example of the latter is an 'important early advice letter on the implementation of the community care reforms sent by Herbert Laming (then Chief Inspector of the SSI); this is often referred to as the "Laming Letter", although its official title is CI (92)34, i.e. the 34th such letter sent by the Chief Inspector [in 1992], (Clements and Thompson, 2007, p.20).

The content of LACs and LASSLs can be found at **www.dh.gov.uk**

There is a brief outline of community care regulations and guidance in Clements (2004, Ch.1).

Students and practitioners should also be familiar with the following publications:

- **Department of Health** (1989) *Caring for People* (Cm. 849). London: HMSO
  This White Paper stated the government's intention that local authorities, health authorities, etc. would be required to publish plans for community care services (see reference to Community Care Plans below).

- **Department of Health** (1990) *Community Care in the Next Decade and Beyond*. London: HMSO
  This contained early policy guidance on the implementation of the NHS and Community Care Act 1990.

- **Department of Health** (1991) *Care Management and Assessment: A Practitioner's Guide*, London: HMSO
  This contains early and important practice guidance. It is an essential reference text. Also see:

- **Department of Health** (1991) *Care Management and Assessment: A Manager's Guide*. London: HMSO

- **Department of Health** (1993) *Empowerment, Assessment, Care Management and the Skilled Worker*. London: HMSO

More recent discussion relevant to community care is contained in the following White Papers:

- **Department of Health** (1998) *Modernising Social Services* (Cm.4169). London: HMSO

- **Department of Health** (2006) *Our Health, Our Care, Our Say* (Cm.6737). London: TSO

- **Department of Health** (2001) Learning Disabilities White Paper – *Valuing People: A New Strategy For Learning Disability for the 21st Century* (Cm. 5086)

Community care law – general considerations

There are four initial points to make:

1) Planning for community care operates at two levels:

   i)   at the community level

   ii) at the individual level.

As you work through these materials, you should try to identify how the legislation provides for this. For example, s.46 (1) of the NHSCCA 1990 requires the local authority to 'prepare and publish a plan for the provision of community care services in their area'. These Community Care Plans are usually published jointly by the social services department and the local health commission. They are normally published annually and there should be consultation with health authorities, housing authorities, voluntary agencies and service user representatives.

2) You also need to identify those parts of the legislation, which give rise to powers and those giving rise to duties on the part of a local authority. A power permits, but does not oblige, an authority to act: the word 'may' is usually used. A duty obliges an authority to act: the word 'shall' is usually used. (However, see 3 below for a further complication.)

3) In addition, it is important to distinguish between a general duty (sometimes referred to as a target duty, as in 'target populations') and a specific duty (individual duty). General duties are expressed broadly, in terms of people in certain categories – an example is s.29 of the NAA (see below). Individual duties, as the term implies, are expressed in respect of a particular person (where an assessment has been completed) – an example is s.2 CSDPA (see below).

This is a very important distinction (not just in community care law). It has been the focus of much case law in community care: generally, authorities can take their finite resources into account in relation to general duties (and often not provide a service); they are much less likely to be able to do so where there is a specific duty.

4) As the earlier quotation from Brayne and Martin implies, community care practitioners need to be very aware of the category into which the service user they are working with falls: this will determine the relevant legislation to be used and, therefore, the powers and duties that apply. Sometimes, of course, a service user may fall into more than one category; or there may be dispute about which one category applies.

As an example of this 'category' issue, home help services could be provided under the following legislation:

- Section 45 HSPHA – a duty to promote the 'welfare of old people'

- Section 2 CSDPA – a duty to provide 'practical assistance' for people who are disabled (within the terms of the definition in s.29 NAA)

- Schedule 8 NHSA – a duty to provide such services for 'a person who is suffering from illness, lying-in, an expectant mother, aged, handicapped as a result of having suffered from illness or by congenital deformity'.

This gives some indication of the complexity of community care legislation. Many practitioners have only a hazy understanding of the key legislation and try to get by on the basis of agency policy.

This is not acceptable for two reasons:

a) they are less likely to be clear about their legal obligations and so won't be able to advise service users appropriately, concerning the services they are entitled to

b) arising from a) they are more likely to make errors in decision-making, which can be contested in the courts and lead to expensive legal defences (thereby further draining scarce resources).

Community care – the legal framework

The core Act in community care is now the NHSCCA 1990. However (as noted above), this Act then links to other legislation, some of which pre-dates the 1990 Act and some of which has been added on since, in a way that is often complicated.

Two key sections in the NHSCCA are s.46 and s.47.

Section 46 provides that, following consultation with a number of specified bodies, each local authority must prepare and publish a plan for the provision of community care services in their area. If you have not seen one of these community care plans, it would be worthwhile doing so.

'Community care services' are defined in s.46(3) as services which a local authority may provide or arrange to be provided under any of the following provisions:

(a) Part III NAA

(b) s.45 HSPHA

(c) s.21 and Schedule 8 NHSA

(d) s.117 MHA.

You will note that the CSDPA – a core piece of disability legislation – is not included in the above list. However, provision made under the CSDPA *would* normally be regarded as part of community care services, not least because of the link between s.29 NAA and s.2 CSDPA (see Example 1 under 'Making connections' below).

Section 47 is the starting point for community care assessments. Section 47 (1) states that 'where it appears to a local authority that any person for whom they may provide or arrange for the provision of community care services may be in need of any such services, the authority –

a) shall carry out an assessment of his needs for those services; and

b) having regard to the results of that assessment, shall decide whether his needs for the provision by them of any such services.'

Two points need to be made about the above:

i) Local authorities don't have to provide services themselves: they may 'arrange for' their provision. In fact, funding arrangements built into community care policy require that most services are not provided by local authorities, but by voluntary and commercial agencies.

ii) While the right (for service users) to have an assessment is fairly clear, the right to service provision itself is less so.

This is because of ambiguities in the language of the legislation to which s.46 links; whether or not the reference is to powers or duties; and the 'strength' of those duties.

It is also because the provision of service is contingent on an assessment and the duty to carry out that assessment is itself full of words requiring interpretation: 'where it appears...', 'having regard to . . . ' and, of course, that very problematic term which is at the centre of much social work practice – 'needs'.

The community care services to which s.46 refers are now outlined in brief, in the order given above (see Vernon, 1998, pp.145–151 for a fuller chronological summary). Also see brief references to each Act in Mandelstam 1998 and, for a very detailed discussion, Mandelstam (2009).

Part III National Assistance Act 1948

You may still hear references to Part III accommodation. This is the Part III being referred to.

There are two key sections in this part:

Section 21 requires a local authority to provide accommodation for people over 18 who because of 'age, illness, disability or any other circumstances are in need of care and attention which is not otherwise available to them . . . '

Section 29(1) requires a local authority to promote the welfare of:

a) the blind and partially sighted

b) the deaf and hard of hearing

c) persons suffering from mental disorder

d) other persons who are substantially or permanently handicapped by illness, injury or congenital deformity.

Both the above sections originally contained powers, which have, in effect, been converted into general duties by directions from the Department of Health in LAC (93) 10. This reinforces the point made above about the importance of policy guidance in government circulars.

Section 45 Health Services and Public Health Act 1968 (HSPHA)

This gives local authorities the power to promote the welfare of old people. DHSS Circular 19/71 identifies the range of services, including 'meals on wheels', home care services, housing adaptations, warden services, etc.

Government guidance indicates that this provision is not for those who are 'substantially and permanently handicapped'. They would be included in the CSDPA (see below).

Section 21 and Schedule 8 National Health Service Act 1977 (NHSA)

This is a complex piece of legislation, referring as it does to the powers and duties of health authorities as well as local authority social services departments.

Schedule 8 mentions three sets of services:

i) services for expectant and nursing mothers (para. 1)

ii) services for the prevention of illness, the care of those who are ill and the after-care of those who have been ill (para. 2); though this provision is vaguely worded, there is a duty to provide after-care services to those who have had a mental disorder, because of a direction under LAC (93) 10

iii) home help and laundry services (para. 3).

Section 117, Mental Health Act 1983

This imposes a duty on health authorities and local authorities to provide after-care services for certain categories of mentally disordered patients who have left hospital, until the authorities 'are satisfied that the person concerned is no longer in need of such services' (s.117 (2)).

The three categories of patient are those who have been detained under:

i) section 3 for treatment

ii) section 37, i.e. a hospital order in criminal proceedings

iii) section 47 or 48 i.e. a transfer order concerning someone who was initially imprisoned.

Section 117 is qualified by the Mental Health (Patients in the Community) Act 1995 on 'supervised discharge' (see Chapter 7).

In the case of *R (Stennett)* v *Manchester City Council* [2002] 2 AC 1127, the House of Lords ruled that 'there is no express power to charge for services provided under it, such services must be provided free of charge' (Jones, 2006, p.451).

> The four provisions above are those specifically referred to in s.46(3) NHSCCA as 'community care services'. However, any community care practitioner must also take account of the following legislation.

Chronically Sick and Disabled Persons Act 1970 (CSDPA)

This was and still is, an extremely important Act. It is a piece of community care legislation (in the sense that a key aim is to support people in their own homes) that pre-dates the NHSCCA by 20 years. The two key sections in it are s.1 and s.2:

Section 1 places a duty on local authorities to:

- inform themselves of the numbers of disabled people in their area to whom s.29 NAA applies;

- publish information about service provision under s.29;

- inform individual people using the authorities services of any additional and relevant services that might meet their needs.

Section 2 places a duty on authorities to provide a range of services to those falling under s.29 NAA.

These services are:

a) provision of practical assistance at home

b) provision of, or assistance in obtaining, wireless, television, library or similar recreational facilities

c) provision of, or assistance in enjoying lectures, games, outings or other recreational facilities outside the home

d) provision of, or assistance in obtaining, travel to participate in services provided under s.29 NAA

e) provision of assistance to adapt home or provide additional facilities for greater safety, comfort or convenience

f) facilitating holidays

g) provision of meals

h) provision of or assistance in obtaining telephone and equipment necessary to enable a person to use it.

The provision of services is subject to the limitations of local authority resources and was considered in the Gloucestershire case (*R* v *Gloucestershire CC, ex p Barry* [1997] AC 584). The courts are reluctant to interfere in local authority decisions about the allocation of scarce resources. See Mandelstam (2009, p.308–315) for further discussion on this complex area.

Disabled Persons (Services, Consultation and Representation) Act 1986 (DPSCRA)

Some sections of this 1986 Act, to do with advocacy, were never implemented. The Act can be broken down into three key elements:

i) Section 4 imposes a duty on local authorities, on a request from a disabled person, or carer, to assess him/her for services under s.2 CSDPA. (This resolved any uncertainty about whether potential service users have a right to assessment: they have. What is far more contentious is their right to services under s.2.)

ii) Sections 5 and 6 impose duties on social services departments and education authorities to carry out assessments etc., of 'statemented' children (i.e. statements of 'special educational needs' under (now) the Education Act 1996) when they approach school leaving age

iii) Section 8 states that the ability of the carer to continue to provide care for a disabled person must be taken into account when making an assessment under any of the following:

- Part III NAA

- s.2 CSDPA

- Sched 8 NHSA

- Part III Children Act 1989.

Carers (Recognition and Services) Act 1995 (CRSA)

This Act reinforces and extends the provision of s.8 DPSRCA to assess the needs of the carer. Where a local authority is making an assessment under s.47(1) (a) NHSCCA, s.1(1) of this Act that, where a carer 'provides or intends to provide a substantial amount of care on a regular basis' for the disabled person being assessed, that carer can ask for an assessment of his/her 'ability to provide and continue to provide care'.

It may be appropriate for community care practitioners to arrange for a separate assessment of the carer (i.e. by another practitioner).

Community Care (Direct Payments) Act 1996 (CCDPA)

This Act empowers (i.e. it does not oblige) local authorities to make payments to community care service users so that they can buy their own services. The service user must be a disabled person and must have had a community care assessment done.

Following the Conservative government's Carers (Recognition and Services) Act 1995, giving carers the right to assessment of their own needs, New Labour continued with the Carers' National Strategy, Caring for Carers (DoH, 1999). The stated aim is to support carers to continue caring, to protect their health and well-being, and giving carers rights to access services in their own rights. Following this, the Carers and Disabled Children Act (CDCA) 2000 gave powers to local authorities to provide services to carers including direct payments, following an assessment. The recent Green Paper *Independence, Well-being and Choice* (2005) further strengthens this role with its focus on carers' rights to social inclusion, employment, leisure and well-being.

Of note, though, is that, according to Lyon (2005), the CDCA (2000) gave local authorities 'power' rather than a 'statutory duty' to provide carers direct payments (DP). Only 25 per cent of local authorities were found to be offering carers direct payments (ADSS Survey 2005 quoted by Lyon, 2005). Hudson (2005) went on to report that there was a high level of dissatisfaction with carer assessment from the carers' perspective.

Carers and Disabled Children Act 2000

This Act of Parliament was promised in the Carers Strategy (1999) and made some important changes to assessment and services for carers. This Act gives carers the right to ask for an assessment of their own needs to help them to continue to care, irrespective of whether the person they are caring for has had or is having their own needs assessment. The assessment is available to any carer who provides or is intending to provide regular and substantial care (this is not clearly defined). The Carers and Disabled Children Act 2000 also allows for the first time social services departments to provide services directly to carers, although whether or not a service is provided is up to the social services.

Carers (Equal Opportunities) Act 2004

This Act was implemented in April 2005. It changes the previous law in a few important ways.

Firstly, it places a duty on social services departments to inform carers of their right to an assessment. Secondly, when the assessment is carried out, the purpose of it is not only to help the carer to continue to care, but should also include a discussion on their wish to start paid work or to continue to work, their wish for further education and their wish to engage in leisure pursuits. Thirdly, carers and their needs have previously only been a duty for social services departments but under this Act, social services departments can ask other public bodies, including local health organisations, to provide services to carers; a request which these bodies have to consider and make a reply.

The above is an extremely brief summary of what, in the narrower sense, constitutes 'community care legislation'. (A broader construction would need to include some social security and housing legislation, for example.)

At the end of this section are some case studies. Prior to that are three brief sub-sections on:

- transferring adult social care
- the importance of case law
- making connections.

Transforming adult social care

Although not a legal framework guidance on how social work and care services should be organised and delivered are currently high on the government's agenda. Via Local Authority Circulars (often referred to as LAC documents) the government signals in very strong terms how it expects local authorities to manage the delivery of social care.

Two very influential LACs of recent times are LAC (2008)1. Transforming Social Care – 17 Jan 2008, and LAC (2009) 1 Transforming Adult Social Care – 5 March 2009. These two documents build on the Department of Health Green Paper, *Independence well being and choice* (2005) and reinforced in the White Paper 'Our Health, our care, our say: a new direction for community services in 2006'.

In effect then, two Local Authority Circulars signalled the move towards 'personalisations'. Here it is envisaged the people will have greater choice and control over the support they receive to live the lives they want. Key to this strategy is the notion of a personal budget whereby a service user is allocated their own budget and given a direct payment. They can then use their budget to plan and coordinate their own care package, in effect purchasing their own care support.

Local authorities have been set targets to achieve an increase in the number of direct payments made so this is seen as a way to promote choice and independence.

It is too early to evaluate the import of this strategy, however it is clear that for some (particularly adults with a physical disability) this strategy has been welcomed. However early evidence suggests that the elderly client often want to take control of their own budget and the purchasing of their care. Of note here is the increasing number of elderly clients with dementia for whom direct payments are clearly a difficult issue.

Indeed with the introduction of the Mental Capacity Act (2005) and the growth in numbers of very elderly and those with dementia it would appear that for many potential service users there will be a crucial need for social work/care support. This new strategy is also being launched during the time of the 'credit crunch' so it will be of great interest to all those involved in social care to see how resources are funded and utilised to provide support for a growing number of potential recipients of care services. In a nutshell can society afford this care, and more accurately will society be prepared to pay for the levels of care required.

The importance of case law

We live in an increasingly litigious society. At the same time as people are more prepared to challenge (often using formal legal processes) the decisions of public authorities, those authorities are – at least sometimes – trying to be more open about decision-making processes and the reasons for their decisions. This trend can be associated with the imperatives in social work to work in partnership with service users, to act in an anti-discriminatory manner and to attempt to empower people. All of this is highly problematic: the very terms are extremely contentious, let alone the practice related to them (for example, see Dalrymple and Burke, 2006).

Challenges to social work decisions (often in the form of judicial review – see Chapter 9) are increasingly important. This certainly applies to community care decisions, partly because the complexity of the law sets traps for the unwary.

The term 'case law', strictly, means law as constructed through judicial decisions, as distinct from statute law (i.e. Acts of Parliament). However, in one sense, the distinction between the two is being blurred: courts are making judgements about the decisions of social workers (and others) which are, in turn, based on statute.

If you are a practitioner in this area you must take into account the following considerations:

- the inter-relationship between different Acts (see below)
- the effect of policy guidance
- the distinction between powers and duties
- the distinction between general and individual duties.

Case law has been extremely influential in determining community care decisions and it is possible to make two generalisations from the courts' decision:

i) It is reasonable to say that service users have a right (corresponding to the local authorities' duty) to have their individual needs assessed. However, the extent to which they can assert a right to particular service provision is much more questionable and often hinges on the perennial issue of scarce resources.

ii) Authorities are more likely to be able to use the scarce resources 'defence' (i.e. for reducing, or not providing, a service) in respect of powers rather than duties and in respect of general duties rather than individual duties.

Some examples of leading cases are given below:

1. *R v Gloucestershire County Council, exp Barry* [1997] AC 584
   This is an extremely important case in which, after earlier hearings in the High Court and then the Court of Appeal, the House of Lords decided that local authorities could take into account resources when determining the needs of, and services to be provided for, disabled people under s.2 CSDPA.

2. *R v Sefton Metropolitan Borough Council, exp Help the Aged and Others* [1997] 4 All ER 532
   This is an extremely complex case heard by the High Court and then the Court of Appeal. It concerns whether a service user's resources may be taken into account when providing, or continuing to support, residential care; but also, whether or not an authority can take its own resources into account, when determining need. In this case (focusing on the NAA rather than the CSDPA), contrary to the Gloucestershire decision, the Appeal Court decided that it could not. This was because of differences in the wording of the legislation.

3. *Avon County Council v Hooper and Another* [1997] 1 All ER 532
   A Court of Appeal hearing, concerning a dispute between a local authority and a health authority focusing on the 'reasonableness' (a key word in judicial review) of a local authority using its power under s.17 HASSASSA to charge for residential services provided under Sched 8 NHSA.

4. *R v Islington London Borough Council, exp Rixon* [1997] 1 Education Law Reports 477
   A High Court hearing involving both community care and education legislation. A central issue was the extent to which authorities are required to take into account policy guidance issued under s.7ALSSA (they must, in short).

The above cases and others are outlined more fully in Mandelstam (2009); and some are also referred to briefly in Brayne and Carr (2008) and Vernon (1998), and also more fully, in Clements and Thompson (2007).

The above are only very brief outlines of some key cases and you are advised to consult the law reports for more detailed accounts. The general thrust of decisions in the House of Lords (e.g. *Re T (A Minor)* (1998) 1 CCLR 352) is that local authorities may, to some extent, take their resources into account in making decisions about community care services, but there are constraints on this (see Clements and Thompson, 2007, pp.88–98) and Mandelstam, 2009):

i)   if eligibility criteria are made more severe, there must be an individual re-assessment before deciding on reductions or withdrawal of services

ii)   resources may be taken into account during assessment and in deciding whether or not to provide a service; however, once a decision is made to provide a service resource issues must not impede or reduce this

iii)   resource availability alone cannot be the determinative factor: the service user's needs must be the paramount consideration (Clements and Thompson note (2007, p.104–5) that local authority allocation panels for nursing and residential homes appear to violate this principle)

iv)   scarce resources cannot be claimed as a reason for not providing resources to someone at severe physical risk (this could contravene the Human Rights Act 1998, specifically Article 2 (duty to protect life) and Article 3 (preventing degrading treatment) – see Chapter 13).

Making connections

Because the NHSCCA only provides a starting point for community care assessments, leading to a complex web of other legislation, it is important to be able to make connections between the various bits.

Here are two examples:

Example 1

As you will have seen above, s.46(3) NHSCCA does not specifically include services under the CSDPA as 'community care services'. However, most commentators would view this central piece of disability legislation as a community care provision. The following connection reinforces this:

i)   Part III NAA is defined by the NHSCCA as providing 'community care services'.

ii)   Part III NAA includes s.29 providing what is now a duty to 'promote the welfare' of certain vulnerable groups.

iii)   Section 2 CSDPA places a duty on authorities to provide a range of services to those falling under s.29 NAA (the former being an attempt, in part, to specify how the rather vague 'promoting welfare' in the latter was to be done).

IV)   There is therefore a clear link between the NHSCCA and the CSDA.

Example 2

i) Community care assessments are initiated on the basis of s.47(1) NHSCCA. However:

ii) Section 47(2) NHSCCA states that, in making the above assessment, if the person concerned appears to be disabled then his/her needs for services under s.2 CSDPA must be assessed.

iii) Section 8 DPSCRA states that the ability of any carer to continue to care must be taken into account in an assessment for s.2 services.

iv) Section 1(1) CRSA reinforces point iii) above, because of its emphasis on the right of a carer to ask for their own assessment, as well as for the disabled person; but it also links back to point i) above, because it refers to the right of carers to ask for their own assessments where a local authority is making assessments under s.47(1)(a).

This section of the book provides only a summary of an extremely complex body of legislation. Some aspects of the legislation are not referred to at all. For further details you should consult the references cited.

However, the summary will go some way to assist you with the case studies below.

Case studies

(These two case studies are taken from Vernon, 1998, pp.179–182.)

In considering the case studies below, ensure that you correctly identify the relevant community care law and the practice issues that arise and their relationship to each other.

CASE STUDY 1

Ranjit is 46. He has had a bad car accident, which has left him paralysed from the waist down. He is still in hospital but his condition is such that he can be discharged. He lives with his wife in a terraced house, which is in poor condition; it is damp and does not have central heating. The bathroom and toilet are on the ground floor but down a small flight of steps at the rear of the house. His wife, who speaks very little English, suffers from angina and high blood pressure.

What are the key considerations in this situation? What action would you take and on what legal basis?

CASE STUDY 2

Alice is 84 years old and lives on her own in a local authority flat. She has been referred to the social services department for the first time by her GP and the case has been allocated to you. She has very bad arthritis and her flat is damp and draughty and has not been modified in any way to help her. She has trouble using the bath and toilet and she cannot get out to collect her pension.

Identify the statutory provisions which you would consider in determining the ways in which you could help Alice continue to live in her own flat. In what circumstances would she be entitled to residential accommodation?

Chapter 9
Decision-making: the legal framework (administrative law)

Overview

In examining the legislation in relation to children, mental health and community care, we have seen how statutes create a legal framework within which social workers and other professionals practise. However, statutes do not exist in a vacuum and the interpretation of statutory provisions is sometimes informed by other rules, which do not appear on the face of the statute but are implied into the Act.

This is the case in relation to decision-making, which is an important generic social work function. The rules we are going to examine in this chapter apply to decision-making by public authorities, a term that includes both central and local government. So when you are making a decision under a particular statutory provision, you need to bear in mind that you have to apply not only the requirements contained in that provision, but also the common law rules discussed in this section. Remember, however, that these are common law rules and that specific statutory provisions may displace them.

These common law rules are sometimes referred to as rules of administrative law. We have tried to present them in a positive way, as they are designed, in part, to promote good decision-making. Many of them are really matters of common sense, which you would apply anyway. The other side of the coin is that if you fail to follow these rules, you will be acting unlawfully and this might expose your authority to legal proceedings. A number of legal procedures may be used to challenge unlawful decisions: these include judicial review, proceedings in a tribunal or a complaint to an ombudsman; there are also complaints (or representations) procedures derived from the Children Act 1989 and the Health and Social Care (Community Health and Standards Act 2003).

In the exercises at the end of this section, we have deliberately chosen examples from areas other than social work to enable you to concentrate on applying the principles to given fact situations.

Objectives

After completing the reading and exercises, you should be able to:

- identify the legal framework for decision-making by public authorities
- have an awareness of the impact of legal requirements on decision-making
- apply the legal rules to novel fact situations

- understand how decisions may be legally flawed and how such flaws may be avoided

- have an awareness of the procedures and remedies available in respect of decisions, which are legally flawed; in particular, be aware of the nature of judicial review.

Principles for decision-making

Administrative law is often seen by public authorities in defensive terms, e.g. in terms of avoiding judicial review, or complaint.

But it can also be seen, more positively, as a guide to good decision-making. The remainder of this section implies these positive principles, but they can be expressed in the following abbreviated terms.

You should:

- identify the law correctly
- make sure you know what your (legal) powers are and do not go beyond them
- follow any statutory criteria (e.g. in the application of terms used in an Act, or in any procedural requirements)
- identify the purpose of the law and act in accordance with it (this is to do with the 'spirit' as well as the 'letter' of the law)
- take into account relevant considerations and do not take into account irrelevant considerations
- follow the requirements of natural justice (for example: letting people have their say; not making up rules after the event; hearing 'both sides'; avoiding bias)
- reach decisions based on the evidence
- act 'in good faith' (this is to do with avoiding discrimination, or even malice or vindictiveness)
- be 'reasonable': there should be some rational line of argument that you can adduce, to support your decision.
- apply the Human Rights Act 1998, which is now relevant to all decisions of 'public authorities' (see Chapter 13).

ESSENTIAL READING

There is relatively little on administrative law in the key social work law texts, but the following extracts are relevant:

Brammer (2009, Ch.2) (especially the brief section on judicial review, pp.41–42)

Brayne and Carr (2008, pp.3–8)

Vernon (1998, pp.159–161)

You are particularly referred to:

Brayne, H. and Broadbent, G. (2002) *Legal Materials for Social Workers* (Ch.1 'Social work and the legal framework'; especially the section on administrative law)

The following discussion on social work accountability also has some relevance to the principles of administrative law:

Braye, S. and Preston-Shoot, M. (2001) *Social work practice and accountability*, in Cull, L.A. and Roche, J. (eds) *The Law and Social Work: Contemporary Issues for Practice*. Basingstoke: Palgrave

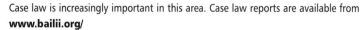

Useful website:
Case law is increasingly important in this area. Case law reports are available from
www.bailii.org/

There is a brief general discussion of judicial review in **Slapper and Kelly** (2006, pp.267–273). There is also relevant material in other general texts on the English legal system e.g. by Elliott and Quinn.

There is an outline of judicial review in **Mandelstam** (2009, pp.101–112) (now in 4th edition); and a much briefer version in **Mandelstam** (1998, pp.123–124).

The remainder of this chapter consists of the following:

• Powers and duties

• The exercise of statutory powers

• Misuse of powers

• Redress

• Judicial review

• Exercises – case studies.

Powers and duties

It is important to distinguish between powers and duties.

• Powers are indicated in statute by words such as 'may'. This indicates that the functions referred to are discretionary, rather than a requirement.

• Duties are indicated in statute by words such as 'shall'. This indicates that the functions referred to are a requirement.

However, this distinction, whilst providing a starting point, is extremely simplistic. Some of the reasons for this are as follows:

• There is also a distinction between general duties and specific duties. General duties (or target duties) are those duties owed to a 'target population', e.g. children 'in need' or other 'vulnerable' groups of the population. Specific duties are duties that are owed to a particular person (usually following an 'assessment'). Specific (or individual) duties are seen as being stronger than the more generalised target duties. Examples of this distinction were given in Chapter 8.

• Powers are sometimes subsequently converted (frequently by government circular) to duties – though not usually the other way round. You need to be alert to this.

• Powers and even duties (the things that social workers and others 'must' do) are contingent on interpretation of statutory terms. These terms can be presented in two categories:

i) statutes frequently state that public service agencies are required to provide a service, but then qualify this with terms such as 'take reasonable steps', 'so far as is practicable', 'appropriate', etc.

    ii)   social work legislation, and social welfare legislation generally, is replete with ambiguous words concerning its subject(s). Examples are:

- 'significant harm' and 'children in need' (Children Act 1989)

- 'mental disorder' and 'health or safety...protection of other persons' (Mental Health Act 1983)

- persons who are 'substantially or permanently handicapped...' (National Assistance Act 1948 and associated community care legislation).

- Law operates in a political and economic context. Social work agencies have finite resources and are often in a position where they know they 'must' do something – but they also know they can't. This can then lead to legal challenges, especially judicial reviews, which are part of the subject of this chapter.

The exercise of statutory powers

The nature of discretion

Where decision-makers are given a discretion under a statute, they must consider the exercise of that discretion in any given case. This means that a decision-maker cannot simply say 'no' without even considering the matter.

Discretion involves choice: a person exercising a discretion may either do something or not do it. A decision-maker must consider the matter before reaching a decision and must make that decision on lawful grounds.

Decision-makers must not 'fetter their discretion': that is, they must not commit themselves to a course of action which prevents them from exercising their discretion. One way this might occur is by having an over-rigid policy. It is perfectly permissible to have a policy, which indicates how a discretion might normally be exercised. This assists good administration by promoting consistency and indicating to applicants how discretion might be exercised. However, a policy must not be mechanically applied and must not be so rigid that it prevents the decision-maker from exercising discretion in any given case. Thus a lawful policy will contain a statement to the effect that this is what will normally happen, but that cases falling outside the policy will still be considered.

For example, in *Findlay* v *Home Secretary* [1985] AC 318, the Home Secretary's policy on early release of those serving prison sentences was held to be lawful on the basis that, although he indicated that certain categories of prisoner would not normally be eligible for early release, he had not shut out the possibility of early release for someone in that category.

Exercising powers

The general principle is that a person can only exercise powers given to him/her. The person must also be aware of the following matters identified by Lord Greene in *Associated Provincial Picture Houses* v *Wednesbury Corporation* [1948] 1 KB 223:

a) legal power must be correctly identified and statutory criteria followed

b) proper purpose of power must be identified

c) relevant considerations must be taken into account and no irrelevant considerations are to be taken into account

d) reasonableness – Lord Greene said that a decision would be unreasonable where it is such that no reasonable authority could ever come to it. (You will come across case law with judgements containing circular and ultimately unhelpful 'reasoning' such as this.)

In *Council of Civil Service Unions* v *Minister for the Civil Service* [1985] AC 374, Lord Diplock regrouped these criteria under three headings:

1) illegality

2) irrationality

3) procedural impropriety.

He also identified a fourth criterion, proportionality, which he said the courts might develop. Particularly under the influence of the Human Rights Act 1998, the courts increasingly expect decision-makers to act in a way that is proportionate – in other words, that they do not use powers excessively, or, more colloquially, they do not use a sledgehammer to crack a nut. This is particularly important when coercive powers are used and is considered further in Chapter 13.

Misuse of powers

Having identified the positive requirements of the law, we need to consider where a decision-maker can go wrong. The cases provide examples. In considering them, think about whether the decision-maker could have acted differently and avoided acting unlawfully.

Illegality

Getting the law wrong: see, for example, *Tameside MBC* v *Secretary of State for Education* [1977] AC 1014. Under s.68 Education Act 1944, the Secretary of State may give such directions to a local education authority 'as appear to him to be expedient' provided he is satisfied that the authority 'have acted or are proposing to act unreasonably'.

The council had put forward a scheme for the implementation of comprehensive schools within its area. This had been approved by the Secretary of State. Following an election, however, the ruling group on the council changed, and the new council proposed to abandon the comprehensive scheme and instead retain grammar schools and operate a selective regime. The Secretary of State gave directions under s.68 requiring the council to implement the comprehensive scheme.

It was held that the directions were unlawful. The local authority had a scheme which was capable of implementation. It could not therefore be said that they were acting unreasonably, and therefore the Secretary of State had no basis for issuing directions.

Improper purpose

Congreve v *Home Office* [1976] QB 629

Under the Wireless Telegraphy Act 1949, a television licence may be issued subject to such terms as the minister may think fit and may be revoked on giving written notice to the recipient.

The minister had announced an increase in licence fees. Congreve, and a number of like-minded people, had bought new television licences before their existing ones expired in order to avoid the increased fee which would be payable if they waited for their licences to reach the expiry date. The Home Secretary wrote to these people stating that they could not renew their licences early and demanding the difference between the fee they had paid and the increased fee.

It was held that the Home Secretary was acting unlawfully. The object of the licensing scheme was to regulate broadcasting and not to make money. The licence holders were acting lawfully in that there was nothing in law to stop them acting as they had.

Neglecting relevant considerations/taking into account irrelevant considerations

Roberts v *Hopwood* [1925] AC 578

A council was empowered to pay 'such wages as it should think fit'. It established a minimum wage and decided to pay the same wage to men and women who were doing the same job.

It was held that the council was acting unlawfully. It had not taken into account the going rate for jobs when deciding upon the minimum wage. Nor had it taken account of the fact that no other council paid men and women at the same rates. Further, in relation to both of these decisions, it had not considered the interests of the ratepayers.

Unreasonableness/irrationality

Backhouse v *Lambeth LBC* [1972] *The Times*, 14 October

The council was empowered to make such reasonable charges for the tenancy of its houses as it determined. In order to evade obligations imposed on it by the Housing Finance Act 1972, and to avoid imposing rises on its tenants, it raised the rent of one house by £18,000. It was held that this was a decision that no reasonable authority could have come to.

Failure to observe procedural requirements

- Rules of natural justice
- Failure to give a hearing at all

Cooper v *Wandsworth Board of Works* (1863) 14 CBNS 180

An Act provided that if a person began to build a new house without giving seven days' notice to the Board, then the Board could demolish that house. Cooper began to build a house, and, without warning, the Board demolished it. It was held that the Board was acting unlawfully. It should have given Cooper notice of its intentions and given him an opportunity to respond before acting.

- Bias

R v *Metropolitan Stipendiary Magistrate ex p Pinochet Ugarte (no. 2)* [2001] 1 AC 119

General Pinochet had challenged attempts to extradite him. His appeal was heard by the House of Lords. In the proceedings in the House of Lords, Amnesty International was allowed to make submissions. One of the judges was Lord Hoffmann, who was a former director of Amnesty International and whose wife had a continuing association with the organisation. The House of Lords decided, by a majority of three to two, that General Pinochet should be extradited. Once Lord Hoffmann's association with Amnesty was discovered, General Pinochet argued that the decision was invalid, on the ground that Lord Hoffmann might not be impartial because of his association with that organisation.

The House of Lords held that the decision was invalid. Even though Lord Hoffmann might not have been in fact biased, his association with Amnesty gave the appearance of bias and this invalidated any decision he had participated in.

- Fair hearing

R v Barnsley MBC ex p Hook [1976] 3 All ER 452

A market stall holder had been observed urinating in a side street one evening after trading had finished and the nearby public lavatories had been closed. The market manager revoked Hook's licence, which meant he was unable to continue to trade. Hook was granted a hearing before a committee of the Council, but the market manager was present throughout and Hook was not allowed to cross-examine him. He was also present while the council committee deliberated. The committee confirmed the market manager's decision.

The Court of Appeal held that this decision could not stand. Hook had not had a fair hearing.

- Failure to observe statutory requirements

Proportionality

R (Daly) v Secretary of State for the Home Department [2001] 2 AC 532

A policy required all prisoners to leave their cells while a search of the cell was being conducted. This was challenged as being in breach of rights under Article 8 (with regard to the right to respect for privacy of correspondence).

It was held that while the right under Article 8 was not absolute and could be restricted, this particular policy was disproportionate – it was not necessary to search cells in the absence of the occupant in all cases. A more selective use of this technique might have been lawful.

Bad faith

An example would be doing something in a deliberately vindictive, or discriminatory, fashion.

As decisions are made by public bodies or individuals holding public offices, such as ministers, it is very rarely that bad faith is even alleged, let alone proved.

Redress

The term 'redress' simply refers to the avenues people can take if they don't agree with decisions made and/or feel they have been poorly treated. Many of these don't involve the use of courts and tribunals. Examples are: complaining directly to the social worker and/or manager(s) concerned; contacting local councillors or the MP; using the complaints procedures in the Children Act 1989 or the Health and Social Care (Community Health and Standards) Act 2003.

Other avenues do involve courts or tribunals or, in the case of the Ombudsman, a formal body set up to deal with maladministration.

Judicial review

This is an increasingly important means for the higher courts to supervise the decisions and actions of public bodies, including social work agencies. The key reference points for the courts (see above) are illegality, irrationality and procedural impropriety, together with proportionality. In addition, you need to be aware that the Human Rights Act 1998 will increasingly feature in judicial review decisions (see Chapter 13).

It is important to note that 'in judicial review the law courts are, in principle at least, ensuring that local authorities have acted within the law, rather than judging the merits of decisions' (Mandelstam, 1998, p.123).

There are four key points to make about judicial review:

i) It can be used to challenge public bodies (e.g. central and local government) exercising public law functions (usually by exercising statutory powers). This will therefore potentially include most social workers in the UK.

ii) Normally the claimant, i.e. the person bringing the challenge, must have 'sufficient interest' in the case. This gives the claimant what is called standing to bring the claim. *NB* It has been legally established that pressure groups with a particular interest may apply for judicial review.

iii) Traditionally, the doctrine of *ultra vires* is central to judicial review. Put simply, *ultra vires* refers to actions undertaken by a public body that go beyond the limits of its powers. Equally, the exercise of administrative powers will be *ultra vires* if it is, for example, procedurally irregular, improperly motivated, or breaches the rules of natural justice.

iv) If the court upholds the view of the applicant, i.e. holds that the decision was unreasonable, unfair or illegal, etc., it will not put a new decision in its place. The most usual outcome will be for the court to require the authority concerned to review its decision – but, in doing so, to ensure that the principles of administrative law are observed.

Orders

There are various orders available to the courts:

A **quashing order** (previously known as 'certiorari'). The High Court may use this to quash decisions of inferior courts, tribunals and other public bodies (including local authority social services departments) which are deemed unlawful.

A **prohibiting order** (previously known as 'prohibition'). This is similar to a quashing order, except that it is pre-emptive, i.e. it stops public bodies making invalid decisions in the first place.

Injunction. This is now a seldom used remedy in judicial review. It orders an authority to do, or not to do, something.

NB The term 'injunction' has general application in legal proceedings and does not just apply in judicial review. For example, injunctions are frequently used in cases of 'domestic violence' (see Chapter 11).

Declaration. A declaration is a statement by the court to let parties know the legality of a situation. For example, there was a declaration, at the High Court stage in the *Barry* case, that Gloucestershire County Council had unlawfully withdrawn services (since overturned).

Other remedies

Ombudsman

There are several versions of Ombudsman but the one social workers are most likely to come into contact with is the Local Government Ombudsman (Commissioner for Local Administration in England). See **www.lgo.org.uk**

There are also a Parliamentary Ombudsman and a Health Service Ombudsman who deal with complaints alleging maladministration by government departments and the NHS respectively (so the latter will be of relevance to social workers in hospitals and Care Trusts). See **www. ombudsman.org.uk**

The key points to make are:

- ombudsmen investigate 'maladministration' (which is not defined in legislation)
- they will normally only investigate once any complaints procedures and other appropriate avenues have been tried (and failed)
- decisions of local ombudsmen are not enforceable in law courts and they do not set precedents
- they can make recommendations (i.e. to local authorities) concerning, for example, financial compensation, service provision, changes to procedures, etc.

Tribunals

The advantages of tribunals over courts are to do with:

- speed
- cost
- informality (e.g. the courts' rules of evidence don't apply as strictly)
- flexibility (they are not bound by precedent)
- expertise (they include people other than lawyers)
- accessibility
- privacy (they aren't as publicised as court cases).

Disadvantages are to do with:

- appeals procedures – there is no uniform approach, or route, following tribunal decisions and their very 'flexibility' also leads to uncertainty
- publicity – lack of publicity can also be a disadvantage, because issues of public concern are not highlighted
- legal aid – is not generally available in tribunal hearings (except for a few types, including employment appeal tribunals and mental health review tribunals).
  (*NB* Legal aid – being both a means of ensuring access to justice and a drain on public expenditure – has always been controversial. Legal aid is no longer available in many types of cases, following the implementation of the Access to Justice Act 1999. For more information see **www.legalservices.gov.uk**)

FURTHER READING

There are references to tribunals at various points in both **Brayne and Carr** (2008) and a section in **Slapper and Kelly** (2009, pp.398–409).

Case studies

These two examples are, deliberately, not social work related, to enable a concentration on the principles of administrative law.

CASE STUDY **1**

The (imaginary) Football Matches (Miscellaneous Provisions) Act 1989 was passed to enable the government to exact a levy from football clubs to reimburse those incurring expenditure as a result of the holding of football matches in their locality.

Section 3 of the Act provides: 'The Secretary of State may, after consulting the Football League, prescribe the appropriate football levy payable to each club for the football league season.'

Section 20 of the Act provides: 'The Secretary of State may prohibit the playing of a particular match if he believes serious disruption to the community would occur should the match be played.'

Without consulting the Football League, the minister set the football levy at £500,000 for each first-division club. He did this because he thought the clubs were making excessive profits, which they ought not to be allowed to keep, and he refused to hear any representations by either the Football League or any of the clubs. He also banned all football matches held on Friday evenings involving London clubs to enable Members of Parliament to catch trains back to their constituencies without having to share them with football supporters.

Discuss the legality of the actions of the Secretary of State.

CASE STUDY **2**

The Secretary of State for Transport has been empowered, under the (imaginary) London Outer Orbital Motorway (Construction) Act 1987 (the 1987 Act) inter alia:

i. *to decide upon the route of the proposed motorway 'as the Secretary of State, in his discretion, shall think fit' (section 2(1)(a)).*

ii. *to make provision for toll charges on the proposed motorway 'at such rate or rates as the Secretary of State shall by Regulation from time to time prescribe' (section 2(1)(b)).*

The Act also states that the Secretary of State, before exercising any section 2(1) powers 'shall consult with all interested organisations and shall consider any representations made to him pursuant to such consultations' (section 3(1)).

Consider the following:

a. *the Secretary of State makes an Order purporting to be made under powers contained in s.2(1)(a) and (b) of the 1987 Act whereby:*

   i. *He decides that the motorway will not pass close to three villages which form part of a constituency where the sitting MP (who belongs to the same party as the minister) has a majority of 23.*

      The minister does this despite the fact that the alternative route is much more expensive. He justifies his decision on the grounds that 'small villages form an important part of Britain's heritage and should, wherever possible, be protected from major road developments'. The three villages in question all have medieval churches which, it is universally recognised, would have to be demolished if the motorway were to pass close to the villages, as the vibrations would cause structural damage.

   ii. *He announces that no tolls shall be payable for the use of the new motorway for the first two years after its opening to the public.*

   iii. *Thereafter, tolls shall be paid at prescribed rates.*

b. *The Secretary of State has, before making such decisions, deliberately not consulted Maidenport Borough Council, through whose area the motorway will pass, on the grounds that the Council is controlled by the 'loony left' who will merely raise spurious objections.*

Chapter 10
Discrimination and the law

Overview

Social workers are committed to anti-discriminatory practice. A considerable body of evidence has shown, over the years, that certain groups within society are subject to discrimination in relation to certain characteristics. Parliament has decided to act by passing legislation to render illegal certain manifestations of prejudice. It is important to appreciate at the outset the limitations of this legislation. It only applies to certain forms of discrimination in certain defined situations.

We thus examine the legislation designed to tackle the issues of discrimination on grounds of sex, race, disability, religion, sexual orientation and age.

Objectives

After completing this chapter you should be able to:

- understand the nature and general characteristics of the anti-discrimination legislation

- recognise the situations covered by such legislation and identify the omissions

- apply the legislation to novel fact situations

- evaluate the effectiveness of such legislation.

ESSENTIAL READING

Brammer, A. (2007, Ch. 14)

Brayne, H. and Carr, H. (2005, Ch. 18)

Further background material on race, sex and disability legislation is contained in:

Brayne, H. and Broadbent, G. (2002) *Legal Materials for Social Workers* (Ch. 3, 'Anti-discrimination law')

FURTHER READING

Cooper, J. (2001) The Disability Discrimination Act 1995, in Cull, L. A. and Roche, J. (eds) *The Law and Social Work: Contemporary Issues for Practice*. Basingstoke: Palgrave

Duff, R. (2001) Racism and social work practice, in Cull, L. A. and Roche, J. (eds) *The Law and Social Work: Contemporary Issues for Practice*. Basingstoke: Palgrave

Hill, H. (2001) *Blackstone's Guide to the Race Relations (Amendment) Act 2000*. London: Blackstone

McColgan, A. (2005) *Discrimination Law: Text, Cases and Materials*. Oxford: Hart

Connolly, M. (2004) *Townshend-Smith on Discrimination Law: Text, Cases and Materials* (2nd ed.). London: Cavendish

Development of the law (in chronological order)

Disabled Persons (Employment) Act 1944

Race Relations Act 1965

Race Relations Act 1968

Equal Pay Act 1970

Sex Discrimination Act 1975

Race Relations Act 1976

Sex Discrimination Act 1986

Disability Discrimination Act 1995

Disability Rights Commission Act 1999

Race Relations (Amendment) Act 2000

Special Educational Needs and Disability Act 2001

The Employment Equality (Sexual Orientation) Regulations 2003

The Employment Equality (Religion or Beliefs) Regulations 2003

Disability Discrimination Act 2005

Racial and Religious Hatred Act 2006

Equality Act 2006

Employment Equality (Age) Regulations 2006

Useful addresses

Equality and Human Rights Commission
Arndale House
The Arndale Centre
Manchester M4 3AQ
Tel: 0161 829 8100 (non-helpline calls only)
E-mail: **info@equalityhumanrights.com**

3 More London
Riverside Tooley Street
London SE1 2RG
Tel: 020 3117 0235 (non-helpline calls only)
E-mail: **info@equalityhumanrights.com**

3rd Floor, 3 Callaghan Square
Cardiff CF10 5BT
Tel: 02920 447710 (non-helpline calls only)
E-mail: **wales@equalityhumanrights.com**

The Optima Building
78 Robertson Street
Glasgow G2 8DU
Tel: 0141 2885910 (non-helpline calls only)
E-mail: **scotland@equalityhumanrights.com**

The remainder of this chapter contains the following seven sections:

- General characteristics
- Sex discrimination
- Racial discrimination
- Discrimination and disability
- Religious discrimination
- Future developments
- Case studies.

General characteristics

The anti-discrimination legislation shares certain characteristics and employs similar concepts, though there exist differences between the Acts in a number of details.

The basic considerations in each Act can be followed through in five stages:

1. What is discrimination?
The term is used in a particular sense in this legislation to mean, essentially, less favourable treatment.

2. Has there been discrimination?
This involves comparison with an actual or hypothetical person.

3. What was the reason for the discrimination?
If it was for reasons other than sex, race or disability, etc., it is lawful as far as the anti-discrimination legislation is concerned, though note that it may still be unlawful under other legislation, e.g. employment laws.

4. Is the discrimination unlawful?
The Acts only make discrimination unlawful in certain defined situations. Discrimination on grounds of race, sex, etc., falling outside these situations is lawful.

5. Can the discrimination be justified?
Even though the discrimination appears unlawful, there may be grounds on which it is justified, for example if it is a genuine occupational qualification under the Sex Discrimination Act, and therefore lawful. The Acts contain exceptions where discrimination is justified, though these are different in each Act.

You will find it helpful in understanding the Acts if you take a structured approach along the lines indicated above. Each of the following sub-sections, on the sex discrimination, race relations, disability and religious discrimination legislation, is set out slightly differently.

Sex discrimination

Sources

Sex Discrimination Acts 1975 and 1986

Equal Pay Act 1970

Article 141 EC Treaty

The Equality Act 2006 inserts a new provision into the Sex Discrimination Act 1975 (as s.76A) requiring public authorities to have due regard to the need to eliminate unlawful discrimination and harassment and to promote equality of opportunity between men and women when carrying out its functions (compare s.71 Race Relations Act 1976 as amended by Race Relations (Amendment) Act 2000 below).

What constitutes discrimination?

Direct discrimination

SDA 1975 s.1(1)(a): 'A person discriminates against a woman if ... on the ground of her sex he treats her less favourably than he treats or would treat a man.'

Indirect discrimination

SDA 1975 s.1 (1)(b): 'A person discriminates against a woman if he applies to her a requirement or condition which he applies or would apply equally to a man but –

i)   which is such that the proportion of women who can comply with it is considerably smaller than the proportion of men who can comply with it and

ii) which he cannot show to be justifiable irrespective of the sex of the person to whom it is applied and

iii) which is to her detriment because she cannot comply with it.'

Victimisation

SDA 1975 s.4(1): 'It is unlawful to victimise a person because she has:

i)   brought proceedings under this Act, or the Equal Pay Act 1970 or

ii) given evidence or information in connection with proceedings under either Act or

iii) done anything in relation to either Act to the discriminator or any other person or

iv) has made allegations of a contravention of either Act unless the allegation was false and not made in good faith.'

Is the discrimination unlawful?

Employment

Discrimination in employment relates to:

i)   arrangements for determining who shall be employed

ii) terms on which a person offers employment to another

iii) refusing or deliberately omitting to offer employment because of a person's sex

iv) the way in which a person offers access to opportunities for promotion, transfer or training or to any other benefits, facilities or services or by refusing or deliberately omitting to afford her access to them

v) dismissing a person or subjecting her to any other detriment.

It is permissible to discriminate in employment in certain situations:

i) Health grounds – especially to comply with the Health and Safety at Work Act 1974

ii) Genuine occupational qualifications (GOQ) – this means that the nature of a job requires a particular sex for one (or more) of the following reasons:

- to preserve decency or privacy

- living-in and separate facilities not available nor reasonable to expect that they are provided

- work in prison, hospital, etc., and when it is reasonable that the job is done by person of particular sex

- provision of personal services promoting education or welfare, etc., which can most effectively be provided by person of particular sex. This is the provision most likely to affect social services agencies. It states that a GOQ may apply where 'the holder of the job provides individuals with personal services promoting their welfare or education, or similar personal services, and those personal services can most effectively be provided by a man' (s.7 (2)(e)). Note that the legal drafting convention is to refer to 'he/him' and, in this case 'man', but that such references should be taken to refer to 'she', etc., unless otherwise stated. This applies even in a statute on sex discrimination!)

- performance of duties outside the UK in a country where law or customs mean that job could not be done by a person of a particular sex

- the job is one of two held by a married couple.

Enforcement is by an Employment Tribunal. In practice, the Act has been most commonly used in employment, despite the fact that it applies to other activities.

The combined effect of the Equal Pay Act 1970 and Article 141 EC Treaty is that men and women should receive equal pay for equal work. To qualify for equal pay, a person must be in the same employment as the person with whom she is comparing herself and engaged on:

- like work (i.e. the same or broadly similar)

- work rated as equivalent

- work of equal value.

The employer may resist a claim if it can be shown that the difference in pay is due to a genuine material factor which is not the difference of sex, e.g. qualifications, additional responsibility.

Education

It is unlawful to discriminate in relation to provision of benefits, services or facilities (though single-sex changing rooms are permissible) and admissions (though single-sex schools are permissible).

Enforcement is by bringing an action in the County Court.

Goods, facilities and services

- It is unlawful to discriminate in the provision of goods, facilities and services by:
- refusing to provide them
- providing them on different terms according to gender.

Facilities and services include:

- access to and use of public places
- accommodation in hotel, boarding house or other similar establishment
- facilities by way of banking or insurance or for grants, loans, credit or finance
- facilities for education
- facilities for entertainment, recreation or refreshment
- facilities for transport or travel.

This includes services of any profession or trade or any local or public authority. Enforcement is by bringing an action in the County Court.

Advertising

It is unlawful to advertise in a way which indicates an intention to discriminate.

Racial discrimination

The Race Relations Act 1976 (RRA) is modelled closely on the Sex Discrimination Act 1975 and provides for discrimination as above, the only difference being that the discrimination is on racial grounds rather than sexual. Eight key sections of the RRA are set out below:

Section 1

i) **Direct discrimination** – i.e. treating a person less favourably 'on racial grounds' than another person (s.1 (1)(a)). This will include segregation on racial grounds (s.1(2)).

ii) **Indirect discrimination** – i.e. applying a 'requirement or condition' to a person which:

   a) is applied unequally to that person's particular racial group, because of its characteristics

   b) cannot be shown to be justifiable 'irrespective of the colour, race, nationality or national origins of the person to whom it is applied'

   c) is to the detriment of that person (s.1(1)(b)).

Section 2

Victimisation also contravenes the legislation. This would include, for example, treating some-one less favourably because they have taken proceedings, or given evidence, under this Act (s.2(1)).

Section 3

The term 'racial grounds' refers to 'colour, race, nationality or ethnic or national origins' (with a corresponding definition for 'racial group') (s.3(1)).

Section 4

It is illegal to have discriminatory arrangements for deciding who should be employed and on what terms; or by refusing or 'omitting to offer' employment (s.4(1)). It is also illegal to discriminate against existing employees, concerning the terms of employment, or promotion, training, benefits, etc., or by dismissing employees (i.e. dismissing them on racial grounds (s.4(2)).

Section 5

Employment may be offered on racial grounds where there is a 'genuine occupational quali-fication' (GOQ) in being a member of a particular racial group (s.5(1)).

There are four categories of GOQ. The one most relevant to social work concerns 'personal services promoting (the) welfare' of a racial group where 'those services can most effectively be provided by a person of that racial group' (s.5(2)(d)).

Three key sections for social services staff are:

s.20 – which refers to 'discrimination in the provision of goods, facilities or services' (s.20(1) specifies the legal requirement to provide services, etc., in 'like manner and like terms' to all racial groups (though s.35 below may provide exception to this). Section 20(2)(g) is the most relevant to social work provision since it refers to 'the services of any profession or trade, or any local or other public authority'.

s.35 – which provides an exception to discrimination on racial grounds (bearing in mind that discrimination can be positive as well as negative) where this is done with the aim of 'affording persons of a particular racial group access to facilities or services to meet the special needs of persons in that group in regard to their education, training or welfare, or any ancillary benefits'.

s.71 – this outlines the general duty of local authorities (as amended by the Race Relations (Amendment) Act 2000 – see box below).

Section 71(1) now reads:

'Everybody . . . specified in Schedule 1A [which includes local authorities] . . . shall, in carrying out its functions, have due regard to the need –

a) to eliminate unlawful racial discrimination; and

b) to promote equality of opportunity and good relations, between persons of different racial groups.'

In practice, the Act has been used most frequently in relation to discrimination in employment (with which Part II, including ss.4 and 5 above, deals), although it also refers, for example, to education (ss.17–19) and housing (ss.21–26).

Concerning the question of employment it is unlawful to discriminate against a person on racial grounds:

i) in the arrangements for determining who shall be offered employment

ii) in the terms in which employment is offered

iii) by refusing or omitting to offer employment

iv) in terms of employment

v) in access to promotion, transfer or training or to other benefits services or facilities

vi) by dismissing or subjecting the person to any other detriment (s.4).

Discrimination is permissible as indicated above, where being of a particular racial group is a genuine occupational qualification, e.g. authenticity in drama, modelling, provision of food and drink (s.5).

Enforcement mechanisms are parallel to those for the SDA:

- on employment matters, complaints are to an Employment Tribunal

- on other matters (e.g. housing, education) complaints are to the county court. Actions should be taken within six months of the alleged discrimination (eight months if to do with education).

Race Relations (Amendment) Act 2000

This Act was implemented in April 2001. It strengthens and extends the scope of the 1976 Act – it does not replace it.

The two major elements in the Act are:

- the extension of protection against racial discrimination by public authorities
- the requirement of a new enforceable positive duty on public authorities (see s.2 which amends s.71 of the 1976 Act).

It also makes other important changes and in doing so, includes areas not previously covered by the 1976 Act, for example:

- it makes Chief Officers of Police liable for acts of discrimination by officers under their command (see ss.1 and 4)
- it allows complaints of racial discrimination in certain immigration decisions to be heard as part of 'one-stop' immigration appeals (see s.6).

Note: the Race Relations (Amendment) Act 2000 is quite complex in the way it intersects with the 1976 Act and with other legislation.

The complete Act can be found (as with other post-1987 legislation) at: **www.opsi.gov.uk/ acts.htm**

Criminal law

Note that the RRA covers civil proceedings (in county courts and employment tribunals) and is not directly concerned with criminal acts.

Below is a very brief summary of the criminal law concerning incitement to racial hatred, racial harassment and racially motivated violence. This can be provided by reference to the following Acts.

Public Order Act 1986

The law concerning incitement to racial hatred is contained in six offences specified by the Act (ss.18–23), in particular:

- section 18 – threatening, abusive or insulting words or behaviour; or displaying threatening, etc., written material, with the intention to (or being likely to) stir up racial hatred.

- section 19 – publishing or distributing written material which is threatening, etc. (the wording parallels the above).

The Attorney General must consent to criminal prosecutions under this provision and this has limited its use.

Crime and Disorder Act 1998

This Act creates a new and important raft of racially aggravated offences, but based on earlier legislation. It deals with racially motivated (physical) violence, as well as harassment. The relevant sections are ss.28 to 32. The offences identified below are 'racially aggravated' if (see s.28(1)):

'(a) either at the time of committing the offence, or immediately before or after doing so, the offender demonstrates towards the victim of the offence hostility based on the victim's membership (or presumed membership) of a racial group; or

b) the offence is motivated (wholly or partly) by hostility towards members of a racial group based on their membership of that group.'

The 'racially aggravated' offences are then outlined in subsection (1) of ss.29 to 32, with reference to existing legislation, as follows:

s.29(1) (a) an offence under s.20 of the Offences Against the Person Act 1861 (malicious wounding or inflicting grievous bodily harm)

s.30(1) an offence under s.1(1) of the Criminal Damage Act 1971 (simple criminal damage)

s.31(1) (a) an offence under s.4 of the Public Order Act 1986 (fear or provocation of violence)

(b) an offence under s.4A of the 1986 Act (intentional harassment, alarm or distress)

(c) an offence under s.5 of the 1986 Act (harassment, alarm or distress)

s.32(2) (a) an offence under s.2 of the Protection from Harassment Act 1997 (harassment)

(b) an offence under s.4 of the 1997 Act (putting in fear of violence)

Racial and Religious Hatred Act 2006

This Act inserts new provisions into the Public Order Act 1986 (as Part 3A, s.29A-N) which create a variety of offences which have as their common element the intention to stir up religious hatred. They broadly parallel the offences of doing acts intended to stir up racial hatred in Part 3 of the Public Order Act.

'Religious hatred' is explained in s.29A as hatred against a group of persons defined by reference to religious belief or lack of religious belief.

Discrimination and disability

Sources

Disabled Persons (Employment) Act 1944 (DPEA) (now largely repealed)

Disability Discrimination Act 1995 (DDA)

Disability Rights Commission Act 1999

Special Educational Needs and Disability Act 2001

Disability Discrimination Act 2005

See also White Paper (1995) *Ending Discrimination against Disabled People* CM2729

Background

At common law, it was lawful to discriminate against a person on grounds of disability.

DPEA dealt with issue of disabled persons in employment in two particular ways:

1. It established a register of disabled workers ('occupationally handicapped'). It divided workers into those who were able to work in ordinary employment and those who could only work in some form of supported or sheltered employment. The DDA has abolished the register.

2. For open employment, employers were required to maintain a quota of disabled employees. For this purpose, certain jobs were designated as particularly appropriate for disabled persons. These provisions have been repealed by the DDA.

General features of the DDA

1. Structure of Act

Part I	definitions of disability
Part II	discrimination in employment
Part III	discrimination in provision of goods, facilities and provision of services
Part IV	education
Part V	public transport
Part VI	National Disability Council (now Disability Rights Commission)

Part VII   supplemental

Part VIII   miscellaneous

In addition there are eight Schedules.

The Disability Discrimination Act 2005 (inserting a new s.49A into the DDA) places a positive obligation on public authorities to promote equality for the disabled (cf similar duties in relation to promotion of equality between different racial groups and in relation to gender).

2. Definitions

i) 'disability'
A person has a disability if he has a physical or mental impairment, which has a substantial and long-term adverse effect on his ability to carry out normal day-to-day activities (s.1).

The definition only applies for the purposes of this Act.

ii) physical or mental impairment
The Disability Discrimination Act 2005 extends the notice of physical impairment to cover debilitating illnesses such as cancer or multiple sclerosis from the date at which they are diagnosed.

There are also provisions in Schedule 1 enabling the Secretary of State to make regulations declaring that certain conditions may be specified as amounting to, or not amounting to, impairment.

iii) substantial and long-term adverse effects
'Substantial' is not, in general terms, further defined in the Act, although the Secretary of State may make regulations stipulating that certain inabilities do or do not amount to substantial adverse effects on ability to carry out day-to-day activities.

Severe disfigurement is to be treated as having a substantial adverse effect, etc., though the Secretary of State may declare that, in certain circumstances, which may include self-inflicted disfigurement, a severe disfigurement is not to be treated as having a substantial adverse effect, etc.

An impairment has long-term effects if:

- it has lasted for at least 12 months

- it is likely to last for 12 months

- it is likely to last for the rest of a person's life.

There are also powers for the Secretary of State to make regulations determining that certain effects are or are not to be treated as long term.

iv) 'normal day-to-day activities'
An impairment is taken to affect the ability of the person concerned to carry out normal day-to-day activities only if it affects one of the following:

- mobility

- manual dexterity

- physical coordination

- continence

- ability to lift, carry or otherwise move everyday objects

- speech, hearing or eyesight

- memory or ability to concentrate, learn or understand

- perception of risk of physical danger.

The Secretary of State may make regulations extending this list or prescribing circumstances in which something falling within this list is not to be taken to affect the ability of a person to carry out day-to-day activities.

v) 'disabled person'
This is a person who has a disability (within the terms of this Act).

3. Discrimination in employment

i) Application of provisions
The anti-discrimination provisions apply in relation to:

- employment policies

- terms of offers of employment

- not offering employment

and for existing employees:

- terms of employment

- opportunities for promotion, transfer or receiving other benefits

- refusing to afford or deliberately not affording opportunities

- dismissing him or subjecting him to any other detriment.

ii) Nature of unlawful discrimination
It is unlawful for an employer to discriminate against actual or potential employees who are disabled by either:

- subjecting them to less favourable treatment on the basis of disability which cannot be justified: s.5(1); or

- failing to make reasonable adjustments to the working environment as are required by s.6 and being unable to justify such failure: s.5(2).

iii) Less favourable treatment
This requires comparison with a person with different or no disability. Once the person has shown that discrimination is due to disability, it is for the employer to justify less favourable treatment. The employer must then show that reason for treatment was both substantial and material to circumstances of the particular case.

In terms of justifying discrimination s.59 provides that in the event of a conflict between this Act and another statute, whether passed before or after this Act, the other statute prevails – for example, an employer is allowed to discriminate in order to comply with duties imposed under the Health and Safety at Work Act 1974.

Note that:

- applying blanket policies would not amount to justification

- making assumptions or acting on basis of stereotypes would not amount to justification

- if material reason for discrimination could have been resolved by a reasonable adjustment and less favourable treatment puts the disabled person at substantial disadvantage (i.e. if complying with s.6 could resolve the matter) then reason will not amount to justification.

iv) Failure to make reasonable adjustments

Section 6 imposes a duty on employers in respect of arrangements for employment or any physical features of the premises which place a disabled person at a substantial disadvantage in comparison with persons who are not disabled. The employer must take such steps as are reasonable to take in all circumstances in order to prevent the effect of putting the disabled person at a substantial disadvantage.

Note that this only applies where an employer is aware that a disabled person is an applicant for employment or where he knows that the applicant or employee is disabled and is likely to be at a substantial disadvantage compared with other persons. The employer is relieved of duties under s.6 where he does not know and could not reasonably be expected to know that the person falls into either of these categories.

Section 6(3) lists examples of adjustments:

- making adjustments to premises

- allocating some of a disabled person's duties to other people

- transferring a disabled person to fill an existing vacancy

- altering a disabled person's working hours

- assigning a disabled person to a different place of work

- allowing a disabled person to be absent during working hours for rehabilitation, assessment or treatment

- giving her/him or arranging to give her/him training

- acquiring or modifying equipment

- modifying instructions or reference manuals

- modifying procedures for testing or assessment

- providing a reader or interpreter

- providing supervision.

The Secretary of State may make regulations explaining or expanding this list. Note also that this list is only for the purposes of this Act.

In determining whether it is reasonable for an employer to take a particular step, s.6(4) provides that regard shall be had to the following:

- extent to which taking a step would prevent disabled persons being at a substantial disadvantage

- extent to which it is practicable for the employer to take a step
- financial and other costs which would be incurred by the employer and extent to which it would disrupt his activities
- extent of the employer's financial and other resources
- availability of financial assistance to the employer.

4. Provision of goods and services

i) Discrimination in provision of goods and services
Similar concepts apply here, in that discrimination against a disabled person in relation to provision of a range of goods and services is unlawful unless the provider can justify that less favourable treatment.

The Act covers goods and services provided by the private and public sectors (including public authorities).

Section 19 gives examples of services covered:

- access to and use of any place which members are permitted to enter
- access to and use of means of communication
- access to and use of information services
- accommodation in a hotel, boarding house or similar establishment
- facilities by way of banking or insurance or for grants, loans, credit or finance
- facilities for entertainment, recreation or refreshment
- facilities provided by employment agencies
- services of any profession or trade or any local or other public authority.

ii) Exclusions
- transport
- manufactured goods
- services provided outside the United Kingdom.

Special Educational Needs and Disability Act 2001
The duties under this Act (which amends Part IV of the Disability Discrimination Act 1995) affect post-16 education and related services for disabled people and students. Note in particular:

i) It is unlawful to discriminate against disabled people or students by treating them less favourably than others. In addition, responsible bodies will be required to provide certain types of reasonable adjustments to provision where disabled students or other disabled people might otherwise be substantially disadvantaged with the exception of the following:

ii) Responsible bodies are required to make adjustments that involve the provision of auxiliary aids and services; and

> iii) They are required to make adjustments to physical features of premises where these put disabled people or students at a substantial disadvantage.

iii) Justifications (see s.20(3) and (4))

- Discrimination is necessary in order not to endanger health or safety of any person (which may include that of the disabled person).

- The disabled person is incapable of entering into an enforced agreement, or giving informed consent.

- Where the provider would otherwise not be able to provide the service to members of the public.

- The (discriminatory) treatment is necessary in order to enable the provider to provide the service to the disabled person or to other members of the public.

- The difference in the terms on which the service is provided to the disabled person and those on which it is provided to other members of the public reflects the greater cost of providing that service.

Section 21 imposes a duty of reasonable adjustment which the provider will be expected to comply with. Where the service provider has practice, policy or procedure which makes it impossible or unreasonably difficult for a disabled person to make use of service which he provides, they must take such steps as are reasonable in circumstances to:

- amend policies, procedures and practices

- remove or alter physical features

- provide reasonable means of avoiding physical features

- provide reasonable alternative means of delivering service.

Also, where auxiliary aid or service (e.g. information on audio tape) would enable a disabled person to make use of a service or facilitate use by a disabled person of such a service, then the provider must take such steps as are reasonable in circumstances of case to provide auxiliary aid (s.21(4)).

Religious discrimination

Equality Act 2006

Part 2 of the Equality Act 2006 outlaws certain forms of discrimination on grounds of religious belief. It is closely modelled on earlier legislation and uses similar concepts. Religion means 'any religion'. Belief means 'any religious or philosophical belief' (s.44).

Discrimination means less favourable treatment (direct discrimination) or applying a provision which, though applying to anybody, puts persons of a particular religion at a disadvantage and cannot be justified by reference to matters other than religion or belief (indirect discrimination) or victimises someone for bringing proceedings under Part 2 (s.45).

Discrimination is prohibited with regard to:

- goods, facilities and services

- premises

- education (unless a school is designated or registered as having religious character or is a faith school)

- exercise of functions by public authorities

- advertisements

- instructing or causing unlawful discrimination.

There is a general exemption for religious organisations and charities with religious objects.

Age discrimination

The Employment Equality (Age) Regulations 2006 (S.I. 2006/1031) came into force on 1 October 2006 and, in general terms, prohibit discrimination on grounds of age in employment and training. These regulations will, due to their restricted scope, have a limited impact on social work pratice, though once issues relating to the age of retirement and pension rights have been fully resolved may have greater relevance.

Questions

As we have seen, discrimination on grounds of sex and race was outlawed by legislation passed in the 1960s and 1970s (though note the limitations in the application of the Acts) and more recently, on grounds of disability and religion.

Do you think that legislation can make a contribution to the prevention of discrimination?

What other forces can reduce discrimination?

How successful do you think the Sex Discrimination Act and the Race Relations Act have been in reducing or eliminating discrimination in their respective fields?

How successful do you think the more recent disability legislation is proving?

Case studies

CASE STUDY *1*

Southshire District Council has a policy at its leisure centre of charging £1.75 admission to its swimming pools, but allows free swimming 'for children under three years of age and persons who have reached the state pension age'.

Mr and Mrs Jones are both aged 61. Mr Jones has retired from employment. In accordance with the Council's policy, when Mr and Mrs Jones went to the swimming pool, because Mrs Jones had reached the state pensionable age of 60 for women, she was allowed in free, but because Mr Jones had not reached the pensionable age of 65 for men, he was required to pay.

Is the Council's policy lawful?

CASE STUDY 2

Bassetshire County Council advertises for care staff between the ages of 25 and 45.

In addition, the social services department recruits home helps by word of mouth only, arguing that this is a very effective method as it is free and that it has also proved very successful.

Are the Council's actions lawful?

CASE STUDY 3

Dennis is a black (Jamaican origin) member of staff in a local authority social services child protection unit. Undertaking a visit to a home where a (white) child is alleged to have been abused, he is told, by the mother, to 'Piss off, I'm not letting one of your sort touch my kid. Go and get someone else.' He is unable to gain entry to the house or see the child.

On returning to the area office, his team manager suggests allocating a white social worker to the case.

What are your comments?

CASE STUDY 4

Sarah is severely disabled, uses a wheelchair and was refused access to her local cinema because she was a 'fire hazard'. What advice would you give?

CASE STUDY 5

Peter has complained to his local bus company that he cannot access their buses with his wheelchair. The Director of the bus company wrote to him stating that there is no requirement for the company to make sure that disabled wheelchair users can access their buses. Is he correct?

CASE STUDY 6

Susan, a qualified solicitor, was told by a prospective employer, a very large firm of London solicitors, that the firm would have liked to employ her but felt that due to her disability, she would need extended periods of time off work for treatment and the firm would not be able to accommodate this sort of disruption to the office routine. Susan considers that she has been discriminated against. What are your comments?

Chapter 11
Law and policy on domestic violence

Overview

So far, the material in this book has concentrated on 'professional law', that is, law that social workers are themselves legally required to put into practice.

This chapter provides an outline of the law and related policy on domestic violence where the primary (civil) law (Part IV of the Family Law Act 1996) is relevant to the work of social work agencies, but not a direct legal responsibility on them.

Objectives

Having read through this chapter, you should be able to:

- summarise various policy approaches to domestic violence
- identify key aspects of the criminal law and, in more detail, the civil law.

ESSENTIAL READING

Bird, R. (2006) *Domestic Violence: Law and Practice* (5th ed.). Bristol: Jordan

Home Office Domestic Violence Mini-site: **www.crimereduction.gov.uk/dv01.htm** and **http://www.homeoffice.gov.uk/crime-victims/reducing-crime/domesticviolence**

Walby, S. (2004) *The Cost of Domestic Violence*. London: TSO

Urbach, C. and Rights of Women (2000) *Domestic Violence Injunction Handbook.* London: Rights of Women (this gives an outline of the substantive law, as well as information on the process of applying for and enforcing, orders. Updates available on-line)

Also see: **Brammer** (2007, pp.148–150) (also note Ch.11 on 'Adult protection')

Brayne and Carr (2008, pp.539–555)

Vernon (1998, pp.98–107)

FURTHER READING

Brogden, M. and Nijhar, P. (2000) *Crime, Abuse and the Elderly*. Cullompton: Willan Publishing

Cull, L. A. (2001) Violence in the home: social work practice and the law, in Cull, L.A. and Roche, J. (eds) *The Law and Social Work: Contemporary Issues for Practice*. Basingstoke: Palgrave

Foreman, S. and Dallos, R. (1993) Domestic Violence, in Dallos, R. and McLaughlin, E. (eds) *Social Problems and the Family*. London: Sage/Open University Press

Greater London Authority (2005) *The Second London Domestic Violence Strategy*. London: GLA. Accessible at **www.london.gov.uk/mayor/strategies/dom_violence/strategy2.jsp**

Home Office (2008) *National Domestic Violence Delivery Plan Annual Progress Report 2007/2008* Available at **www.crimereduction.homeoffice.gov.uk/domesticviolence/domestic violence069.htm**

Hooper, C.A. (1996) Men's violence and relationship breakdown: Can violence be dealt with as an exception to the rule? in Hallett C. (ed.) *Women and Social Policy: An Introduction*. London: Prentice Hall

McCann, K. (1985) Battered women and the law: the limits of legislation, in Brophy, J. and Smart, C. (eds), *Women-in-Law: Explorations in Law, Family and Sexuality*. London: Routledge

Mullender, A. (1996.) *Rethinking Domestic Violence: The Social Work and Probation Response*. London: Routledge (Note in particular the section on the 'bad news' about the social work response, pp.72–80.)

Kershaw, C., Nicholas, S. and Walker, A. (2008) Crime in England and Wales 2007/2008. *Home Office Statistical Bulletin No.07/08*. London: Home Office

Walby, S. and Allen, J. (2004) Domestic Violence, sexual assault and stalking: Findings from the British Crime Survey. *Home Office Research Study No.276*. London: Home Office

Useful Addresses
Rights of Women
52–54 Featherstone Street
London
EC1Y 8RT
Tel: 020 7251 6577
E-mail: **info@row.org.uk**
Website: **www.rightsofwomen.org.uk**

Women's Aid Federation of England
PO Box 391
Bristol BS99 7WS
Tel: 0117 944 4411 – administration
0808 2000 247 – national helpline
E-mail: **info@womensaid.org.uk**
Website: **www.womensaid.org.uk**

NB This manual does not outline the law on divorce (which is contained in the Matrimonial Causes Act 1973) and separation and related areas such as family property and child support. You are referred to general texts on 'family law' for this. (This term includes not only domestic violence law and divorce and separation, but also adoption, wardship, child abduction and the public law and private law aspects of the Children Act 1989.)

For example, see:
Standley, K. (2006) *Family Law* (5th ed.). Basingstoke: Macmillan

Black, J., Bridge, J., Bond, T. and Gribbin, L. (2007) *A Practical Approach to Family Law*. (8th ed.). Oxford: Oxford University Press

The rest of this chapter provides:

- a brief discussion of policy relating to domestic violence

- an outline of the criminal law

- a more detailed outline of the civil law, particularly focusing on Part IV of the Family Law Act 1996.

Key legislation

Domestic violence is, by its nature, something that cuts across a number of areas of law. Below is listed some of the key legislation.

Family Law Act 1996 Part IV Family Homes and Domestic Violence
Enables 'associated persons' to make civil law applications for non-molestation and occupation orders.

Protection from Harassment Act 1997
Creates two criminal offences:

1. Harassment (s.2)

2. Putting people in fear of violence (s.4)

It also provides civil remedies designed to prevent stalking.

Human Rights Act 1998
Creates duty on public authorities to uphold rights under the European Convention on Human Rights. The rights particularly relevant in the context of domestic violence are:

Article 2 – right to life

Article 3 – prohibition on torture and inhuman treatment

Article 8 – right to respect for privacy and family life

Education Act 2002
Places a duty on Local Education Authorities to safeguard and promote the welfare of children.

Homelessness Act 2002
Puts those who are homeless or liable to become homeless by reason of violence or threats of violence from another person into the category of priority need.

Adoption and Children Act 2002
Amends s.31 Children Act 1989 to include 'impairment suffered from seeing or hearing the ill treatment of another'.

Sexual Offences Act 2003
Creates range of offences of sexual violence with adults and children: see DfES LAC (2004) 17 Sexual Offences Act 2003.

Female Genital Mutilation Act 2003
Makes further provision to criminalise this practice.

Domestic Violence Crime and Victims Act 2004
Improves the legal protection for victims of domestic violence. Provides for mandatory reviews following any domestic homicide (s.9).

Serious Organised Crime and Police Act 2005
Provide that all offences carry a power of arrest without warrant.

Childcare Act 2006
This requires local authorities to improve the well-being of young children in their area. It also requires authorities to reduce inequalities between young children with regard to a number of

matters, including their physical and mental health and emotional well-being and prevention from harm and neglect.

Equality Act 2006

Places new duty on public authorities to promote equality of opportunity between men and women in all areas of policy and service delivery. It is the counterpart of the duty under the Race Relations (Amendment) Act 2000 of promoting racial equality.

Brief discussion of policy

A brief survey of policy positions on domestic violence is given below, but it is worth reflecting, first of all on the very term itself.

Domestic violence is not a new problem. Throughout history, domestic violence has been a feature of family life and part of a wider problem of violence against women. What is new in terms of policy is that domestic violence is no longer viewed as acceptable: it is no longer an assumption that family members have the 'right' to do or say what they like in their own home.

Currently a number of government policy initiatives, involving several departments, aim to improve service responses to victims of domestic violence. These initiatives include multi-agency strategic responses across social services and housing, the NHS and mental health services, the voluntary sector and the criminal justice system.

Understanding domestic violence

In order to understand fully the issue of domestic violence, it is useful to focus not on specific incidences but on patterns of power and control that underlie that behaviour.

In terms of the incidence of crime, domestic violence is one of the greatest problems facing the criminal justice system, accounting for a quarter of all violent crime. Crime statistics and research (see below) both show that domestic violence is a gendered issue. It is predominantly experienced by women and perpetrated by men. Women experience domestic violence regardless of race, ethnicity, religion, class, sexuality, mental or physical ability or lifestyle. The government states that one in four women experience domestic violence at some time in their lives. There were 102 female and 23 male victims of domestic homicide in 2000–01. Women also are at greater risk of repeat victimisation and serious injury (Walby, 2004). See **www.crimereduction.gov.uk/dv01.htm**

Although gender does play a role in domestic violence, it does not mean that all victims will be female and all perpetrators will be male. Domestic violence occurs in lesbian, gay, trans-gender relationships and against men in heterosexual relationships. It does mean, however, that the gender of victim and offender influences patterns of response. For example, women victims may be more likely to be frightened, repeatedly abused and more likely to be murdered. Male victims may be less likely to access services fearing ridicule should their disclosure involve violence from a woman.

Murder statistics

Every year since 1991, an average of 97 women have been killed by a current or former partner, which constitutes 42 per cent of all women killed. On average 28 men are killed annually by a current or former partner – 7 per cent of all men murdered (Walby and Allen, 2004).

Defining domestic violence

The government's 'core' definition of domestic violence is:

> *Any incident of threatening behaviour, violence or abuse (psychological, physical, sexual, financial or emotional) between adults who are or have been intimate partners or family members, regardless of gender or sexuality.* Home Office: **www.crimereduction.gov.uk/dv01.htm**

The definition is wide enough to incorporate issues such as forced marriage, female genital mutilation, 'honour killings' and elder abuse when committed in the family or by an intimate partner.

An adult is any person over 18 years. Violence involving people under 18 is classified as child abuse and dealt with by separate policies and legislation. However, children are affected by domestic violence; many are traumatised by what they witness or overhear, and frequently direct child abuse occurs alongside domestic violence.

Family members are defined as mother, father, son, daughter, brother, sister and grandparents, whether directly related, in-laws or step-family.

ACTIVITY 11.1

Defining domestic violence has always been problematic. No definition will ever be sufficient to understand the complexities of domestic violence.

It is useful to reflect on the following:

- *Domestic violence is rarely a one-off incident; it can be seen as a pattern of controlling behaviour through which the abuser seeks power over the victim.*

- *Focusing on individual acts is necessary for determining thresholds for some agencies, e.g. the police. However, the focus on individual acts often presents an incomplete picture, particularly in terms of the effects of abuse. The criminal law generally operates in terms of individual responsibility. This is one reason why the Domestic Violence, Crimes and Victims Act 2004 is so important in the case of domestic homicides.*

- *When a focus on individual acts is necessary, it is common to view different types of abuse hierarchically. Physical abuse is perceived as 'more serious' than emotional abuse. (Many abused women describe the psychological effects of domestic violence as having a more profound effect than physical violence, even when there has been life-threatening or disabling physical abuse.)*

Questions
1. *What types of abuse fall into the categories noted in the definition of domestic violence?*
2. *Should we use the term 'victim' or 'survivor'? 'Violence' or 'abuse'?*
3. *What are the 'family factors' that influence the prevalence of domestic violence?*
4. *Why do women stay with/leave an abusive partner?*
5. *What do women gain from leaving/staying?*
6. *What are the practical implications for those who choose to stay/leave?*

Law, policy and practice on domestic violence falls into a number of connected categories:

1. Promotion of the protection of the victim (and any dependants) at risk of violence through effective use of the civil law, policy and practice, and holding perpetrators of violent/abusive behaviour accountable for their behaviour.

2. Promoting prevention of interpersonal and gender-based violence through public awareness and primary prevention programmes, as well as through an effective legal framework that will punish the perpetrator.

3. Development of the provision of a range of effective, flexible and reliable services to meet the needs of all victims and their dependants.

4. Promotion of the clear public message that society will no longer tolerate domestic violence.

These policy categories form part of a coordinated multi-agency approach to domestic violence and affect all levels of local government, criminal justice, social welfare and voluntary agencies.

In relation to the principles outlined above, it useful to consider the following:

*   Each victim has a unique set of circumstances that can affect how s/he responds to the violence.

*   Effective interventions that support the victim and increase choices, and build on positive coping strategies that have already developed.

*   Interventions have the potential to be dangerous or even fatal if insufficient priority is given to safety issues. Victim safety must be the overriding priority.

*   The focus of service providers should be what can be offered to increase safety, not just assessments of what is or is not being done.

Questions

This is only a brief discussion on policy strands and theories concerning domestic violence. In reading through this material and other information, consider the following questions:

1. What are your views on the causes of domestic violence?

2. Are there stereotypical images of perpetrators and victims of domestic violence?

3. What policies are appropriate and how should they be developed? By whom?

4. What might work in reducing the prevalence of domestic violence?

5. How do the social factors, not only gender but also class, economic position, race, disability, religion and sexual orientation impact on people's views on, and experiences of, domestic violence?

Below is an outline of the two branches of relevant law – firstly, the criminal law and, in rather more detail, the civil law.

Criminal Law

Domestic violence involves violent crime and significantly impacts on homicides. It is, however, widely accepted that domestic violence is under-reported and studies suggest that women will experience an average of 35 incidents before seeking help (Walby and Allen, 2004).

Domestic violence affects victims, their families and the wider community, regardless of race, geography or social background. One in four women and one in six men will be affected in their lifetimes, with women suffering higher rates of repeat victimisation and serious injury (Walby and Allen, 2004).

This is an extremely brief summary of some key points. The principal legislation on the range of assaults is still the Offences against the Person Act 1861, now supplemented by the Criminal Justice Act 1988.

Broadly, there are four offences of assault, of ascending gravity:

- common assault and battery (s.39 Criminal Justice Act 1988)
- assault occasioning actual bodily harm (ABH) (s.47)
- malicious wounding or inflicting grievous bodily harm (GBH) (s.20)
- malicious wounding or causing GBH with intent (s.18).

Following the Serious Organised Crime and Police Act 2005, there is a power of arrest with regard to all these offences. Definitions of each 'level' tend to vary, but common assault could be something as trivial as a push (though the 'triviality' will depend on who is being pushed and who is doing the pushing); ABH will involve some discernible 'hurt or injury' such as a cut or bruise; GBH is a really 'serious injury' to the body. The Sexual Offences Act 2003 creates a range of offences of sexual violence.

Domestic violence can result in death, which is covered by the common law offence of murder, which is the intentional killing of another human being.

If the police are contacted following an incident of domestic violence, arrest will be more likely when:

- there is evidence of a physical injury, especially if serious
- violence seems likely to recur
- there are witnesses (including older children)
- there is corroborating evidence of physical struggle.

As noted above, not all domestic violence is of a physical nature; the police and other agencies are increasingly aware of this, though other forms of abuse such as psychological damage, are less tangible and tend to present less strongly evidentially in court.

Note the following three points concerning police intervention:

i) If charged, following an incident, the perpetrator may be kept in custody until the hearing, or they are released on bail (not going near the home may be a condition of bail).

ii) Evidence obtained at the scene may be used to prosecute the victim. The Crown Prosecution Service may still be able to prosecute domestic violence cases even if a victim does not wish to proceed.

iii) If found guilty, a range of sentences is possible for the perpetrator, from being 'bound over to keep the peace', to a fine, to a community penalty, to imprisonment.

The above is only a very brief summary of the criminal law on domestic violence and further information may be sought from criminal law textbooks and directly from personnel in the Community Safety Units that most police services now have.

It is worth reflecting on the following points:

- The law is one thing, but policy and practice determine how it operates; this is as much to do with (gendered) attitudes as with the substantive law.

- In prosecuting without the main witness, the CPS is taking responsibility away from the victim and giving social and professional networks the right to intervene and challenge the abusive and violent behaviour of the perpetrator. Does this protect the short-term and long-term interests of the victim?

- How can sentencing properly reflect the long-term and cumulative effects of domestic violence?

Civil law

This section provides:

1) An outline of the current legislation, that is Part IV, Family Act 1996, including:

    - potential applicants

    - occupation orders

    - non-molestation orders

    - without notice orders

    - powers of arrest

    - amendments to the Children Act 1989.

2) Brief comments on other relevant civil law:

    - Children Act 1989

    - Child Support Act 1991 (as amended)

    - Housing Act 1996.

The current legislation: Part IV of the Family Law Act 1996 (FLA) as amended by the Domestic Violence, Crime and Victims Act 2004.

The FLA received Royal Assent in July 1996. Part IV, dealing with domestic violence, was implemented in October 1997.

NB Part II of the FLA deals with divorce and separation. It has not been implemented and there are no plans at present to do so. You need to be careful about this because some older law texts refer to planned implementation in early 1999.

Part IV of the FLA reduced the complexity and unfairness of the previous domestic violence law and procedures by repealing the following legislation:

- Domestic Violence and Matrimonial Proceedings Act 1976

- Matrimonial Homes Act 1983

- Domestic Proceedings and Magistrates' Court Act 1978 (ss.16–18).

The FLA also makes important amendments to other legislation including the Children Act 1989. It has itself been amended by the Domestic Violence, Crime and Victims Act 2004 and the Civil Partnership Act 2004.

1. Potential applicants

'Cohabitants' or 'associated persons' can apply for one, or both, of the two orders (see 2 below). 'Associated persons' are defined in s.62(3) and include those who:

- are or have been married to each other
- are or have been civil partners of each other
- are or have been cohabitants
- live or have lived in the same household (other than simply as 'the other's employee, tenant, lodger or boarder')
- are relatives
- have (or had) agreed to marry each other
- have (or had) entered into a civil partnership agreement.

Note the following observations:

a) These categories will be open to interpretation, but they extend the previous range of applicants (i.e. married couples and cohabitants) and would include, for example, gay and lesbian couples and relatives such as brother/sister, child/parents and grandchild/grandparents.

b) Section 43 states that children under the age of 16 may apply for an order provided that: they have leave of the court and the court is satisfied that 'the child has sufficient understanding to make the proposed application'.

2. Orders

There are two principal orders available under Part IV of the FLA:

- occupation orders
- non-molestation orders.

a) Occupation orders

These orders are dealt with under ss.33–41. Prior to the drafting stages of the FLA, the Law Commission recognised two classifications of occupation orders:

- Declaratory orders, e.g. declaring existing occupation rights; extending them beyond divorce, etc.
- Regulatory orders, which regulate the occupation of the home and will include termination of occupation rights prohibiting parties from entering the home; requiring one party to allow the other entry to and/or remain in the home, etc.

This is a broad classification, but within that, there are five types of occupation order. Their application depends on the legal position of the applicant.

There is no need for social workers to know the details of each type, but they should at least know that they exist. They are:

a) where the applicant has an estate or interest, etc., or has home rights (s.33)

b) where the applicant is a former spouse or former civil partner with no existing right to occupy (s.35)

c) where the applicant is a cohabitant or former cohabitant with no existing right to occupy (s.36)

d) where neither spouse or civil partner is entitled to occupy (s.37) (e.g. where there is an eviction order, or the couple are squatting)

e) where neither cohabitant or former cohabitant is entitled to occupy (s.38).

Grounds for making an occupation order

In deciding whether or not to make an order, the court must 'have regard to all the circumstances'. The factors to be included will vary, dependent on which of the five orders applies, but the considerations, which will always apply (see s.33(6)), are:

- the housing needs and housing resources of each of the parties and of any relevant child

- a 'relevant child' is defined in s.63(2) as
  - any child who is living or might reasonably be expected to live with either party to the proceedings

  - any child in relation to whom an order under the Adoption Act 1976, the Adoption and Children Act 2002 or the Children Act 1989 is in question in the proceedings

  - any other child whose interests the court considers relevant

- the financial resources of the parties

- the likely effect of any order (or not making an order) on the 'health, safety well-being of the parties and of any relevant child'

- 'the conduct of the parties in relation to each other and otherwise' ('otherwise' would include, e.g., towards any children).

The FLA does not prioritise these (or any other) considerations; the weight given to each one will, itself, depend on the circumstances.

However, in order to help the court decide between these competing factors, considerations may be given (in the case of *all* the types of orders) to the question of 'significant harm'.

The court must make an order if 'the applicant or any relevant child is likely to suffer significant harm attributable to conduct of the respondent' if an order is not made (s.33(7)).

The exception to this (i.e. where the court must not make an order) is where:

- the respondent or any relevant child is likely to suffer significant harm if the order is made

- and the harm likely to be suffered 'is as great as, or greater than, the harm attributable to conduct of the respondent which is likely to be suffered by the applicant or child if the order is not made'.

This is the balance of harm test: the court must consider and balance the interests of all those involved (see s.33(7), s.35(8), s.36(8), s.37(4) and s.38(5)).

'Harm' is defined (in s.63(1)) as 'ill-treatment or the impairment of health' in relation to adults; for children (i.e. under 18) the definition is identical to that in s.31 of the Children Act 1989.

The effect and length of occupation orders

The effect of an occupation order will vary. This will partly depend on any existing rights to the property and whether the parties are (or were) spouses, or cohabitants – and, therefore, which order is sought.

The effects of an occupation order may include:

- enforcing the applicant's entitlement to remain in occupation

- regulating both parties' occupation (e.g. saying what the arrangements for sharing are, where this is possible)

- prohibiting, suspending, or restricting the respondent's right to occupation

- requiring the respondent to leave the house (in essence, an 'ouster order')

- excluding the respondent from a defined area around the house.

The length, as well as the effect, of an occupation order, will vary according to which of the five relevant sections applies:

i) s.33 (i.e. where the applicant has an estate or interest or 'home rights').

The order will be 'for a specified period, until the occurrence of a specified event, or until further order'. In other words, the order should not last for an indeterminate period – it should continue until a specified date, or 'event' (e.g. another court hearing), or until another order is made; neither is it a final order – it could always be changed in a subsequent court hearing.

ii) s.35 (where one former spouse or former civil partner, with no occupation rights, applies). Such an order:

- will be for a specified period, not exceeding six months

- may be extended on one or more occasions, for a specified period, not exceeding six months.

iii) s.36 (i.e. where one cohabitant, or former cohabitant, with no occupation rights, applies). Such an order:

- will be for a specified period, not exceeding six months

- may be extended, on one occasion only, for a specified period, not exceeding six months (note the difference from s.35).

iv) s.37 (i.e. where neither spouse or former spouse or civil partner or former civil partner has occupation rights – e.g. where there is an eviction order, or the couple are squatting).

The maximum period of the order is as for s.35, i.e. one year. However, because this would apply, for example, in circumstances where the parties' entitlement to occupy had been terminated by an eviction order, or they were squatters, it is much less likely that the order(s) would continue to be in effect for this maximum period of a year – they would probably be out before then.

v) s.38 (i.e. where neither cohabitant, or former cohabitant, has occupation rights). The comments on s.37 apply similarly.

NB Reference must be made to ss.33, 35, 36, 37 and 38 for the precise powers contained in each section. The above is only an outline.

b) Non-molestation orders

Fortunately, these orders are not as complex as the 'occupation order' types because:

- no distinction is made between spouses and cohabitants
- 'entitlement to occupy' is irrelevant.

Non-molestation orders are dealt with in s.42. The key points to note are:

- As with occupation orders, 'associated persons' may apply; similarly, any party to existing family proceedings may apply.
- Though 'molestation' is not defined, the Law Commission stated that 'it includes, but is wider than violence (and) encompasses any form of serious pestering or harassment'. In deciding whether to make an order, the court will consider 'all the circumstances' including the need to secure the health, safety and well-being of the applicant and any relevant child.
- A non-molestation order may be made in proceedings brought for that purpose, or in existing family proceedings; in the latter case, an application does not have to be made at all – the court could make an order 'of its own motion'.
- The order is an injunction to stop the respondent doing whatever it was that damaged the 'health, safety and well-being', etc.
- It may be made 'for a specified period or until further order'. If made in family proceedings, the order ceases to have effect if those proceedings are withdrawn or dismissed.

Under the Domestic Violence Crime and Victims Act 2004, breach of a non-molestation order becomes a criminal offence in its own right, with a possible maximum penalty of five years' imprisonment.

c) Without notice orders

A without notice order (formerly known as an *ex parte* order) is one made in proceedings of which the respondent has been given no notice. Clearly, this is a serious step to take, particularly with occupation orders (especially ouster orders, i.e. removing the respondent from the home). However, considerations of justice (being allowed to 'have your say') may compete with those of safety.

Case law had developed to indicate that what were then *ex parte* orders would be exceptional, in cases of real urgency, where notice could not be given.

However, this case law has now been superseded by the statutory provision in s.45. The court may make a without notice order (an occupation order and/or non-molestation order), having 'regard to all the circumstances', including:

- any risk of significant harm to the applicant or a relevant child, attributable to conduct of the respondent, if the order is not made immediately

- whether it is likely that the applicant will be deterred or prevented from pursuing the application if the order is not made immediately

- situations where the respondent is believed to be aware of the proceedings, evading service of notice of proceedings and the applicant, or relevant child, will be 'seriously prejudiced' by any delay.

If an order is made, the respondent should be allowed a full hearing 'as soon as just and convenient'.

4. Powers of arrest

The previously fragmented law and practice have now been consolidated in s.47. The key points are:

- where either an occupation order or non-molestation order is made, the court must attach a power of arrest if it appears that 'the respondent has used or threatened violence against the applicant or a relevant child' unless it considers they would be adequately protected without it

- such a power of arrest may be attached to a without notice order if, in addition to the above, there is a risk of 'significant harm to the applicant of child, attributable to conduct of the respondent', if this action is not taken immediately

- the period to which the power of arrest applies may be shorter than for the order itself

- if a power of arrest has not been attached, the applicant may still apply to the court for the issue of an arrest warrant if, in their view, the order has been breached.

In essence, these provisions are likely to lead to a higher number of orders with attached powers of arrest. If the order is breached, the applicant could then contact the police and request that the respondent be arrested.

Questions
1. Could the civil law be used more widely to provide protection for victims by means of an injunction excluding the perpetrator and providing early intervention in domestic violence?
2. Does the civil law send out the same messages as the criminal law to:
   a) the perpetrator?
   b) the public at large?

---

5. Amendments to the Children Act 1989

Section 52 and Schedule 6 of the FLA amend the previous legislation on interim care orders (ICO) and emergency protection orders (EPO) in the Children Act (ss.38 and 44 respectively). This allows for an 'exclusion requirement' to be made. The key points are:

- an exclusion requirement can only be made if the court is already satisfied that the grounds for making an ICO or EPO are met, i.e. it is an ancillary order

- the court must be satisfied that the exclusion of the 'relevant person' (i.e. whoever is deemed to be causing the 'significant harm' which provides the grounds for the ICOs and EPOs) will lead to the child(ren) no longer suffering significant harm

- the exclusion requirement can only be made if another person in the house (who may or may not be a parent) is 'able and willing' to provide reasonable care and consents to the inclusion of the requirement

- the comments on 'without notice orders' and 'powers of arrest' above apply to exclusion requirements

- the requirement does one or more of the following:

   a) requires the 'relevant person' to leave the house in which the child(ren) live

   b) prohibits that person from entering the house

   c) excludes that person from a defined area of the house

- 'undertakings' may be accepted by the court, instead of making an exclusion requirement (i.e. an undertaking, in these circumstances, to leave or stay away). Such an undertaking is 'enforceable as if it were an order', but does not carry a power of arrest. (Undertakings can also be made in relation to occupation orders and non-molestation orders – see s.46).

This is a very important amendment to the Children Act. Previously a person causing significant harm to a child could be assisted in obtaining 'alternative accommodation', only if they intended to leave, i.e. it was voluntary (Schedule 2, para. 5); it is now the case that the abuser may be required to leave, rather than the child.

Note also the amendment to s.31 Children Act 1989 made by s.120 Adoption and Children Act 2002, which adds 'impairment suffered from seeing or hearing the ill treatment of another' to the definition of 'harm'.

> The Protection from Harassment Act 1997 was introduced to control 'stalking'. It was not drafted with domestic violence in mind, but has had some impact on it.
>
> The 1997 Act is a hybrid, in that it 'creates an offence of harassment which is the subject of the criminal law and also provides civil remedies for the restraining of and damages for such offences' (Bird, 2006, p.49).

Other relevant aspects of civil law

There are numerous other Acts of Parliament that could be relevant to domestic violence situations, but the three identified here are:

- Children Act 1989

- Child Support Act 1991 (as amended by the Child Support Act 1995 and the Child Support, Pensions and Social Security Act 2000)

- Housing Act 1996 (and the Homelessness Act 2002).

Children Act 1989

This comprehensive piece of legislation includes the following (among many other things):

- 'Section 8 Orders'. There are four types: orders relating to residence and contact ('access') and prohibited steps and specific issue orders. These orders regulate the arrangements for children between people holding 'parental responsibility' and can be made in divorce and matrimonial proceedings, but also could be made in respect of proceedings under Family Law Act 1996.

- Part III and Schedule 2, which deal with local authority services to families and children, e.g. day care, family centres and 'accommodation' for children. These are not compulsory measures.

- Parts IV and V, which deal with care proceedings and child protection measures such as emergency protection and child assessment orders. These are compulsory measures, which require court decision.

- Schedule 2, para. 5 of the Act allows a local authority to assist someone who is ill-treating a child at particular premises to leave those premises (this can include payments of money, e.g. for rent).

However, this can only be done if it is in the person's intention to leave – they can't be forced. The Family Law Act 1996 (s.52 and Sched. 6) implements a new s.38A(1) to the Children Act, making it possible to compulsorily exclude an abuser, when an interim care order is made, and a new s.44A in relation to emergency protection orders.

Child Support Act 1991

This was implemented (April 1993) via the Child Support Agency. It is very contentious, partly because continuing responsibility of a 'non-custodial' parent to make child care payments departs from 'clean break' divorce principles, but also because amounts ordered from 'absent parents' have been claimed to be excessive.

Payments are based on formulae, with set amounts related to:

1. basic needs of the child (income support level)

2. ability of the absent parent to pay

3. means of the parent with care.

Single parents living on means-tested benefits (income support, family credit, disability working allowance) may be ordered to recover maintenance from the absent parent, via the CSA. Other single parents cannot be ordered to do so.

The Act allows such parents not to authorise the CSA to recover maintenance if 'there would be a risk of her, or any child living with her, suffering harm or undue distress as a result' (s.6 (2)(b)).

See generally **www.csa.gov.uk**

A report by Sir David Henshaw in July 2006 recommended changes to the current system of child support, which the government has broadly accepted. See **www.dwp.gov.uk/child maintenance/henshaw_report.asp**

The government consulted further and produced a White Paper 'A new system of child maintenance' (Cm6979 (2006). This ultimately led to the Child Maintenance and Other Payments Act 2008. When fully implemented, this will abolish the CSA and replace it with a new body, the Child Maintenance and Enforcement Commission, which will be a non-departmental public body.

The Commission will seek to encourage and support parents in making voluntary arrangements. It will have wide-ranging powers of enforcement and debt management to ensure that children are properly maintained.

Housing Act 1996

Part VII of this Act is the primary legislation on homelessness, but has been extended by the Homelessness Act 2002. Previously it was Part III of the Housing Act 1985 and, prior to that, the Housing (Homeless Persons) Act 1977. An applicant is 'homeless' within the definition of this Act if he/she has no accommodation (anywhere in the world) which the person is entitled to occupy and which is 'reasonable' to occupy. It is not 'reasonable', if likely to lead to domestic violence (actual or threatened) towards the applicant, or someone who might reasonably be expected to reside with them.

However, preventing homelessness by enabling victims to remain in their homes is a key policy objective for local authorities, e.g. by taking action against a person who is in breach of a tenancy agreement, providing genuine alternative accommodation or installing additional security measures to the home to prevent a violent partner from entering the property.

If someone applies for housing as a homeless person, the housing authority must decide whether they are:

- homeless or threatened with homelessness and
- eligible for assistance and
- in priority need and
- not 'intentionally homeless'.

The authority will also consider whether the applicant has a 'local connection' and ascertain that no other suitable accommodation is available in their district.

A Department of the Environment report (1991) stated 'rehousing of women and children' in violent situations should not be delayed in the hope that they would be 'taken back' by partners if they had sought emergency housing in refuge.

Section 145 of the 1996 Act inserts a new para. 2A into Sched. 2 of the Housing Act 1988 which allows local housing authorities to secure possession orders in cases of domestic violence. A parallel provision for housing associations is contained in s.149.

Chapter 12

Housing (homelessness) legislation

Overview

Housing law and policy is an extremely wide and complex area. A key trend in housing policy is that towards owner occupation; this has been promoted by legislation such as the Housing Act 1980, providing the 'right to buy' council housing. A frequent area of concern for property owners is that of mortgage difficulties, where the best advice is to contact the building society or bank concerned – with the social worker, in appropriate circumstances, acting as intermediary and/or advocate.

Many people with whom social workers come into contact are not property owners, however. As Brayne and Carr note (2005, pp.652–3), the key issues for them are:

a) obtaining a property

b) keeping the property (i.e. security of tenure)

c) making sure it is fit to live in (i.e. repair and disrepair)

d) not having to pay too much for it (i.e. rent control)

e) homelessness.

Homelessness

The principal purpose of this chapter is to advise on recommended reading.

The primary legislation on homelessness is now contained in the Housing Act 1996 (Part VII) as amended by the Homelessness Act 2002.

Previous legislation was contained in the (now repealed) Housing (Homeless Persons) Act 1977 and subsequently the Housing Act 1985 (Part III).

Texts which refer to this latter legislation will therefore have out-of-date information, but may be useful for the following two reasons:

- they may contain references to case law that are still relevant (though note that the Human Rights Act 1998 will have an impact on the development of case law – see Chapter 13).

- they may be interesting and useful in getting an understanding of the development of law, policy and practice in this area.

The simplest way to understand homelessness legislation is by identifying a number of criteria that the applicant has to satisfy in order for the full housing duty to be effected. These are:

- Is the applicant homeless or threatened with homelessness? (ss.175–177)

- Is the applicant eligible? (s.186), for example, generally, people from abroad are not eligible. (The National Assistance Act 1948 and the Children Act 1989 provide fallback legal responsibilities to adults and children respectively.)

- Is the applicant in priority need? (s.189) Four categories are identified:

  i) a person with dependant children living with them, or who might reasonably be expected to live with them

  ii) a person who is homeless through flood, fire or disaster

  iii) a person and anyone who might reasonably be expected to live with them, who is vulnerable because of old age, mental illness or disability, physical disability or other special reason

  iv) a woman who is pregnant or the woman with whom the person is living or might reasonably be expected to live is pregnant.

- Is the applicant intentionally homeless? (s.191) Homelessness law and policy have led to a great deal of case law, but, above all, on the issue of intentionality.

- Does the applicant have a local connection? (s.199)

The Homelessness Act 2002 received Royal Assent in February 2002 and was implemented on 31 July 2002. The impact of this Act is still becoming apparent.

The Homelessness Act 2002 amends and extends Part VII of the Housing Act 1996. Key features are as follows (section references are to the 2002 Act unless otherwise stated):

- Sections 1–4 impose a duty on each housing authority to review the extent of homelessness in its area and to publish a homelessness strategy in consultation with other departments of the local authority, and with voluntary agencies.

- Regulations have been implemented which extend the priority needs groups beyond those identified in s.189 of the 1996 Act. These groups are:

  - homeless 16 and 17 year olds, except those for whom a local authority has a responsibility under the Children (Leaving Care) Act 2000

  - care leavers aged 18 to 21

  - people the local authority consider to be vulnerable as a result of fleeing violence or threats of violence

  - those considered to be vulnerable as a result of an institutionalised background such as local authority care, the armed services or prison.

- Section 5 extends s.192 of the 1996 Act so that accommodation may be provided for persons not in priority need, who are not intentionally homeless.

- Section 6, in effect, extends the 'full housing duty' beyond the two years required in the 1996 Act; there is now no time limit.

- Section 10 extends the definition of violence in s.177 of the 1996 Act (which is a criterion of 'priority need') beyond domestic violence, by adding the phrase 'or other violence'.

- Section 12 applies to homelessness situations in which children are involved, but where the applicant is ineligible for assistance, or is intentionally homeless. This inserts a new s.213A into the 1996 Act which requires referral to the local authority social services department in such circumstances.

There is a Code of Guidance with the 2002 Act which can be accessed at the website of the Department for Communities and Local Government: **www.communities.gov.uk/ publications/housing/homelessnesscode**

The following chapters from a key social work law text contain information on homelessness legislation, but also other housing-related information, such as rent law, eviction and repossession, repair problems, etc.

Brayne and Carr (2008, Ch. 21)

Government publications

In addition to the 1996 and 2002 Acts, useful supplementary reading from central government is contained in:

Government Response to the ODPM Select Committee's Report: Homelessness Inquiry (Cm. 6490) ODPM, 2005

Websites

Further information on housing law and policy generally (which goes far beyond 'just' homelessness) can be found on the government website: **www.communities.gov.uk/housing**

As a counterpoint to 'official' statements of government policy it is worth checking out the Shelter website: **www.shelter.org.uk**

Academic texts

A key text on homelessness legislation is:

Arden, A., Hunter, C. and Johnson, L. (2006) *Homelessness and Allocation* (7th ed.). London: Legal Action Group

Also see:

Lowe, S. (1997) Homelessness and the Law, in Burrows, R. et al. (eds) *Homelessness and Social Policy*. London: Routledge

There is detailed information on housing law generally in:

Arden, A. and Dymond, A. (2007) *Manual of Housing Law* (8th ed.). London: Sweet and Maxwell

Burnet, D. (2006) *Introduction to Housing Law*. London: Cavendish

Cowan, D. (1999) *Housing Law and Policy*. Basingstoke: Macmillan (See Ch.7 for a discussion of homelessness legislation. *NB* This book contains a critique of housing law, pp. 13–41, which puts it into a political and ideological context.)

Robson, G. and Roberts, D. (2006) *A Practical Approach to Housing Law*. London: Cavendish

TV play

It is worth watching the following influential TV play, which deals with homelessness and which led directly to the formation of the housing charity Shelter. *Cathy Come Home* (1966) Directed by Ken Loach, written by Jeremy Sandford. This has been released by the British Film Institute on video and DVD (Reference: BBC Worldwide Ltd (2003) 1 035673 005514)

Useful addresses

Shelter
(National Campaign for the Homeless)
88 Old Street
London EC1V 9HU
Tel: 0845 458 4590
E-mail: **info@shelter.org.uk**
Website: **www.shelter.org.uk**

Department for Communities and Local Government
Eland House
Bressenden Place
London SW1E 5DU
Tel: 020 7944 4400
E-mail: **contactus@communities.gov.uk**
Website: **www.communities.gov.uk**

Chapter 13
The Human Rights Act 1998

Overview

The Human Rights Act 1998 came into force on 2 October 2000. It puts an obligation on 'public authorities' to act in accordance with those 'Convention rights' (from the European Convention on Human Rights) contained in Schedule 1 of the Act. The term 'public authorities' includes the courts and tribunals, and also central government departments, the police, local authorities and other bodies providing a public service.

The Act applies both to rules of law themselves and to the way they are used. It therefore has an impact on the delivery, and nature of, services provided by social work agencies.

In any references to (social work) law you need to be aware that there are different laws, jurisdictions and legal processes in the four countries of the United Kingdom.

The comments below apply to England. One aspect of the process of devolution is that Convention rights are already built in to the legislation for Wales and Scotland, by virtue of the Government of Wales Act 1998 and the Scotland Act 1998 respectively; though, because of the different levels of law-making power in these two countries, the Convention rights will not apply in the same way.

After reading this chapter and associated materials you should be able to:

- state the operating principles of this Act
- outline the content of the Act
- understand the significance of key features in the Act (e.g. 'declaration of incompatibility')
- develop and maintain an understanding of the significance of the Human Rights Act for social work policy and practice.

ESSENTIAL READING

Wadham, J., Mountfield, H. and Edmundson, A. (2007) *Blackstone's Guide to the Human Rights Act 1998* (4th ed.). Oxford: Oxford University Press

There is now a huge literature on human rights, both general and with regard to particular issues. The texts listed below are particularly recommended.

The following key social work law text contains an overview of the HRA:

Brammer (2009, pp.43–55)

Brayne and Carr (2008, pp.71–83)

Also see:

Johns, R. (2007, Ch.2)

Background material is contained in:

Brayne, H. and Broadbent, G. (2002) *Legal Materials for Social Workers.* (Ch. 2, 'Human Rights Law')

Also see:

Schwehr, B. (2001) Human rights and social services, in Cull, L.A. and Roche, J. (eds) *The Law and Social Work: Contemporary Issues for Practice.* Basingstoke: Palgrave

FURTHER READING

Foster, S. (2008) *Human Rights and Civil Liberties.* (2nd ed.). Harlow: Pearson Longman

Home Office (1997). *Rights Brought Home: The Human Rights Bill*, Cm 3782, HMSO (The text of this White Paper is contained in Appendix 3 of Wadham and Mountfield, 2003)

Drabble, R., Maurici, J. and Buley, T. (2004) *Local Authorities and Human Rights.* Oxford: Oxford University Press, especially Chapters 1, 2, 3 and 10

There are references to the Human Rights Act in many other law texts. An example is:

Holland, J.A. and Webb, J.S. (2006) *Learning Legal Rules: A Student's Guide to Legal Method and Reasoning* (6th ed.). Oxford: Oxford University Press (Ch. 9)

There are articles on the Human Rights Act 1998 in journals such as:

European Human Rights Review
European Law Review
Legal Action
Public Law.

Also see the *Human Rights Law Reports.*

As the impact of the Act develops, following implementation, you are also likely to see more frequent reference to it in main stream social work journals.

The following websites contain helpful information on the HRA:

Equality and Human Rights Commission
www.equalityhumanrights.com

European Convention on Human Rights:
www.echr.coe.int/NR/rdonlyres/D5CC24A7-DC13-4318-B457-5C9014916D7A/0/ EnglishAnglais.pdf

European Court judgements:
www.echr.coe.int/ECHR/EN/Header/Case-Law/HUDOC/HUDOC+database

The website of the British Institute of Human Rights is also useful: **www.bihr.org**

The remainder of the chapter is organised under the following headings:

* Introduction

* Key operating principles

* The Convention rights

* The interpretative duty

* Statements of compatibility and declarations of incompatibility

* Areas of social work services that might be affected.

Introduction

The Human Rights Act 1998 (HRA) is very short – it contains only 22 sections and four schedules – but its impact on social work is fundamental. The main provisions of the HRA came into force on 2 October 2000. The effect of this is that UK courts at all levels will be required to take into account the European Convention on Human Rights (ECHR).

The ECHR is an international treaty, which was signed on 4 November 1950 and came into force on 3 September 1953, under the auspices of the Council of Europe.

The ECHR is concerned with the identification and protection of certain fundamental rights and freedoms (the right to life itself; protection of private life; right to a fair trial, etc.). You will probably be aware that UK citizens have been able (since 1966) to assert such rights by application to the European Court of Human Rights (ECtHR) in Strasbourg. They can still do so, but these rights have been 'brought home' by requiring UK courts to interpret law and make decisions compatibly with the ECHR, or, in some cases, state that they are unable to do so.

> The European Court of Human Rights in Strasbourg should not be confused with the European Court of Justice in Luxembourg. The former deals with human rights legislation; the latter deals with European Union law.

The HRA legislation will challenge both 'liberal' and 'conservative' traditions in law (and to some extent public policy generally).

The classical liberal position is that citizens should be free to do what they wish, provided it is not illegal, damaging to others, etc. (This is a convenient position, correspondingly, for those who have wished to limit state intervention.) 'The shift from the traditional permissive approach of civil liberties, characterised by the idea that we are free to do anything which is not explicitly unlawful, to the positive rights of the HRA 1998 is likely to be difficult to ignore' (Holland and Webb, 2006, p.308).

The conservative tradition in law is embedded (many would say) in the politics of the judiciary; but it is also inherent in certain aspects of legal procedure, especially precedent. The English courts will no longer simply be able to interpret cases – which will include disputes about the actions of social workers – in terms of earlier domestic decisions, on a hierarchical basis. They will have to go beyond the boundaries of English law and consider decisions of the ECtHR; but also, more generally and profoundly, they will be required to consider the philosophical principles behind the Convention rights.

The HRA will impact on social work agencies and other 'public authorities' primarily in response to the decisions of the courts. It is to be hoped that some of the working principles in social work (anti-discriminatory practice, empowerment, etc.) are conducive to the HRA and that social workers individually will be in sympathy with this new legislation. However, challenges to social work decisions are likely to be as much to do with the issue of scarce resources and agency policy generally, as with the views of individuals.

The HRA states that its purpose is 'to give further effect to rights and freedoms guaranteed under the European Convention on Human Rights'. This will be done in three ways:

i) by obliging courts to decide all cases before them (whether brought under statute or common law) compatibly with Convention rights unless prevented by primary or secondary legislation (s.6(1)(2)(3))

ii) by introducing a new obligation on courts to interpret existing and future legislation in conformity with the Convention wherever possible (s.3)

iii) by requiring courts to take relevant case law from the ECtHR into account in any proceedings (s.2(1)).

There are other formal statements on human rights, two of the best known being:

United Nations Convention on Human Rights (1948)
This is not a code of law, and has not been incorporated into the law. It does, however, contain important statements of principle (many of which correspond to those in the ECHR) against which public policy may be judged. The Convention articles are set out in Brayne and Broadbent (2002, pp.69–72).

United Nations Convention on the Rights of the Child (1989)
The UN publishes every five years a report on the extent to which countries' policies meet the principles in this Conventions but (unlike the ECHR) no redress is available. The journal *Childright* often contains articles linked to this Convention.

For further information go to: **www.unicef.org/crc/**

There are also UN Conventions on the rights of disabled people (1974) and on the elimination of discrimination against women (1981).

Unlike the fields of sex, race and disability, there was initially no Human Rights Commission. The Parliamentary Joint Committee on Human Rights reported that there was a compelling case for the establishment of such a commission in England and Wales, in order to place the HRA at the heart of the public authorities' policies; the committee's view is that local authorities and health trusts tend to act defensively to avoid litigation, but no more. *The Case for a Human Rights Commission* (2003) by the Joint Committee on Human Rights is available at: **www.publications.parliament.uk**

The Equality Act 2006 established a new Equality and Human Rights Commision which became operational in 2007.

Key operating principles

The courts will make such decisions on the basis of certain principles (though these principles may not be explicitly stated in court). Briefly, (for a further discussion see Wadham and Mountfield) these principles are:

i) **The rule of law**
No matter how desirable a particular aim, government and its agents cannot interfere with a Convention right unless the basis for doing so is set out in an ascertainable law. As you will see under C below, the theme of 'interference' is central; and much of social

work is about 'interference' (albeit, one hopes, legitimate) in people's lives. The Children Act 1989, the Mental Health Act 1983, community care legislation, etc., are precisely the sort of 'ascertainable law' referred to above.

ii) **Legitimate aims**

One defence for a public authority against a claim that it has contravened a Convention right is that of 'legitimate aim'. For social workers this will often be 'yes, we did interfere in your private life, but we did so in order to protect you/others from danger or secure your/others' welfare'.

iii) **Proportionality**

Any interference with a Convention right must not only have a legitimate aim, in order to be defended in an action using the HRA; it must also not be excessive. The idea of not 'taking a sledgehammer to crack a nut' is relevant here. This is important for social work; for example, many child abuse enquiries have criticised the manner in which child protection procedures have been executed, through 'dawn swoops', excessive police presence, domineering attitudes in conferences, etc.

The margin of appreciation

Running alongside the above principles is the idea of a 'margin of appreciation'. Different countries have varying legal traditions and public policy aims. This idea allows the courts in different countries some latitude to interpret the ECHR and evaluate public policy decisions, in accordance with those traditions and aims. Clearly there is a tension here: to some extent signatory countries will 'go their own way'; but they must not go so far as to depart from the principles of the Convention, or the decisions of the Strasbourg court.

The Convention rights

Please note the following points:

- The HRA has not simply declared the ECHR to be part of English law. Instead, elements of the ECHR have been selectively incorporated, as 'Convention Rights' under s.1 of the Act.

- Those elements of the ECHR which have been incorporated into the HRA are expressed, in full, in Schedule 1 of that Act.

- The extent of Convention rights varies. There are three key groups:

  i) Absolute rights, from which no departure is permitted. For example, Article 3 (preventing torture) and Article 4 (preventing slavery/forced labour) are absolute. Because these rights are not restricted, they cannot be balanced against any public interest.

  ii) Limited rights, i.e. rights, which are limited in certain defined circumstances. However, the existence of these limitations or specific exceptions is not balanced against considerations of public interest. Article 5 (the 'right to liberty and security of person') is an important example. This sets out six circumstances, to do with 'lawful arrest, detention etc.' where someone's liberty can be curtailed. Examples are given below.

  iii) Qualified rights, i.e. rights which are expressed positively, but are subject to restriction clauses which enable consideration of the balance between individual rights and the public interest. An apparent violation of a qualified right will be justified if a particular action is prescribed by law, pursues a legitimate aim, is necessary in a democratic society, fulfils a pressing need and is proportionate. Examples are Articles 8–11. To illustrate this, Article 8 ('the right to respect for private and family life') is set out in full below, under 'Qualified rights'.

There are also two other categories of rights – derogated rights and designated reservations – with only one example of each as far as England and Wales is concerned:

iv) 'Derogated' rights. A government may make a statement of derogation – in effect that it is not going to adhere to a Convention right. This is permitted by Article 15 of the ECHR, which refers to suspension of rights 'in time of war or other public emergency threatening the life of the nation'.

v) The only derogations entered by the UK government (see HRA s.14 (1)(a)) are to Article 5(3). This refers to bringing defendants to trial 'promptly', etc., and is in contradiction to detention powers in the successive Prevention of Terrorism Acts and, more recently, the Anti-Terrorism, Crime and Security Act 2001 and Terrorism Act 2005. The whole issue of detention of terrorism suspects without trial remains controversial.

vi) there is also the concept of 'designated reservations' (see HRA s.15) which enables signatory states to limit challenges under the ECHR.

There is one reservation by the UK government: the part of Article 2 of Protocol 1, requiring education to be provided according to parents' religious wishes, has been accepted only to the extent that it is compatible with efficient instruction and training and reasonable public expenditure.

The HRA 1998 has selectively identified Articles 2–12 and 14 of the ECHR together with Articles 1–3 of the First Protocol and Articles 1 and 2 of the Sixth Protocol. (These 'Protocols' are later additions to the ECHR.)

This encompasses all the major substantive rights in the ECHR, subject to the derogation and reservation referred to above. However, Article 1 of the ECHR is not included in Schedule 1 of the Act. This is referred to, misleadingly, as 'introductory only' in some government, and other, guides. Article 1, in full, runs as follows: 'Obligation to respect human rights. The High Contracting Parties [i.e. the signatories to the ECHR] shall secure to everyone within their jurisdiction the rights and freedoms defined in Section 1 of this Convention.'

This Article currently forms the basis for the actions against member states as a whole (i.e. not just 'public authorities') in Strasbourg, for failure to secure rights and freedoms for everyone in their jurisdiction through adequate legislation, so it is significant that it has been omitted from the HRA.

A summary of the Convention rights

Please note that the listing below does not state each Article in full. A full version of the Articles adopted in the HRA is contained in Schedule 1. It is essential (as with any other legislation) that you read each Article in full in order to understand it properly.

Article 2   Everyone's right to life shall be protected

Article 3	No one shall be subjected to torture or inhuman or degrading treatment or punishment
Article 4	No one shall be held in slavery or be required to perform forced or compulsory labour
Article 5	Everyone has the right to liberty and security of person
Article 6	Everyone is entitled to a fair and public hearing within a reasonable time by an independent and impartial tribunal established by law
Article 7	No one shall be subject to retroactive penalties of law
Article 8	Everyone has the right to respect for their private and family life, home and correspondence
Article 9	Everyone has the right to freedom of thought, conscience and religion
Article 10	Everyone has the right to freedom of expression
Article 11	Everyone has the right to freedom of peaceful assembly and freedom of association with others, including the right to form and join trade unions for the protection of their interests
Article 12	Men and women of marriageable age have the right to marry and found a family
Article 14	The enjoyment of the rights and freedoms set forth in this Convention shall be secured without discrimination on any ground.
	(*NB* this is not a free standing 'anti-discriminatory' right but rather concerns how the other rights in the Convention should be determined and upheld.)
Article 1 of Protocol 1	Everyone is entitled to the peaceful enjoyment of his/her possessions
Article 2 of Protocol 1	No person shall be denied the right to education
Article 3 of Protocol 1	There shall be free elections at reasonable intervals by secret ballot, under conditions which ensure the free expression of the opinion of the people in the choice of the legislature
Article 1 of Protocol 6	Abolition of the death penalty (but Article 2 permits the death penalty in time of war).

Qualified rights

As noted above, some Convention rights are absolute, but many are qualified (or limited). In order to illustrate this, the full text of Article 8, which is a qualified right, is given below:

Article 8	*Right to respect for private and family life*
	1. Everyone has the right to respect for his private and family life, his home and his correspondence.
	2. There shall be no interference by a public authority with the exercise of this right except such as is in accordance with the

> law and is necessary in a democratic society in the interests of national security, public safety or the economic well-being of the country, for the prevention of disorder or crime, for the protection of health or morals, or for the protection of the rights and freedoms of others.

This Article, along with Articles 3, 5 and 6, is one of the most likely to have a direct impact on social work practice. It has implications for all of the legislation and associated policy and practice outlined in this manual.

The interpretive duty

The impact of the HRA on public authorities will be driven through the mechanism of the interpretive duties in ss.2, 3 and 6.

Section 6

Section 6 applies to 'public authorities'. This includes courts and tribunals, but will also include (for example) social work/social care agencies 'whose functions are . . . of a public nature' (s.6(3)(b)).

The HRA states that 'it is unlawful for a public authority to act in a way which is incompatible with a Convention right' (s.6(1)).

However, this section goes on to say that a public authority will not have acted unlawfully if because of primary legislation, or related provisions, it could not have acted any differently (s.6(2)(a) and (b)).

NB This is important and links to the 'declaration of incompatibility' discussed below.

Section 2

Section 2 states (s.2(1)) that a court or tribunal 'determining a question which has arisen in connection with a Convention right' has to take into account any judgements, etc., from the European Court of Human Rights, etc.

Section 3

Section 3(1) states that: 'So far as it is possible to do so, primary legislation and subordinate legislation must be read and given effect in a way which is compatible with the Convention rights.' (An example of primary legislation is the Children Act 1989 and subordinate legislation, the regulations on children's homes, reviews, complaints, etc.)

However, this section goes on to say that it does not affect the 'validity, continuing operation or enforcement' of any incompatible primary or subordinate legislation (s.3(2)(b) and (c)).

NB This too is important and links to the 'declaration of incompatibility'.

Sections 2 and 3 taken together will have two key effects:

i) The Convention must be given effect and Strasbourg case law integrated.

   This will require a new form of judicial reasoning (a major reason for delay in implementing the HRA was so that there could be judicial training on this) requiring a considered balance between:

- individual rights and freedoms

- the general public interest.

Briefly, the judicial decision-making process will require the following series of questions (and some answers):

a) What is the (Convention) right (or rights) in question?

b) What is the alleged interference and is it prescribed by law?

c) What objectives are served – is the interference necessary?

ii) The traditional notion of precedent (in part, a hierarchical deference by lower courts to the decisions of higher courts) will be abrogated to the extent that the courts are required to give effect to Convention rights. The UK courts will no longer simply be able to refer to past decisions of the Appeal Court, or House of Lords, to decide present cases: ss.2 and 3 require a consideration of Strasbourg case law as well. The weight put on Strasbourg decisions will vary: for example, more recent cases, unanimous or majority decisions and decisions of the plenary Court are more likely to be influential.

Statements of compatibility and declarations of incompatibility

Statement of compatibility

Where government bills are passing through Parliament, s.19 of the HRA requires ministers to issue a statement of compatibility (before the second reading of the Bill concerned) to the effect that the Bill's provisions are compatible with the Convention rights.

The minister may also 'make a statement to the effect that although he is unable to make a statement of compatibility the government nevertheless wishes the House to proceed with the Bill' (s.19(1)(b)).

It is unlikely that ministers will routinely and frequently state that new legislation is incompatible. It would, at the least, be embarrassing and contradictory to have on the one hand implemented the HRA and on the other to ignore it all the time. Ultimately this could be political suicide, but this depends on so many factors, including the size of the government majority.

Declaration of incompatibility

This is a declaration by a court (see s.4) that a particular provision of primary legislation is incompatible with a Convention right. In effect, what the court would be saying is: 'Yes, this public authority did contravene a Convention right but it was correctly using the relevant primary legislation: it had no option. We will therefore criticise the legislation itself and not the authority.'

There are several points to note:

i) While all courts must adhere to the HRA, only some courts have the power to make a declaration of incompatibility: the House of Lords, the Court of Appeal and the High

Court, for example, can (see s.4(5)), but the 'lower courts', e.g. magistrates' courts, county courts and the Crown Court, can't.

ii) If a higher court makes such a declaration, this does not mean that the legislation concerned is 'set aside' (i.e. doesn't apply any more). Parliamentary sovereignty is preserved by virtue of s.3(2)(b) and (c), which confirm the 'validity, continuing operation [and] enforcement' of incompatible primary and subordinate legislation.

iii) Where declarations are made, there is a 'fast track' procedure (s.10) available to government to amend the legislation concerned.

The effect of a declaration of incompatibility is to send a message to Parliament (or, in practical terms, the government) in a very public way, to the effect that despite the court's best efforts, the legislation in question cannot be made compatible with the Convention rights. This may generate public interest and promote debate on changes that might be made to achieve compatibility. The House of Lords has said that making a declaration of incompatibility should be regarded as a last resort only where it has proved impossible to read the legislation in a way which is compatible with the Convention rights (see *R v A* [2002] 1 AC 45). However, the courts must not indulge in 'judicial law making' by abusing their powers under s.3 (see *In re S* [2002] 2 AC 291). There is a fine line between interpretation and law making where the courts will have to police themselves.

Areas of social work services that might be affected

What the HRA does in practical terms for the day-to-day running of social services is to provide:

- a new ground for judicial review (to be added to those summarised in Section 9) based on an alleged breach of s.6(1)

- a new test for unlawful action or decisions (which could lead to private law proceedings alleging a failure of statutory duty)

- a duty to act positively to further people's human rights.

In addition, it may also be possible for someone to use the Act by citing a public authority's illegal action as a defence in any proceedings, which it may itself bring.

Some brief examples of the possible effect of the HRA are given below. But firstly four key terms are referred to.

Victims

Section 7 of the HRA states that a person can bring proceedings against a public authority alleging illegality under s.6(1), but only if he or she 'is (or would be) a victim of the unlawful act' (s.7(1)). This is reinforced in s.7(7) (which refers to Article 34 of the Convention), which identifies a 'victim' as a 'person, non-governmental organisation or group of individuals' directly affected by an alleged violation.

In addition the question of 'standing' (i.e. who can bring proceedings) in judicial review is raised in s.7 (7): 'If the proceedings are brought on an application for judicial review, the applicant is to be taken to have a sufficient interest in relation to the unlawful act only if he is, or would be, a victim of that act.'

The definition of 'victim' and the issue of 'sufficient interest' mentioned in s.7(7), is likely to be the subject of arcane legal controversy.

There are two essential points to make concerning social work:

i) Service users who are directly affected by social workers actions and omissions will be 'victims' and can cite the Convention rights in Schedule 1 in making their case. Case law tends to indicate that this notion of 'victim' can include people who are closely and personally representative of those who are/were affected and also people who are potentially affected by a proposed action.

ii) A key area of controversy is likely to be in judicial review. As noted in Chapters 8 and 9, this is an increasingly important area for social services. As in other aspects of public service, public interest groups (e.g. Age Concern, MIND, Family Rights Group, etc.) have often instituted proceedings on behalf of others (in HRA-speak: 'victims').

An example of this is cited in Chapter 8: *R* v *Sefton Metropolitan Borough Council, ex parte Help the Aged* [1997] 4 All ER 532.

There is likely to be dispute about the 'standing' of such bodies to use the Convention rights in the HRA to represent the interests of others, because these bodies are not, themselves, 'victims'. In effect this means that where judicial reviews are brought by such groups they would be able to raise points about 'irrationality' and 'unlawfulness' (i.e. the earlier grounds for judicial review) but not any Convention points. This is likely to be an area for future litigation.

Limitation periods

Section 7(5) provides that proceedings against a public authority using the HRA must be made within one year of the 'act complained of' though the court can extend this period if they consider it 'equitable having regard to all the circumstances' (s7(5)(b)).

However, this normal limitation period is subject to any rule which imposes a shorter time limit (the usual time limit for judicial review is three months).

'Vertical' legislation

The HRA is an example of 'vertical' legislation, that is, it is concerned with the issue of rights and obligations between individuals on the one hand and the state or public bodies on the other.

It is much less likely to be used as 'horizontal' legislation – i.e. concerned with rights and obligations between two or more individuals (divorce legislation is an example).

However, it will have an indirect impact on this aspect of private law, because it will affect the way courts (as 'public authorities') exercise their discretion and take decisions affecting rights between individuals.

'Public authority'

This is defined (s.6) as a 'court or tribunal' but also (in that circular fashion frequently used in legislation) 'any person certain of whose functions are of a public nature'.

The question of who is the 'public authority', i.e. who is 'responsible' for social work decisions and actions, is going to be important, particularly in an era of contracted out functions.

It is clear that local authority social services departments and voluntary agencies providing social services, would be public authorities. The position of bodies providing contracted out services has proved to be controversial. It is clear that a social services authority commissioning such services would be a public authority. The position of the provider of such services is less easy to determine. In YL v Birmingham City Council (2008) 1AC95 the House of Lords decided that a private care home accommodating publicly funded (under s21 National Assistance Act 1948) residents was not a public authority for the purposes of the Human Rights Act. However, this decision has been reversed by s145 Health and Social Care Act 2008.

The effect of the HRA on social services

As with all aspects of the operation of the HRA there will be jurisdictional questions (i.e. which court(s) should be used in particular instances). Sometimes this will be part of existing proceedings; for example, Mental Health Review Tribunals are likely to be required to deal with Article 5 (liberty and security of the person); magistrates' courts dealing with family proceedings will be concerned with Article 8 (respect for family and private life); and so on.

Whatever court is used, there will be a number of effects on social services agencies (see s.8 on 'judicial remedies'). For example:

i) a particular authority may have damages/compensation and/or court costs awarded against it (the damages, etc, being paid to the successful complainant)

ii) in cases of judicial review any one or more of the relevant orders may be made (i.e. quashing, prohibiting and mandatory orders and declarations) against the particular authority, i.e. it will have to do/not do something, reconsider its actions, etc.

iii) proceedings using the HRA, very importantly, will have an impact on authorities generally (even if not directly involved) where, for example, the Department of Health issues policy guidance following an important test case.

Examples

The examples below refer to Articles 3, 5, 6 and 8. These are the most likely to apply to social work agencies but this does not mean that others will not apply.

Article 3

'No one shall be subjected to torture or to inhuman or degrading treatment or punishment.'

This is an absolute right. This Article may be used to bring actions against punitive or harsh residential care regimes.

It could also be used against enforced medical treatments. An example (see Chapter 7) could be some of the proposed (community-based) treatments in the White Paper on mental health law reform. There could be an impact concerning bullying in educational establishments.

While the thrust of the HRA tends to be towards the curtailment of state ('public authorities') intervention, it is very important to note that it could have the opposite effect. For example, a case was reported (Z v *United Kingdom* (2002) 34 EHRR 3) in which the European Court of Human Rights found that Bedfordshire County Council had breached Article 3 because it allowed four children to suffer parental neglect over a five-year period, before taking them into care. Inaction may lead to legal censure, as well as (illegal) action.

Article 5

'Everyone has the right to liberty and security of the person.'

This is a limited right. Article 5 goes on to cite exceptions, including:

- 'lawful arrest or detention' concerning (alleged) offences

- 'the detention of a minor by lawful order for the purpose of educational supervision' or bringing him 'before the competent legal authority'

- 'the lawful detention of persons for the prevention of the spreading of infectious diseases, of persons of unsound mind, alcoholics or drug addicts or vagrants'.

The most widespread impact of Article 5 will be to do with criminal justice, both before and after conviction. Many social workers operate at the interface between social welfare and criminal justice and will need to be aware of this.

But many social work powers in *civil* proceedings are likely to be relevant in this respect since they curtail civil liberties – for example, emergency protection orders; the use of 'compulsory' sections under the Mental Health Act 1983; and even the use of (supposedly) 'voluntary' powers, such as the reception into care of elders under the National Assistance Act 1948. The tensions in social work between issues of 'control' and concerns about 'welfare' exactly mirror the controversies likely to be raised by the HRA.

Any area of public service that curtails liberty (even though for 'legitimate' reasons); or that blurs the boundary between institutional care/control and the community, or between civil and criminal proceedings (the Crime and Disorder Act 1998 being a good example) is likely to be affected by proceedings using Article 5.

Article 6

'Right to a fair trial.'

In civil and criminal proceedings 'everyone is entitled to a fair and public hearing within a reasonable time by an independent and impartial tribunal established by law'.

Again, this will be a key concern for any public authorities (including the courts themselves) involved with criminal justice, but it will also have an impact on civil proceedings such as care order applications.

The main facets of a 'fair hearing' are:

- prior disclosure of all relevant material

- the right to 'have your say' – which will include legal representation and could include such matters as the provision of an interpreter

- aiming to ensure that parties are on an equal footing (there is a power imbalance in care proceedings for example, where local authorities are 'repeat players' – they know the rules, parents and others might not)

- a reasoned judgement prior to the HRA criminal and civil legislation has, increasingly, required courts to give reasons for their decisions; this is now likely to be reinforced.

Many of the implications of the above for social work practice are obvious. But there may be some implications that are not so immediately evident – for example, the reference to hearings 'within a reasonable time' may be used (reinforcing the no-delay principle in s.1(2) of the Children Act 1989) to complain against protracted family proceedings.

This Article may have implications for without notice (formerly *ex parte*) hearings, i.e. where proceedings do not have one of the main parties present (so they can't be heard, making it 'unfair'). This could apply, for example, to without notice applications in domestic violence hearings, or for an emergency protection order.

While the notion of a 'fair trial' clearly refers to the work of the courts and tribunals, ECHR case law has also included administrative and not just judicial decision-making forums. For social workers this could, potentially, have implications for reviews, case conferences, etc., and issues to do with their fairness, independence and impartiality and the promptness of decision-making.

Article 8

'Everyone has the right to respect for his private and family life, his home and his correspondence.'

This right is qualified by laws concerning national security, public safety, crime and disorder, protection of health, etc. Article 8 is likely to be a key focus of concern for social services agencies.

Some examples of areas that might be affected are:

- care and supervision in residential establishments
- the (proposed or actual) closure of residential homes
- the use of any compulsory powers involving the removal of people from their own homes
- the use of non-compulsory powers could also apply, raising the issue of informed consent
- the curtailment or removal of services and/or increased costs of services (this is relevant not only for the service user him/herself, but also for carers)
- any forms of compulsory examination or treatment
- failure on the part of public authorities to protect the interests of vulnerable people (including their removal from home; cf. the case example above under Article 3).

Cases could be brought, using Article 8 (and others) not only by service users against social services agencies, but also by social workers against their own employing body.

Chapter 14
Miscellaneous

This chapter contains information on a number of disparate aspects of law related to social work. The intention here is simply to provide a very brief outline with recommendations on further reading and, where appropriate, websites.

The topics referred to are:

nationality, asylum and immigration law

data protection legislation

the Public Interest Disclosure Act

Freedom of Information Act

social security law.

Nationality, asylum and immigration law
Introduction

Concern and controversy about immigration and related issues are not new. The first legislation designed to limit entry to the UK was the Aliens Order (known as the Aliens Act) of 1905, prompted by the arrival of many Jewish immigrants escaping the pogroms in Eastern Europe; and there is a history going back at least to the 12th century of often violent xenophobic outbursts.

Working with asylum seekers is now very much a part of social work, to the extent that many local authorities and voluntary agencies have formed specialist teams. About 80 per cent of asylum seekers are women and children; they are usually destitute, and often traumatised by their experiences, which may include armed conflict, torture and exploitation. There is an increasing number of unaccompanied children (raising issues around the duty to identify and to provide services for children in need).

The aim of this section is to identify the relevant legislation and to refer to some practice issues. This area of law has become more complex over the last few decades, especially with the newer legislation on asylum seekers; what follows, therefore, is emphatically not a detailed or comprehensive guide to the law, for which you would need to seek legal advice.

Current legislation

Before identifying the current legislation on asylum seekers it is relevant to mention the following two Acts:

- The British Nationality Act 1981 – this remains the key legislation on citizenship despite having been amended. Brayne and Carr (2005, p.727) identify the circumstances in which a person will be regarded as a British citizen.

- The Immigration Act 1971 – this Act (which became law in 1973) brought 'new permanent primary migration for the Indian sub-continent, the Caribbean and Africa to the United Kingdom finally to a halt' (Spencer 1997,p.43) though the rights of dependants were preserved, and they continued to arrive.

The previous categories of 'alien' and 'British Subject' were abandoned and replaced by 'patrials' and 'non-patrials'. Patrials were free from restrictions and were defined as British or Commonwealth citizens who were born or naturalised in the UK or who had a parent (or grandparent in the case of British citizens) who had been born or naturalised in the UK. The distinction between patrial and non-patrial was essentially a racially divided one, since the former were more likely to be white and the latter black. However, this term is no longer used following the repeal of s.2 Immigration Act 1971. More modern texts talk in terms of those subject to immigration control and those not.

The 1971 Act, alongside the Immigration and Asylum Act 1999 (itself amended by the Nationality, Immigration and Asylum Act 2002 and the Immigration, Asylum and Nationality Act 2006) and the Immigration Rules, outlines the circumstances under which leave to enter or remain may be granted (see Brayne and Carr, 2005, p.728).

Asylum seekers

Unlike most legislation, the statutes on asylum seekers apply in the same way in the four countries of the UK (i.e. England, Wales, Scotland and Northern Ireland).

The 1999 Act is the primary legislation on asylum seekers but the following earlier legislation is relevant:

- The Asylum and Immigration Appeals Act 1993. The major features of this act are:
  - the incorporation of obligations under the 1951 Geneva Convention
  - the provision of a right of appeal against refusal of asylum within strict limits
  - the requirement for all asylum seekers to be fingerprinted
  - the power to detain asylum seekers awaiting a decision on an asylum claim.
- The Asylum and Immigration Act 1996, the major features of which are:
  - the establishment of a 'white list' of countries considered not to pose a serious risk of persecution
  - the blocking of asylum seeker applications from those who had travelled through a safe third country
  - entitlement to welfare benefits restricted to asylum seekers who made an immediate application on arrival in the UK
- The Immigration and Asylum Act 1999. This Act is extremely complex and detailed; what follows is the identification of some major features (the details of this and other post-1980 legislation can be found at **www.opsi.gov.uk**). Central features of the Act are:
  - the establishment of a National Asylum Support Service (NASS) based in Croydon. Social workers should not advise asylum seekers on asylum-related matters; that role is reserved to NASS, which is now the only permitted government-funded mechanism for addressing the economic needs (but not other needs such as health, education and community care) of asylum seekers

- support is provided to asylum seekers who are destitute, or likely to become so in 14 days. This support may be accommodation-only, vouchers-only (for which shops do not give change), or both

- appeals against decisions of NASS are to the Asylum Support Adjudicators.

- The Asylum and Immigration Act 2002 contains the following powers:

  - the Home Secretary may require the asylum seeker to return to any third country through which they have passed and to appeal from there

  - to establish overseas centres where asylum can be claimed before arrival in the UK (claims may be made by children as well as adults in which case the Refugee Council must be informed)

  - those claiming asylum may be required to report to the police; and to live at a specified address for 14 days, to receive an induction programme

  - very significantly, the planned withdrawal of all support from an asylum seeker who does not seek asylum at the first opportunity

- The Immigration, Asylum and Nationality Act 2006:

  - makes changes to the rules relating to appeals against, e.g., refusals of clearance to enter

  - creates new powers to acquire information, e.g. passenger lists, and also regulates the types of evidence that may be used to verify, e.g., identity

  - alters the powers of local authorities when dealing with persons subject to immigration control with regard to housing and services.

Definition of 'refugee'

The Geneva Convention Relating to the Status of Refugees 1951 defines a refugee as a person who:

- 'owing to well-founded fear of being persecuted for reasons of race, religion, nationality, membership of a particular social group or political opinion, is outside the country of his nationality and is unable or, owing to such fear, is unwilling to avail himself of the protection of that country;

- or who, not having a nationality and being outside the country of his former habitual residence as a result of such events, is unable or, owing to such fear, is unwilling to return to it.'

(For more information see **www2.ohchr.org/english/law/refugees.htm**)

Implications of the Human Rights Act 1998

Legislation should be interpreted to meet the Articles attached to the Human Rights Act 1998; see s.3. NASS is a public authority and therefore bound by the Articles in the Human Rights Convention. Areas where breach is possible are:

- Article 2 (the right to life), e.g. where an asylum seeker is removed to a country where he is likely to face the death penalty.

- Article 3 (prohibition of inhuman or degrading treatment, punishment or torture), e.g. where there is removal to a country where racial harassment or torture are likely.

- Article 5 (right to liberty and security of person) provides for regular reviews of and speedy challenges to detention.

- Article 6 (right to a fair trial) the independence of the Asylum Support Adjudicators may be questioned, since they are appointed and financed by the Home Office.

- Article 8 (right to respect for private and family life) asylum seeker dispersal policies may contravene this by disrupting family support.

Service provision

Social workers may not provide services to asylum seekers only for reasons of destitution – that role rests with NASS.

However, it is clear now that, where other welfare considerations are apparent, social work provisions may apply: the Children Act 1989 (both in terms of assessing children 'in need' and the s.47 duty to investigate possible need for child protection); the NHS and Community Care Act 1990 and associated community care legislation (starting with the s.47 duty to assess); and the Mental Health Act 1983.

Educational and health services should also be provided by the relevant authorities. Local authority children and family services, rather than NASS, provide support to unaccompanied children. Many unaccompanied children will be children 'in need' and therefore qualify for services under Part III and Schedule 2 of the Children Act; some will be accommodated (s.20).

There are notable exceptions to the ability to provide services, because of restrictions in the Immigration and Asylum Act 1999 and associated amendments (see Brayne and Carr, 2008, p.737 for a list of restrictions). See also the Immigration, Asylum and Nationality Act 2006.

ESSENTIAL READING

There are very helpful chapters in the two standard social work law textbooks:

Brammer (2009, Ch.13 – Asylum)

Brayne and Carr (2008, Ch.21 – Nationality, immigration and asylum issues)

Note, however, that neither contains the Immigration, Asylum and Nationality Act 2006. This, and the explanatory notes with it, can be found at: **www.uk-legislation.hmso.gov.uk/acts/acts2006a.htm**

FURTHER READING

Home Office (1998) *Fairer, Faster and Firmer – A Modern Approach to Immigration and Asylum* (Cm. 4018). London: TSO (the White Paper that led to the Immigration and Asylum Act 1999)

Home Office (2002) *Secure Borders, Safe Haven: Integration with Diversity in Modern Britain* (Cm. 5387). TSO

Home Office (2005) *Controlling our Borders: Making Migration Work for Britain* (Cm. 6472). London: TSO

William, S., Knafler, S. and Pierce, S. (2004) *Support for Asylum Seekers: a guide to legal and welfare rights*. London: Legal Action Group

Background reading
Those interested in understanding more about the background to immigration law and policy should see:

Clayton, G. (2008) *Textbook on Immigration and Asylum Law* (3rd ed.). Oxford: Oxford University Press

Spencer, I. (1997) *British Immigration Policy since 1939: the making of multi-racial Britain.* London: Routledge

Winder, R. (2004) *Bloody Foreigners: the story of immigration to Britain*. London: Little Brown

Data protection legislation – law on access to personal records

Key legislation

- **Data Protection Act 1998**

The Act was implemented on 1 March 2000, and amalgamates previously separate regulation on:

i) computerised records

ii) manually held records.

Also relevant to an understanding of the 1998 Act are the following regulations (in the form of a statutory instrument):

- **Data Protection (Subject Access Modification) (Social Work) Order 2000 (S.I. 2000/415)**

The 1998 Act repeals the previous Acts and regulations though you will still find references to them. The repealed Acts, etc., are:

- on computerised records:

    - Data Protection Act 1984

    - Data Protection (Subject Access Modification) (Social Work) Order 1987

- on manually held records:

    - Access to Personal Files Act 1987

    - Access to Personal Files (Social Services) Regulations 1989 (and Department of Health circular LAC (89) 2).

However, it is important to note here that the operation of the 1998 Act is built on eight principles (contained in Part 1 of Schedule 1). Very briefly, these principles are that personal data:

1. will be 'processed fairly and lawfully' (further conditions are set out on this in Schedules 2 and 3)

2. will be obtained only for 'specified and lawful purposes' and will not be used for other 'incompatible' purposes

3. will be 'adequate, relevant and not excessive' for the purpose(s) concerned

4. will be 'accurate and, where necessary, kept up to date'

5. will not be kept for 'longer than is necessary'

6. will be processed 'in accordance with the rights of data subjects under the Act'

7. will be kept secure through 'appropriate technical and organisational measures'

8. will not be transferred to countries 'outside the European Economic Area' unless adequate protection is ensured.

Brayne and Carr, (2008, Ch.4)

Further reading, containing the text of the Act itself and commentary on its general application (within which social work/social care agencies play a relatively small part), is contained in:

Carey, P. (1998) *Blackstone's Guide to the Data Protection Act 1998.* London: Blackstone
The range of agencies with responsibilities (as 'data controllers') under the Act is extremely wide, including not only social services, health and education authorities, but also, for example, banks, credit reference agencies and postal ordering services. The above guide is, consequently, equally wide ranging. There is a brief and very clear outline of the implications of the Act for social work agencies in the following text:

Clements, L. and Thomson, P. (2007) *Community Care and the Law* (4th ed.). Legal Action Group (pp.724–34)

There is also information available on the following government websites:

www.ico.gov.uk

www.homeoffice.gov.uk

www.dh.gov.uk/PolicyAndGuidance/OrganisationPolicy/RecordsManagement/ DataProtectionAct1998Article/fs/en?CONTENT_ID=4000489&chk=VrXoGe

This last website address refers to the Department of Health guidance on the Act, issued in March 2000.

The Public Interest Disclosure Act 1998

This is a piece of employment legislation which protects workers who 'blow the whistle' about wrongdoing. It mainly takes the form of amendments to the Employment Rights Act 1996 and makes provisions about the kinds of disclosures which may be protected; the circumstances in which such disclosures are protected; and the persons who may be protected (DTI Employment Relations – Guide to the Public Interest Disclosure Act 1998 – **www.berr.gov.uk**).

A good guide to this can be found on the DTI website referenced above.

Who does the Act cover?

The Act protects most workers in the public, private and voluntary sectors. The Act does not apply to genuinely self-employed workers (including charity trustees and charity volunteers), police officers or the intelligence services.

How does the Act protect workers?

The Act protects workers in a number of ways, for example:

● if an employee is dismissed because he has made a protected disclosure, that will be treated as unfair dismissal

- in any event workers are given a new right not to be subjected to any 'detriment' by their employers on the ground that they have made a protected disclosure, and to present a complaint to an employment tribunal if they suffer detriment as a result of making a protected disclosure.

Disclosing to a regulatory body

The Act makes special provision for disclosures to 'prescribed persons'. These include the following:

General Social Care Council

Matters in respect of which the person is prescribed

Matters relating to the registration of social care workers under the Care Standards Act 2000

General Social Care Council
Goldings House
2 Hay's Lane
London SE1 2HB
Tel: 020 7397 5100
Fax: 020 7397 5101
Website: **www.gscc.org.uk**

Care Council for Wales

Matters in respect of which the person is prescribed

Matters relating to the registration of social care workers under the Care Standards Act 2000.

Care Council for Wales
South Gate House
Wood Street
Cardiff CF10 1EW
Tel: 029 2022 6257
Fax: 029 2038 4764
E-mail: **info@ccwales.org.uk**
Website: **www.ccwales.org.uk**

Scottish Social Services Council

Matters in respect of which the person is prescribed

Matters relating to the registration of the social services workforce by the Scottish Social Services Council.

Scottish Social Services Council
Compass House
11 Riverside Drive
Dundee DD1 4NY
Tel: 01382 207101
Fax: 01382 207215
E-mail: **enquiries@sssc.uk.com**
Website: **www.sssc.uk.com**

Children's Commissioner for Wales

Matters in respect of which the person is prescribed

Matters relating to the rights and welfare of children

Children's Commissioner for Wales
Oystermouth House
Phoenix Way
Llansamlet
Swansea SA7 9FS
Tel: 01792 765600
Fax: 01792 765601
E-mail: **post@childcomwales.org.uk**
Website: **www.childcom.org.uk**

Reading: **Ells, P. and Dehn, G.** (2001) Whistleblowing: Public Concern at Work, in Cull, L.A. and Roche, J. (eds) *The Law and Social Work: Contemporary Issues for Practice.* Basingstoke: Palgrave, pp.105–119

Freedom of Information Act 2000

This Act, much of which came into force on 1 January 2005, has changed the basis on which information is held by public authorities. It creates a general right of access for individuals to information held by public authorities, a term covering, for example, central and local government. It requires public authorities to have a publication scheme explaining how information will be made available.

There are a number of exemptions from disclosure: of particular relevance to social work practice are personal information (s.40), information provided in confidence (s.41), information which is unable to be disclosed because of a legal prohibition (for example, information covered by the Official Secrets Act) (s.44) and information accessible by other means (s.21).

The Freedom of Information Act and the Data Protection Act are complementary. The following chart (taken from Macdonald and Jones, *The Law of Freedom of Information*, p.351) explains the three main differences:

Freedom of Information Act 2000	Data Protection Act 1998
Applies only to information held by public authorities	Applies to personal data processed by all data controllers whether public authorities or not
Any person may apply for information on any other person	Only living individuals may apply and only for information about themselves
Generally speaking, only non-personal information may be obtained if it relates to a living individual	Only covers personal data relating to living individuals

Central and local government all have freedom of information statements.

Macdonald, J., Crail, R. and Jones, C.H. (eds) (2009) *The Law of Freedom of Information*. Oxford: Oxford University Press (contains a huge amount of information on the law in this area).

Another useful source is the website of the Information Commissioner: **www.ico.gov.uk**

Another site with much information on issues related to this is the site of the pressure group the Campaign for Freedom of Information: **www.cfoi.org.uk**

The legal structure of social security

Overview

The principal purpose of this brief section is to advise on recommended reading. An outline of information on social security law is not provided. However, you should be aware of the following two points:

i) The various tasks of social security have been devolved (between 1989 and 1993) via the Department of Social Security (now Department of Work and Pensions) to five 'next steps' agencies (see Ling, 1994). These agencies are:

- Benefits Agency

- Child Support Agency

- Contributions Agency

- I.T. Services Agency

- Resettlement Agency.

ii) There is a range of primary legislation providing the framework for social security, for example:

- Child Support Act 1991

- Social Security Contributions and Benefits Act 1992

- Social Security Administration Act 1992

- Job Seekers Act 1995

- Welfare Reform and Pensions Act 1999

- Tax Credits Acts 1999, 2002.

However, it is important to recognise that this primary legislation does only provide a framework and that there is a complex of secondary legislation, in the form of regulations, which provide the detailed criteria for decision making and benefit levels. It is these **details** that directly affect people's lives.

FURTHER READING

The key authoritative legal text on social security is:

Wikeley, N., Ogus, A.I. and Barendt, E.M. (2002) *The Law of Social Security* (5th ed.). London: Lexis Nexis

However, in day-to-day terms, benefits guides such as the following are of more practical use:

- Child Poverty Action Group, *Child Support Handbook*

- Child Poverty Action Group, *Welfare Benefits and Tax Credits Handbook*

- Disability Alliance, *Disability Rights Handbook*

- Child Poverty Action Group, *Rights Guide to Non-Means Tested Benefits*

  Each one is updated annually. For details see www.cpag.org.uk

Department of Work and Pensions

This department was formed on 8 June 2001 from parts of the former Department of Social Security and parts of the former Department for Education and Employment. (This change is to do with the process of 'joining up' policies on education, work and income maintenance.)
www.dwp.gov.uk

Other useful addresses:

Child Poverty Action Group
94 White Lion Street
London N1 9PF
Tel: 020 7837 7979
E-mail: **staff@cpag.org.uk**
Website: **www.cpag.org.uk**

Disability Alliance
Universal House
88–94 Wentworth Street
London E1 7SA
Tel: 020 7247 8776
E-mail: **office.da@dial.pipex.com**
Website: **www.disabilityalliance.org**

Concerning the organisational and policy changes in the administration of the benefits system, referred to above, see:

Hill, M. (1994) Social security policy under the Conservatives, in Savage S. et al. (eds) *Public Policy in Britain*. Basingstoke: Macmillan

Ling, M. (1994) The new managerialism and social security, in Clarke J. et al. (eds) *Managing Social Policy*. London: Sage

More recent overviews are contained in:

Ditch, J. (ed.) (1999) *Introduction to Social Security: Policies, benefits and poverty*. London: Routledge

McKay, S. and Rowlingson, K. (1999) *Social Security in Britain.* Basingstoke: MacMillan

However, note that the above are primarily social policy texts and do not contain details on social security legislation.

Appendix

This appendix includes some suggestions as to the issues that might be considered when answering the questions posed at various points in the manual. Outline or full answers have not been provided as there is no single way of approaching or answering issues that arise in practice. Much depends on evaluation of the evidence or interpretation of the information that has been given. One area where accuracy is necessary (and so there is a right or wrong answer) is in the actual words used in Acts of Parliament. You should always check the primary source to ensure that you are working from the correct version (and bear in mind that Acts may be amended by later legislation).

Chapter 2 – Interpreting rules

Activity 2.1

1. Links back to the earlier discussion of the rule of law. Even though this exercise involves rules rather than laws, are the principles to be applied the same?

2. This is concerned with many ideas. A first is to do with the aims of rules and the importance of identifying what the rule is designed to do. A common problem for lawmakers is to pass an Act with one particular purpose in mind only to find that, while achieving its desired results, it also has undesirable consequences. The exercise provides an example of this in the episode with the salmon. A second idea relates to law as a reaction to a particular event or concern – a 'knee jerk' reaction rather than a measured one in some cases. The impetus for the passing of a law may be a response to perceived public concern, a desire to be seen to do something. You might like to think about criminal justice policy in this context. A third idea relates to the complexity of many social issues and the need for creative thinking in order to address the range of concerns rather than any particular one. In the context of politics, think about the difficulties involved in trying to legislate for a range of social issues rather than any single issue. Think also about this quotation in the context of the mother's rules. Is she aiming at the 'right' target? Should she be thinking of a different approach?

3. As well as trying to formulate a description of what a rule is (guidance? standards? – this has implications for q.5 below), you may also think about other issues relating to rules. Who is able to make rules? (in this scenario both mother and father make rules – whose rules prevail?) To whom do rules apply? Why do people obey rules? How are they enforced? How are disagreements about rules resolved?

If you want to relate the discussion to legal rules, in what ways are legal rules different from other rules?

You might also think about the values the rules are promoting – as with legal rules, the values underlying the rules are not made explicit. In promoting a particular set of values over others, what judgements are being made about what is important? Are the value positions supported by the rule consistent? You might think about power relationships and the way that rules alter those relationships.

One issue that you might think about is that the mother has failed to specify what will happen if Johnny breaches one of her rules. Why is it important to know what the outcome of breaking rules might be? Does it influence behaviour? Is it as important a factor as the likelihood (in this instance) of being caught? How might the lack of a specified outcome lead to inconsistency in application?

4. Incident 1 – this involves a question of interpretation. At first sight Johnny is correct – but could the broom be regarded as an extension of Johnny? Think about different ways of interpreting the same words, perhaps looking literally at the words used or looking at their purpose and interpreting them more broadly as a consequence.

Incident 2 – Johnny has obeyed the rule, but what does this tell us about the rule? Did it achieve the results the mother wanted? Do rules need exceptions in order to achieve their objectives? How could the mother have addressed this situation?

Incident 3 – This concerns evidence. Is there sufficient to say that Johnny entered the larder and ate the jam? He appears to have had unique opportunity yet denies it. You might explore issues of proof here – is it for Johnny to prove he didn't take it or the mother to prove he did? Why does this matter? Also, how much evidence do we need before we can say he took it? You could test it by applying the normal civil or criminal standards of balance of probabilities (is it more likely than not that Johnny took it?) or beyond reasonable doubt (are we sure Johnny took it?). Does it matter which standard we apply?

Incident 4 – There is a clear breach of the rule, but what happens next? Is the mother justified in inflicting punishment on Johnny? If so, what form/severity of punishment would be justified?

5. a) Reasonableness is clearly a flexible standard – what one person (e.g. father) regards as reasonable may not be regarded as reasonable by another (e.g. Johnny). Where the concept at the heart of a rule is couched in these terms, is it really a rule? (Think back to your answer to q.3.)

b) How is this 'rule' to be interpreted? By whom? What happens if there are conflicting interpretations?

c) By not setting down any clear standard, has the father excluded any possible creative or mischievous interpretation such as that seen in the incidents with the broom and the salmon in q.4?

6. It is much easier to criticise a rule devised by someone else than it is to devise one!

7. a) Do we have rules that are simply understood rather than being stated? What if a person takes a different view of the unstated rule? How can it be challenged? Who decides what the unstated rule is and whether it has been broken? Why might it be easier to have unwritten rules in a family context rather than in the context of society as a whole? Even where we have rules that are stated, do they have implicit values?

b) It might be instructive to compare your response with that of your friends or fellow students!

Activity 2.2

The answers to these questions depend on the way in which you interpret the Act. Following on from the previous exercise, think about how you could put forward an argument for an offence being committed and how you might counter that argument in order to show that an offence is not committed. In some cases, it may not be possible to come up with a counter-argument, as the matter is clearly resolved one way or another.

Many, though not all, of the examples are drawn from the parliamentary debates on the legislation.

a) The letter appears to fall under s.1(1)(a)(ii); the question is whether it is A's purpose (as required toward the end of s.1(1)) to cause distress, etc. – this depends on whether liability depends on what he thinks his purpose is or whether a court can infer his purpose (which he may deny) from his actions.

If spoken over the telephone, the Malicious Communications Act would not apply, as a telephone call is not a 'letter or other article' under s.1(1).

b) This would appear to fall under s.1(1)(b); again the issue would be C's purpose in sending the item.

c) This could fall within s.1(1)(a)(ii), even though not something that might conventionally be understood as a communication. It fits the words of the Act and if so is capable of amounting to an offence under it. You might consider whether it is the most appropriate legislation for this type of conduct.

d) This falls under s.1(1)(a)(iii) and will amount to an offence as long as the purpose requirement is satisfied.

e) The issue here again falls under s.1(1)(a)(iii). Here the question is whether the stated purpose of the sender is the determining factor or whether the reaction of the recipient is the decisive factor in deciding whether the causing of distress was the sender's purpose. Bear in mind here that the offence is committed if the sender has as his purpose the causing of distress, etc. – actual distress is not required.

f) The question here is whether this falls within s.1(1)(a)(i) and whether the purpose of causing distress is satisfied.

g) This appears at first sight to fall within s.1(1)(a)(ii), but might be redeemed by the effect of s.1(2) – legal proceedings are generally regarded as a legitimate way of enforcing a demand.

h) This, however, is not saved by s.1(2). While the demand is one that Nigel had reasonable grounds for making, the use of the threat was not a proper means of enforcing the demand. The offence is made out by virtue of s.1(1)(a)(ii).

i) The package would appear to fall within s.1(1)(b), but Pat is not liable as, not knowing what the contents of the package are, he cannot satisfy the purpose requirement in s.1(1).

j) Much depends on your view of the publications in question. If you are thinking about whether s.1(1)(b) is satisfied, bear in mind that the word 'grossly' qualifies the word offensive. Who would decide whether a publication was 'grossly offensive' if the matter went to court?

Chapter 4 – Children's legislation

Activity 4.1

Case study 1

Think about the evidence you have here in the context of the requirements of the Children Act. Think also about the sources of such evidence – from parents, grandparents, the children themselves and other professionals. How are you going to weigh the evidence from each of these sources? What are the best interests of the child here?

In terms of parental responsibility, think about the application of ss.2, 3 and 4 and apply this to Josie, Dennis and the grandparents. Think also about the process by which parental responsibility could be acquired.

With regard to potential action by the local authority, think about whether the children are 'in need' under s.17. Think through the various permutations of Josie being ill either at home or in hospital; whether Josie can continue to care for the children; whether anyone else is in a position to care for them. Could any support be provided for the family? Would a care order be appropriate? Where would be the best place for the children to live? Consider the matters in schedule 2, and remember throughout that, as far as the Children Act is concerned, the focus is the care and well-being of the children, not the parents, etc.

Case study 2

Look at the evidence here, including the circumstances, the nature of the injuries and the wishes of the parents and child. Is this a 'child in need' under s.17, in which case appropriate support might be provided, or is this a child at risk of significant harm, requiring consideration of Part IV? Consider also both the immediate response to the situation and also the longer term solution.

Chapter 7 – Mental health law: an outline

Case study 1

Common practice for Community Mental Health Teams would be to gradually build up the amount of s.17 leave of a detained patient in order to see if they are able to use the leave productively and to monitor whether there is any change in his mental health. Leave can be either short- or long-term and is at the discretion of the responsible medical officer (usually the team consultant psychiatrist).

Generally one of the aims of allocating a key worker under the CPA system would be to take practical steps with George and his sister to improve the living situation or to assess what support may be necessary in the community. An important element of the key worker's involvement is to build some rapport with George to enable their continued involvement on discharge. They would also discuss any benefits that support or medication could offer and risks involved if George were to relapse, in order to try to reduce the risk of relapse.

If necessary use of s.25A or s.7 guardianship could be considered to provide a statutory structure for accommodation, access and appointments to reduce risk of relapse following discharge from hospital.

Chapter 8 – Community care law: An introduction

The two case studies in this chapter are wide ranging in the nature of the issues the clients present. Answers are not provided here as the relevant aspects of the legislation are covered in the chapter and you need to look carefully at these sections. These case studies are deliberately written to provoke discussion and thought and not to provide model answers.

Chapter 9 – Decision-making: the legal framework
Case study 1

In the first instance, the fixing of the levy, the minister appears to be acting unlawfully in two ways. First, the purpose of the levy is to reimburse those living in the area, not to make judgements about the profits that are being made. An alternative way of looking at this is that the minister has taken into account irrelevant consideration when reaching a decision. Secondly, the Football League has not been consulted as required in the legislation.

On the second matter, the banning of matches on Friday evenings, the minister is acting unlawfully, as the power is only to be exercised to prevent serious disruption to the community, and it cannot be said that the train journeys of Members of Parliament fall into this category. The minister therefore does not have the power to make an order in this way. It could also be seen as using the power for an improper purpose.

Case study 2

a. i. The minister appears to be acting unlawfully in taking into account irrelevant considerations (the marginal seats). The question is whether the minister's stated purpose is the true purpose behind the decision. Also consider whether the decision, however laudable on conservation grounds, is lawful given the terms of the Act in question.

ii. The minister appears to be acting unlawfully in that s.2(1)(b) appears to require that tolls are levied. There appears to be no power to create a situation where tolls are not payable. An alternative view might be that setting the toll at £0 is still a 'rate' under s.2(1)(b) and might therefore be lawful.

iii. This would appear to be lawful as the use of the term time to time suggests that it is possible that rates might change.

b. This decision would appear to be unreasonable in that no reasonable minister would defy a statutory requirement on these grounds.

Chapter 10 – Discrimination and the law

In approaching these questions, you need to take a structured approach by first identifying whether there is discrimination; whether it appears to be unlawful or whether the discrimination falls into one of the classes where discrimination is allowed. Remember that you are looking at these questions purely in terms of the anti discrimination legislation – other legislation may be relevant in the situations described.

Case study 1

The exemptions are on the face of them lawful as they do not discriminate between individuals on grounds of gender, race, disability or religion. However, in discriminating between the pensionable ages of a woman and man there is less favourable treatment of Mr Jones on grounds of sex of a kind that is not capable of being justified.

Case study 2

The imposition of age restrictions may be a form of indirect discrimination under the Sex Discrimination Act if, for example, they disadvantage women who may not be eligible because of the ages in question being the principal child-bearing ages. Is there something about the job that requires a person between the stated ages? When the Employment Equality (Age) Regulations came into force on 1 October 2006, discrimination of this type on grounds of age in the context of employment became unlawful.

In advertising by word of mouth, there is an issue about equality of opportunity, and if any person can show that because of that person's race, gender, etc., this type of activity causes them to be less favourably treated than a person of a different group classified by race, sex, etc., then it will be unlawful. Bear in mind also that public authorities (such as a local authority) are under a positive duty to promote equality between persons of different race, etc., by virtue of the Race Relations Act 1976 as amended by the Race Relations (Amendment) Act 2000, and to promote equality between men and women by virtue of the s.76A Sex Discrimination Act 1975 as inserted by the Equality Act 2006.

Case study 3

Would the manager be acting unlawfully as Dennis would be treated less favourably because of his ethnicity? Is the determining factor under this legislation the response of the mother?

Case study 4

There appears to be discrimination here but the question is whether it is justified or whether reasonable adjustments can be made to facilitate access.

Case study 5

The Disability Discrimination Act 2005 will require those operating public transport to make it accessible to the disabled. See ss. 19–21 of the 1995 Act as amended by the 2005 Act.

Case study 6

This is one of those cases where the question is whether the discrimination is justified or whether reasonable adjustments could be made to accommodate Susan's disability. Think about the sorts of adjustments that could be made in this case and ask whether they are ones it would be reasonable to expect the employer to carry out.

Recommended reading

Every attempt has been made to cite the most recent edition of these texts, but please inform us of any new editions.

NB Because law is constantly changing it is imperative that you use up-to-date sources. This includes electronic data as well as books and journals.

Highly recommended reading:

Brammer, A. (2009) *Social Work Law* (3rd ed.) Harlow: Longman

Brayne, H. and Carr, H. (2008) *Law for Social Workers* (10th ed.). Oxford: Oxford University Press

Further recommended reading is set out below.

As a supplement to Brammer and Brayne and Carr it would be worth buying the following book, which contains 32 short chapters, by various authors, on different aspects of social work law:

Cull, L.A. and Roche, J. (eds) (2001) *The Law and Social Work*: *Contemporary Issues for Practice*. Basingstoke: Palgrave.

Also see the following general texts on social work law:

Ball, C. and McDonald, A. (2002) *Law for Social Workers: An Introduction* (4th ed.). Aldershot: Ashgate

Braye, S. and Preston-Shoot, M. (1997) *Practising Social Work Law* (2nd ed.). Basingstoke: Macmillan

Brayne, H. and Broadbent, G. (2002) *Legal Materials for Social Workers.* Oxford: Oxford University Press

Dalrymple, J. and Burke, B. (2006) *Anti-Oppressive Practice: Social Care and the Law* (2nd ed.) Maidenhead: Open University Press

Johns, R. (2007) *Using the Law in Social Work (Transforming Social Work Practice)* (3rd ed.). Exeter: Learning Matters

In addition to the above, the following are a few examples of law-related texts which may be useful to social work students:

Carson, D. (1990) *Professionals and the Courts: A Handbook for Expert Witnesses*. London: Venture Press

Darbyshire, P. (2008) *Darbyshire on the English Legal System* (9th ed.) London: Sweet and Maxwell

Elliott, C. and Quinn, F. (2008) *English Legal System* (9th ed.). Harlow: Pearson Longman

Fox, M. and Bell, C. (1999) *Learning Legal Skills* (3rd ed.). Oxford: Oxford University Press

Holland, J.A. and Webb, J.S. (2006) *Learning Legal Rules: A Student's Guide to Legal Method and Reasoning* (6th ed.). Oxford: Oxford University Press

Martin, E.A. and Law, J. (ed.) (2009) *A Dictionary of Law* (7th ed.) Oxford: Oxford University Press

Partington, M. (2008) *Introduction to the English Legal System* (4th ed.). Oxford: Oxford University Press

Slapper, G. and Kelly, D. (2009) *The English Legal System* (9th ed.). London: Routledge-Cavendish

Stewart, W. (2006) *Collins Internet-Linked Dictionary of Law* (3rd ed.). London: Collins

Twining, W. and Miers, D. (1999) *How to do Things with Rules: A Primer of Interpretation* (4th ed.). London: Lexis Nexis (now Cambridge University Press)

Some examples of key texts on substantive social work and related law are:

Allen, N. (2007) *Making Sense of the New Adoption Law* (2nd ed.) Lyme Regis: Russell House Publishing

Allen, N. (2005) *Making Sense of the Children Act 1989* (4th ed.). Chichester: John Wiley

Ashton, G. R. (2009) *Elderly People and the Law* (2nd ed.). London: Lexis Nexis Butterworths

Ball, C. et al. (2001) *Young Offenders: Law, Policy and Practice* (2nd ed.). London: Sweet and Maxwell

Bartlett, P. and Sandland, R. (2007) *Mental Health Law, Policy and Practice* (3rd ed.). Oxford: Oxford University Press

Bird, R. (2006) *Domestic Violence: Law and Practice* (5th ed.). Bristol: Family Law

Connolly, M. (2004) *Townshend-Smith on Discrimination Law: Text, Cases and Materials.* (2nd ed.). London: Cavendish

Drabble, R. et al. (2004) *Local Authorities and Human Rights.* Oxford: Oxford University Press

Foster, S. (2008) *Human Rights and Civil Liberties* (2nd ed.) Harlow: Pearson Longman

Gostin, L. (1986) (updating service) *Mental Health Services – Law and Practice.* London: Shaw and Sons (reference)

Jones, R. (2001) *Mental Health Act Manual* (8th ed.). London: Sweet and Maxwell

Jones, R. (2008) *Mental Health Act Manual* (11th ed.). London: Sweet and Maxwell

Mandelstam, M. (1998) *An A–Z of Community Care Law.* London: Jessica Kingsley

Mandelstam, M. (2009) *Community Care Practice and the Law* (4th ed.). London: Jessica Kingsley

McConville, M. and Wilson, G. (2002) *The Handbook of the Criminal Justice Process.* Oxford: Oxford University Press

Muncie, J. and Wilson, D. (2004) *Student Handbook of Criminal Justice and Criminology.* London: Routledge-Cavendish

Osborne, S. et al. (eds) (2009/10) (updated annually). *Welfare Benefits and Tax Credits Handbook* (11th ed.). London: Child Poverty Action Group

Ryan, M. (1999) *The Children Act 1989: Putting it into Practice* (2nd ed.). Aldershot: Ashgate

Sargeant, M. (ed.) (2004) *Discrimination Law*. Harlow: Pearson Longman

Wadham, J., Mountfield, H., Edmundson, A. and Gallagher, C. (2007) *Blackstone's Guide to the Human Rights Act 1998* (4th ed.). Oxford: Oxford University Press

White, R. (ed.) (1991) (updating service) *Clarke, Hall and Morrison on Children*. London: Lexis Nexis (also available on CD-ROM)

White, R., Carr, P. and Lowe, N. (2008) *The Children Act in Practice* (4th ed.). London: Lexis Nexis

NB Law changes rapidly. Please use the most up-to-date edition of any text, if possible. Please note that, as well as textbooks, there are other sources of written information.

Reference texts

Jones, R.M. (ed.) (1993) (regularly updated). *Encyclopaedia of Social Services and Child Care Law*. London: Sweet and Maxwell (reference only).

Journals

We also draw your attention to relevant journals, such as the *British Journal of Social Work*. The magazine *Community Care*, is weekly and frequently has short articles concerned with social work law. The following are examples of journals which have more detailed articles in this area:

- *Journal of Law and Society*
- *Journal of Social Welfare and Family Law (JSWFL)*
- *Legal Action*
- *New Law Journal*

The value of journals, as opposed to textbooks or monographs, is in the currency of the information that they can provide. They contain articles, news of legal developments, book reviews, etc. Some contain useful case notes and may even be the only source for a report.

Electronic journals

Journals are increasingly available, not only in printed form, but also electronically.

Newspapers

Just like social work, law is constantly changing and developing and it is extremely important for you to keep up with this by reading newspapers. Newspapers such as the *Times* and *Independent* have good law coverage, which includes law reports. The *Guardian* also has regular features and news items relating to aspects of social work law. Recent editions are available via the Internet.

Databases

Electronic sources are an increasingly important and useful means of finding out about developments in social work law. The resources are an integrated part of the provision of legal information.

Journals and newspapers should be used to find out about recent developments in a topic and to update information found in handbooks, review articles and textbooks.

Databases provide a searchable index to relevant material. Each entry will provide sufficient bibliographic information to allow you to track down an item for subsequent reading. They usually include an abstract; some provide the full text.

- **Westlaw**
  Contains case law, legislation, journal archives, commentary, news and business information. Case coverage dates back to 1865 and includes the European Court of Justice.

- **Lawtel**
  Contains informed summaries and some full text of parliamentary legislation, reported and unreported cases, bills, Green and White Papers and EU legislation. The daily update provides a constant overview of new developments.

- **Lexis Nexis**
  Lexis Nexis (formerly Butterworths) is a well-known legal publisher. This source provides access to their legal services including All England Direct (law reports) and Halsbury's Laws, (which is the authoritative text on Acts of Parliament).

Preparation and evaluation of a recognised search strategy using subject terms and phrases with recognised links should be undertaken prior to using these sources.

Websites

Most companies, organisations and regulatory bodies have Internet sites, which may provide links to other sources. Recent Acts of Parliament, statutory instruments (SIs) and *Hansard* (the official record of debates in both Houses of Parliament) are also available from government sites. You may find the following websites useful:

- **Acts of Parliament and Statutory Instruments**
  This website provides the full text of all Acts of Parliament and statutory instruments (SIs) from and including 1988. Most social work regulations are in the form of SIs. The website list is presented numerically, so you would need the SI number (e.g. SI 2000/415). **www.uk-legislation.hmso.gov.uk/acts.htm**

- **Legislation in progress**
  The following website contains a great deal of information about government and parliamentary procedures. It will help you keep up to date with parliamentary bills (which are intended to become Acts of Parliament). When you go to this website click on index, then B (for Bills). **www.parliament.uk/bills/bills.cfm** A useful site containing legislation, cases and other legal material is **www.bailii.org/**

- **Government circulars**
  Government circulars are a means for central government departments (normally the Department of Health for social workers) to advise local authorities and other agencies

on the implementation of law and policy. Current circulars are listed on the following website, which also provides the full text of recent circulars: **www.dh.gov.uk/en/ Publicationsandstatistics/Lettersandcirculars/LocalAuthorityCirculars/ AllLocalAuthority/index.htm**

Also see:

Department of Health – **www.dh.gov.uk**

Department for Work and Pensions – **www.dwp.gov.uk**

Department for Children, Schools and Families – **www.dcsf.gov.uk**

Ministry of Justice – **www.justice.gov.uk**

Department for Communities and Local Government – **www.communities.gov.uk**

and generally **www.direct.gov.uk**

References

Adcock, M. (1991) Significant Harm: Implications for the exercise of statutory responsibilities, in Adcock, M. et al. (eds) *Significant Harm: its management and outcome*. Croydon: Significant Publications

Allen, N. (2007) *Making Sense of the New Adoption Law* (2nd ed.). Lyme Regis: Russell House Publishing

Allen, N. (2005) *Making Sense of the Children Act 1989* (4th ed.). Chichester: John Wiley

Arden, A. and Dymond, A. (2007) *Manual of Housing Law* (8th ed.). London: Sweet and Maxwell

Arden, A. and Hunter, C. and Johnson, L. (2006) *Homelessness and Allocations* (7th ed.). London: Legal Action Group

Ashton, G.R. (2009) *Elderly People and the Law* (2nd ed.). London: Lexis Nexis Butterworths

Bainham, A. (2005) *Children – The Modern Law* (3rd ed.). Bristol: Family Law

Ball, C. et al. (2001) *Young Offenders: Law, Policy and Practice* (2nd ed.). London: Sweet and Maxwell

Ball, C. and McDonald, A. (2002) *Law for Social Workers: An Introduction* (4th ed.). Aldershot: Ashgate

Barber, P., Brown, R. and Martin, D. (2008) *Mental Health Law in England and Wales.* Exeter: Learning Matters

Bartlett, P. and Sandland, R. (2007) *Mental Health Law, Policy and Practice* (3rd ed.). Oxford: Oxford University Press

Bevan, H. (ed.) (2007) *The Adoption and Children Act 2002*, London: Lexis Nexis Butterworths

Bird, R. (2006) *Domestic Violence: Law and Practice* (5th ed.). Bristol: Family Law

Black, J., Bridge, J., Bond, T. and Gribbin, L. (2007) *A Practical Approach to Family Law* (8th ed.). Oxford: Oxford University Press

Brammer, A. (2009) *Social Work Law* (3rd ed.). Harlow: Longman

Braye, S. and Preston-Shoot, M. (1997) *Practising Social Work Law* (2nd ed.). Basingstoke: Macmillan

Brayne, H. and Broadbent, G. (2002) *Legal Materials for Social Workers.* Oxford: Oxford University Press

Brayne, H. and Carr, H. (2008) *Law for Social Workers* (10th ed.). Oxford: Oxford University Press

Bridge, C. and Swindells, H. (2003) *Adoption: the Modern Law.* Bristol: Family Law

Brogden, M. and Nijhar, P. (2000) *Crime, Abuse and the Elderly*. Cullompton: Willan

Brown, K. (2006) *Vulnerable Adults and Community Care*. Exeter: Learning Matters

Brown, R. (2009) *The Approved Social Worker's Guide to Mental Health Law* (2nd ed.). Exeter: Learning Matters

Burnet, D. (1999) *Introduction to Housing Law*. London: Cavendish

Carey, P. (1998) *Blackstone's Guide to the Data Protection Act 1998.* London: Blackstone

Carson, D. (1990) *Professionals and the Courts: A Handbook for Expert Witnesses*. London: Venture Press

Clayton, G. (2008) *Textbook on Immigration and Asylum Law* (3rd ed.). Oxford: Oxford University Press

Clements, L. and Thompson, P. (2007) *Community Care and the Law* (4th ed.). London: Legal Action Group

Connolly, M. (2004) *Townshend-Smith on Discrimination Law: Text, Cases and Materials* (2nd ed.). London: Cavendish

Cooper, J. (ed.) (2000) *Law, Rights and Disability.* London: Jessica Kingsley

Cooper, J. (2001) The Disability Discrimination Act 1995, in Cull, L. A. and Roche, J. (eds) *The Law and Social Work: Contemporary Issues for Practice*, Basingstoke: Palgrave

Cowan, D. (1999) *Housing Law and Policy*. Basingstoke: Macmillan

Cretney, S., Masson, J. and Bailey-Harris, R. (2003) *Principles of Family Law*. London: Sweet and Maxwell

Cull, L.A. and Roche, J. (eds) (2001) *The Law and Social Work*: Contemporary Issues for Practice. Basingstoke: Palgrave

Dalrymple, J. and Burke, B. (2006) *Anti-Oppressive Practice: Social Care and the Law*. (2nd ed.) Maidenhead: Open University Press

Darbyshire, P. (2008) *Darbyshire on the English Legal System* (9th ed.). London: Sweet and Maxwell

Department of Health (2005) *Independence well-being and choice: our vision for the future of social care for adults in England*. Cm6499. London: HMSO

Ditch, J. (ed) (1999) *Introduction to Social Security: Policies, benefits and poverty*. London: Routledge

Drabble, R., Maurici, J. and Buley, T. (2004) *Local Authorities and Human Rights*. Oxford: Oxford University Press

Duff, R. (2001) Racism and social work practice, in Cull, L. A. and Roche, J. (eds) *The Law and Social Work: Contemporary Issues for Practice*. Basingstoke: Palgrave

Elliott, C. and Quinn, F. (2008) *English Legal System* (9th ed.). Harlow: Pearson Longman

Ells, P. and Dehn, G. (2001) Whistleblowing: Public Concern at Work, in Cull, L.A. and Roche, J. (eds) *The Law and Social Work: Contemporary Issues for Practice.* Basingstoke: Palgrave

Foreman, S. and Dallos, R. (1993) Domestic Violence, in Dallos, R. and McLaughlin, E. (eds) *Social Problems and the Family.* London: Sage/Open University Press

Foster, S. (2008) *Human Rights and Civil Liberties* (2nd ed.). Harlow: Pearson Longman

Fox, M. and Bell, C. (1999) *Learning Legal Skills* (3rd ed.). Oxford: Oxford University Press

Goldson, B. (ed.) (1999) *Youth Justice: Contemporary Policy and Practice.* Aldershot: Ashgate

Goldson, B. (ed.) (2000) *The New Youth Justice.* Lyme Regis: Russell House Publishing

Gordon, R. and Mackintosh, N. (1996) *Community Care Assessments: A Practical Legal Framework* (2nd ed.). London: Sweet and Maxwell

Gordon, W., Cuddy, P. and Black, J. (1999) *Introduction to Youth Justice* (2nd ed.). Winchester: Waterside Press

Gostin, L. (1986) (updating service) *Mental Health Services – Law and Practice.* London: Shaw and Sons

Greig, D.N. (2002) *Neither Bad nor Mad: The Competing Discourses of Psychiatry, Law and Politics.* London: Jessica Kingsley

Griffiths, G. and Roberts, G. (1995) *The Law and Elderly People* (2nd ed.). London: Routledge

Hall, W.C. (1991) *Clarke Hall and Morrison on Children.* London: Lexis Nexis Butterworths

Herbert, M. (1993) *Working with Children and the Children Act: A Practical Guide for the Helping Professionals.* Leicester: BPS Books

Hill, H. (2001) *Blackstone's Guide to the Race Relations (Amendment) Act 2000.* London: Blackstone

Hill, M. (1994) Social security policy under the Conservatives, in Savage S. et al. (eds) *Public Policy in Britain.* Basingstoke: Macmillan

Hoggett, B. (2005) *Mental Health Law* (5th ed.). London: Sweet and Maxwell

Hoggett, B. (2006) *Hoggett: Parents and Children* (5th ed.). London: Sweet and Maxwell

Holland, J. A. and Webb, J.S. (2006) *Learning Legal Rules: A Student's Guide to Legal Method and Reasoning* (6th ed.). Oxford: Oxford University Press

Hooper, C.A. (1996) Men's violence and relationship breakdown: Can violence be dealt with as an exception to the rule? in Hallett, C. (ed.) *Women and Social Policy: An Introduction.* London: Prentice Hall

Hudson, B., Dearey, M. and Glendinning, C. (2005) A new vision for adult social care: scoping service users' views, *Research Works*, 2005–02, Social Policy Research Unit, University of York, York

Johns, R. (2007) *Using the law in Social Work (Transforming Social Work Practice)* (3rd ed.). Exeter: Learning Matters

Johns, R. and Sedgwick, G. (1999) *Law for Social Work Practice: Working with Vulnerable Adults.* Basingstoke: Macmillan

Jones, R. (2001) *Mental Health Act Manual* (8th ed.). London: Sweet and Maxwell

Jones, R. (2008) *Mental Health Act Manual* (11th ed.). London: Sweet and Maxwell

Jones, R.M. (ed.) (1994) *Encyclopaedia of Social Services and Child Care Law.* London: Sweet and Maxwell.

Ling, M. (1994) The new managerialism and social security, in Clarke, J., Cochrane, A. and McLaughlin, E. (eds) *Managing Social Policy.* London: Sage

Lowe, S. (1997) Homelessness and the Law, in Burrows, R. et al. (eds) *Homelessness and Social Policy.* London: Routledge

Lyon, J. (2005) A systems approach to Direct Payments: a response to friend or foe? Towards a critical assessment of Direct Payment, *Critical Social Policy*, 2592: 240–252.

Macdonald, J., Craill, R. and Jones, C.H. (eds) (2009). *The Law of Freedom of Information.* Oxford: Oxford University Press

Mandelstam, M. (1998) *An A–Z of Community Care Law.* London: Jessica Kingsley

Mandelstam, M. (2009) *Community Care Practice and the Law* (4th ed.). London: Jessica Kingsley

Mansell, W., Meteyard, B. and Thomson, A. (2004) A *Critical Introduction to Law* (3rd ed.). London: Cavendish

Martin, E.A. and Law, J. (ed.) (2009) *A Dictionary of Law* (7th ed.). Oxford: Oxford University Press

McCann, K. (1985) Battered women and the law: the limits of legislation, in Brophy, J. and Smart, C. (eds) *Women-in-Law: Explorations in Law, Family and Sexuality.* London: Routledge

McColgan, A. (2005) *Discrimination Law: Text, Cases and Materials.* Oxford: Hart

McConville, M. and Wilson, G. (2002) *The Handbook of the Criminal Justice Process.* Oxford: Oxford University Press

McDonald, A. (2000) *Community Care Law.* Norwich: University of East Anglia

McKay, S. and Rowlingson, K. (1999) *Social Security in Britain.* Basingstoke: MacMillan

Mullender, A. (1996) *Rethinking Domestic Violence: The Social Work and Probation Response.* London: Routledge

Muncie, J. (2009) *Youth and Crime* (3rd ed.). London: Sage

Muncie, J. and Wilson, D. (2004) *Student Handbook of Criminal Justice and Criminology.* London: Cavendish

Muncie, J., Hughes, G. and McLaughlin, E. (eds) (2002) *Youth Justice: Critical Readings.* London: Sage

Newburn, T. (2007) Youth crime and youth culture, in Maguire, M., Morgan, R. and Reiner, R. (eds) *The Oxford Handbook of Criminology* (4th ed.). Oxford: Oxford University Press

Osborne, S. et al. (eds) (2009) (updated annually). *Welfare Benefits and Tax Credits Handbook 2009/10* (11th ed.). London: Child Poverty Action Group

Partington, M. (2008) *Introduction to the English Legal System* (4th ed.). Oxford: Oxford University Press

Pitts, J. (1999) *Working with Young Offenders* (2nd ed.). Basingstoke: Macmillan

Rashid, S.P. et al. (1996) *Mental Health Law* (3rd ed.). Norwich: University of East Anglia

Robson, G. and Roberts, D. (2006) *A Practical Approach to Housing Law*. London: Cavendish

Ryan, M. (1999) *The Children Act 1989: Putting it into Practice* (2nd ed.). Aldershot: Ashgate

Sargeant, M. (ed) (2004) *Discrimination Law*. Harlow: Pearson Longman

Schwehr, B. (2001) Human rights and social services, in Cull, L.A. and Roche, J. (eds) *The Law and Social Work: Contemporary Issues for Practice*. Basingstoke: Palgrave

Selznick, P. (1979) Legality, in Campbell, C. and Wiles, P. (eds) *Law and Society: Readings in the Sociology of Law*. Oxford: Martin Robertson

Shaw, M. et al. (1991) *Children in Need and their Families; A New Approach*. Department of Health/University of Leicester

Slapper, G. and Kelly, D. (2009) *The English Legal System* (9th ed.). London: Routledge-Cavendish

Spencer, I. (1997) *British Immigration Policy since 1939: the making of multi-racial Britain*. London: Routledge

Standley, K. (2006) *Family Law* (5th ed.). Basingstoke: Macmillan

Stewart, W. (2006) *Collins Internet-Linked Dictionary of Law* (3rd ed.). London: Collins

Swindells, H. and Heaton, C. (2006) *Adoption: The Modern Procedure*. Bristol: Family Law

Taylor, M. and MacDonald, A. (1995) *The Law and Elderly People*. London: Sweet and Maxwell

Titterton, M. (2005) *Risk and Risk taking in Health and Social Welfare*. London: Jessica Kingsley

Triseliotis, J. et al. (1997) *Adoption: Theory, Policy and Practice*. London: Cassell

Twining, W. and Miers, D. (1999) *How to do Things with Rules: A Primer of Interpretation* (4th ed.). London: Butterworths (now published by Cambridge University Press)

Unsworth, C. (1987) *The Politics of Mental Health Legislation*. Oxford: Clarendon Press

Urbach, C. and Rights of Women. (2000) *Domestic Violence Injunction Handbook*. London: Rights of Women

Vernon, S. (1998) *Social Work and the Law* (3rd ed.). London: Lexis Nexis

Wadham, J., Mountfield, H., Edmundson, A. and Gallagher, C. (2007) *Blackstone's Guide to the Human Rights Act 1998* (4th ed.). Oxford: Oxford University Press

Walby, S. (2004) *The Cost of Domestic Violence*. London: TSO

Walby, S. and Allen, J. (2004) *Domestic Violence, sexual assault and stalking: Findings from the British Crime Survey Home Office Research Study No.276*. London: Home Office

White, R. (ed.) (1991) (updating service) *Clarke, Hall and Morrison on Children.* London: Lexis Nexis

White, R., Carr, P. and Lowe, N. (2008) *The Children Act in Practice* (4th ed.). London: Lexis Nexis

Wikeley, N., Ogus, A.I. and Barendt, E.M. (2002) *The Law of Social Security* (5th ed.). London: Lexis Nexis

Willman, S., Knafler, S. and Pierce, S. (2004) *Support for Asylum Seekers: a guide to legal and welfare rights*. London: Legal Action Group

Winder, R. (2004) *Bloody Foreigners: the story of immigration to Britain*. London: Little Brown

Index